Long Ago and Far Away

Hollywood and
the Second World War

Robert Fyne

THE SCARECROW PRESS, INC.
Lanham, Maryland • Toronto • Plymouth, UK
2008

ROWMAN & LITTLEFIELD PUBLISHERS, INC.

Published in the United States of America
by Scarecrow Press, Inc.
A wholly owned subsidary of
The Rowman & Littlefield Publishing Group, Inc.
4501 Forbes Boulevard, Suite 200, Lanham, Maryland 20706
www.scarecrowpress.com

Estover Road
Plymouth PL6 7PY
United Kingdom

British Library Cataloguing in Publication Information Available

Library of Congress Cataloging-in-Publication Data

Fyne, Robert.
 Long ago and far away : Hollywood and the Second World War / Robert Fyne.
  p. cm.
 Includes bibliographical references and index.
 ISBN-13: 978-0-8108-6124-4 (hardcover : alk. paper)
 ISBN-10: 0-8108-6124-0 (hardcover : alk. paper)
 1. World War, 1939–1945—Motion pictures and the war. 2. Motion pictures in
propaganda—United States—History. I. Title.
D743.23.F96 2008
940.53'1—dc22   2007050198

∞™ The paper used in this publication meets the minimum requirements of American
National Standard for Information Sciences—Permanence of Paper for Printed Library
Materials, ANSI/NISO Z39.48-1992.
Manufactured in the United States of America.

All photos in the book supplied by Photofest

This book is for Jo-Ann,
who deserves much more.
Mon bijou précieux,
mon étoile brillante.

Contents

Chapter One

We've Never Been Licked
1941–1945

"It was the best of times, it was the worst of times."—Charles Dickens's antistrophic appraisal of everyday life prior to the unsettling events that eventually propelled eighteenth-century France into a long period of conflict, turmoil, and mayhem in *A Tale of Two Cities*

"Ever read *Guadalcanal Diary* by Richard Tregaskis? That was a bestseller and I read it!"—Amherst undergraduate Jonathan Fuerst (Jack Nicholson) arguing with his roommate, Sandy (Art Garfunkel), about belles-lettres in Mike Nichols's scathing 1971 depiction of sexual mores, *Carnal Knowledge*

On Thanksgiving Day 1941, many American families—clustered around a holiday table—still felt unclear about their nation's future. Why wouldn't they? Now in the ninth year of President Roosevelt's revolutionary New Deal—a complex organization of alphabet agencies designed for social and economic reform—the country witnessed a dramatic drop in the unemployment rate as eager recruits swelled the ranks of the Civil Works Administration (CWA), Civilian Conservation Corps (CCC), and the Work Projects Administration (WPA). Certainly this innovative surge created a better lifestyle, but off in the distance—in faraway Asia and Europe—another world war raged. Nazi Germany occupied many European nations, Imperial Japan swallowed up huge regions of China, and Stalin's Russia verged on collapse as *Wehrmacht* (German armed forces) troops approached Moscow. How long, many Americans pondered, before this conflict involved the United States? When would the homeland's youth—like their fathers before them—leave their families, enter the military, and fight on foreign soil?

1

Certainly, this global situation seemed bleak as each day's newspaper headlines bemoaned the British Empire's precarious state, Vichy France's fascist
directives, and prime minister Hideki Tojo's Far East saber-rattling policies—
while back in the States the right-wing isolationists, spearheaded by their hero
Charles Lindbergh, argued neutrality with the interventionists. At the same
time, magazine articles, radio commentators, and motion-picture newsreels
added more information about Axis expansionist goals. And, of course, Hollywood feature films—the most popular form of entertainment—depicted one
scene after another in an array of preparedness titles, warning audiences that
war was lurking around the corner. No wonder many holiday guests, munch-
ing sweet potatoes, turkey breast, and pumpkin pie, seemed apprehensive
about the future. While much of the Great Depression's misery had dissipated
and a bouncy song proclaimed "We're in the Money," the looming overseas
conflict worried everyone. On most people's minds a simple question
gnawed: were they living in the best or worst of times?

A few days later all speculation ended when Japanese air squadrons attacked the Pacific fleet moored at Pearl Harbor. Within hours, Americans
heard the news. Casualties were high at the Hawaiian outpost, and the threat
of invasion alarmed the nation. Spurious sightings of Japanese vessels rattled
West Coast residents, unsubstantiated rumors of fifth-column activities
frightened everybody, and railroad stations, jammed with thousands of servicemen hurrying back to their bases, bulged at their seams. The following
morning President Roosevelt, with Congress applauding his Day of Infamy
proclamation, declared war on the Japanese Empire and warned about the uncertain days ahead. In the meantime, the Axis Pact—spearheaded by Germany and Italy—issued their formal declaration, and by week's end dozens
of nations officially joined one side or the other. Clearly, these events removed any ambiguity. Without question, the worst of times had arrived.

Almost overnight, the nation prepared. Young men flocked to recruiting
stations, civil-defense leaders implemented precautionary policies, manufacturers retooled for military armament, mayors of large coastline cities decreed
blackouts, consumer rationing appeared, Boy Scouts organized scrap drives,
public schools doubled as air-raid shelters, and in California studio executives
stepped forward. With FDR's imprimatur, the motion-picture industry, now
on a wartime footing, produced feature films that fostered morale, reassuring
every American that the nation—with God's blessing—would emerge victorious from the global conflict. For the next four years, Hollywood created numerous photodramas that heralded the Allied cause, extolled democratic institutions, and applauded America's fighting men—while at the same time
vilifying Axis leaders, denouncing expansionist policies, and disparaging the
enemies' combat forces. Collectively, these war-related, black-and-white ti-

tles, with their two-dimensional characterizations, stereotypical plotlines, and clichéd dialogue, reminded audiences of their nation's commitment to victory. All of these pictures, of course, with their subliminal storylines, were propaganda films.

For Hollywood, this call to colors was old hat because many of the studios, especially Warner Bros., had already released feature films that in one way or another contained anti-German or anti-Japanese sentiments. In 1938 MGM's *Test Pilot*, with Clark Gable in the aviator's seat, argued for a strong bomber fleet; in Paramount's *Men with Wings*, an American airman, Fred MacMurray, died fighting for China against Japan; in RKO's *Hawaii Calls*, a young crooner, Bobby Breen, helped U.S. officials wreck a German and Asian undercover operation, stealing plans for the island's fortification; and in Columbia's *Smashing the Spy Ring*, Ralph Bellamy broke up an espionage gang nabbing U.S. military secrets. But in 1939, Warner Bros. declared war on Germany with its blatant *Confessions of a Nazi Spy*, an elaborate denunciation of Third Reich agents working on American soil. Likewise, Producers Distributing Corporation's *Beast of Berlin* warned about Hitler's persecution of Jews, Catholics, and non-Aryans in graphic concentration-camp scenes.

One year later, in 1940, the furnace reached full blast. MGM's *Escape*, *They Met in Bombay*, and *The Mortal Storm*; United Artists' *Foreign Correspondent* and *The Great Dictator*; Fox's *The Man I Married* and *Four Sons*; and Paramount's *Mystery Sea Raider* denounced Nazi Germany in unequivocal language. By 1941 Warner Bros.' *Dive Bomber*, *Underground*, *Sergeant York*, and *International Squadron*; Paramount's *I Wanted Wings*; Fox's *Man Hunt*; and United Artists' *Sundown* warned audiences that war with Germany and Japan was just around the corner. After all, Joel McCrea, in the concluding minutes of *Foreign Correspondent*, pleaded with his countrymen to "keep those lights burning—cover them with steel, ring them with guns, build a canopy of battleships and bombing planes around them. Hello, America, hang on to your lights; they're the only lights left in the world!"

So in the broadest of terms, December 7 did not surprise most Hollywood producers. In a matter of hours numerous department heads huddled in smoke-filled rooms, plotting their next move. For these experienced moviemakers, this Sunday-morning Hawaiian attack ended all sugarcoating. Now cameramen received blunt instructions. Remove the kid gloves, load up your equipment, and go after the Axis Pact with both barrels. By war's end, this high-powered industry—even with unprecedented shortages and ambiguous U.S. Office of War Information (OWI) directives—delivered approximately four hundred motion pictures that in one form or another were outright propaganda films. Both entertaining and persuasive, these feature stories and optimistic storylines—as President Roosevelt often bragged—became an important component of morale.

Sizing up the situation, a New York City journalist (Joel McCrea) and his girlfriend (Laraine Day) keep a sharp eye on some fifth columnists operating near the Dutch coastline in Alfred Hitchcock's 1940 Foreign Correspondent. *Courtesy of United Artists.*

Like all moving pictures, propaganda films were easily categorized. Some screenplays concentrated on the Japanese offensive—depicting American troops assaulting heavily fortified South Pacific islands. Others focused on the European theater—showing the GIs' eastward advance toward Berlin. Still others extolled the Russian and Chinese armies—newfound allies—as these nations, often using rudimentary equipment, fought their invaders. Many described home-front life, reminding audiences about fifth columnists, black marketeering, food points, blackouts, housing shortages, and meatless Tuesdays. Musicals and comedies entered the fray, with popular songsters taunting the Japanese with "You're a Sap, Mr. Jap, to Make a Yankee Cranky" or rallying against the Nazis with "Let's Knock the Hit out of Hitler," offering some levity to a war-weary nation. At the same time, the American cowboy saddled up against the Axis, often in anachronistic plots, where galloping horses raced across the plains and caught up with foreign saboteurs. And, finally, Saturday-afternoon serials, those once-a-week cliffhangers, and Technicolor cartoons, featuring such staples as Popeye, Donald Duck, and Mighty Mouse, took potshots at their nemeses, Hitler, Tojo, and Mussolini.

For Hollywood directors, the Oriental enemies, with their distinctive facial features, became easy to caricature, ridicule, and malign. Soon, dozens of anti-Japanese pictures appeared, depicting the soldiers as diminutive, banzai-spouting automatons, wearing Coke-bottle eyeglasses, ready to commit hara-kiri at the drop of their funny-looking hats. Hastily produced B-potboilers— *A Yank on the Burma Road*, *Secret Agent of Japan*, and *Remember Pearl Harbor*—indicted the nation for treachery, while *Two-Man Submarine*, *Corregidor*, and *Manila Calling* reminded edgy audiences that the United States, now gearing for offensive war, would emerge triumphant. Why not? As another B-title reaffirmed, *We've Never Been Licked*.

Certainly, these "B for budget" screenplays, with their seven-day shooting schedules, unknown actor rosters, and painted backdrops, promised victory in every frame. But these sixty-minute motion pictures lacked the complexity of their big brothers, the feature films.

Full-length titles such as *Guadalcanal Diary*, *Gung Ho*, *Thirty Seconds Over Tokyo*, and *Flying Tigers* glamorized America's fighting men, led by tough, wiry officers, routing the Japanese on remote islands or blasting their aircraft over Chinese skies. Other photodramas—*Wing and a Prayer*, *Destination Tokyo*, and *God Is My Co-Pilot*—destroyed the Oriental foe on land, sea, and air. Occasionally a few movies, *The Purple Heart*, *Wake Island*, *Bataan*, and *Cry Havoc!* among them, detailed unavoidable setbacks, but even in defeat these titles demonstrated U.S. determination. Major Brian Donleavy, the Wake Island marine commandant, rejected the Japanese surrender offer, radioing to the superior force, "Come and get us," while another leatherneck in *Air Force* defiantly bragged, "Send us more Japs!" Even Robert Taylor, trapped behind enemy lines on the Bataan Peninsula, blasted some encroaching Japanese soldiers moments before his death, screaming, "We're still here; we'll always be here!"

Without question, Hollywood portrayed the Japanese foes as sadistic, inhuman, bestial animals, a nation of fanatics lacking compassion, dignity, or decency, happy to kill American prisoners of war, torture civilian workers, or rape captured nurses. Frequently called monkeys, rodents, rats, or snakes, these Orientals—like the epithets used to describe them—required immediate extermination. For the German enemy, however, different criteria prevailed. Caucasian by birth and admirers of Beethoven, Bach, and Mozart, this ethnic group spoke a language similar to English and enjoyed food found on most U.S. tables. Haughty, well dressed, and punctual, this European foe, for the most part, resembled a clown, buffoon, or simpleton. Feature films such as *To Be or Not to Be, Once upon a Honeymoon, Hotel Berlin,* and *Five Graves to Cairo* depicted *Wehrmacht* officers as silly, inept, and boastful men who constantly tugged at their suede gloves, polished their monocles, clicked their heels, uttered Heil Hitler salutes, and goose-stepped on the parade ground—while behind their backs Allied soldiers blew up bridges, rescued their friends, and captured strategic strongholds.

Why joke about a military force that committed unremitting atrocities, deported millions of civilians to death camps, and indiscriminately bombed major cities? Why depict the Nazis in such superficial terms? Was it to downgrade their power and minimize the threat? Or was Hollywood following a propaganda tenet: make your enemy look foolish and useless and downplay his strengths and accomplishments? In *Casablanca,* a supercilious Nazi major (Conrad Veidt) locked horns with an American expatriate, Rick Blaine (Humphrey Bogart) about civilian control in the Vichy-occupied city. Proud as the proverbial peacock, the German—fingering a small black book—bragged about his research, "We have a complete dossier on you." Without missing a beat, Rick's deadpan retort, "Are my eyes really brown?" derided the *Wehrmacht* officer, rendering his meticulous record keeping ineffective. Or how about a Nazi major's (Raymond Massey) serious comportment when an Allied officer (Ronald Reagan) mockingly explained a secret bombsight's design, detailing the "thermotrockle's" interaction with the "dermodyne" in *Desperate Journey*?

Not every motion picture contained laughs. Some titles portrayed Nazism's darker side. Somber screenplays—such as *The Moon Is Down, Edge of Darkness, Hitler's Children,* and *This Land Is Mine*—lacked humor but, instead, detailed the New Order's draconian occupation policies, portraying civilian deaths in Norway, a public flogging of a young German girl, and an execution of a simple French schoolteacher. Similar storylines, *Hangmen Also Die, Hitler's Madman, Hostages, The Seventh Cross,* and *Action in the North Atlantic* reiterated Nazi brutality with their depictions of village reprisals, concentration-camp crucifixions, and strafing unarmed mariners. In all, these anti-Germany propaganda films seemed evenly divided. On the one hand, the Third Reich was ridiculed in zany comedies such as *Hitler—Dead or Alive,*

That Nazty Nuisance, and *The Devil with Hitler*; on the other hand, this Teutonic enemy was vilified as harsh, unrelenting, and cruel in such unsmiling productions as *The Cross of Lorraine*, *Joan of Paris*, and *Above Suspicion*.

While Japanese and German belligerents received most of Hollywood's propaganda efforts, a few shows took swipes at their Axis partner, Italy, but in muted format. Historically, Benito Mussolini aligned his nation with Hitler, hoping to capitalize on the führer's lebensraum conquests, only to witness, a few years later, the Allied invasion and subsequent homeland surrender. For America's filmmakers, this abrupt change of sides involved finessing a delicate situation. Initially, a few pictures—*Casablanca*, *Sahara*, and *Five Graves to Cairo*—depicted Italian combatants as passive conscripts, men oblivious to *Il Duce*'s the-grandeur-that-was-Rome mentality. Basically friendly, almost comical, these nationals seemed interested in enjoying robust meals, sipping hearty vino, and chasing pretty women instead of obeying military directives. After Italy's capitulation, two additional screenplays—*The Story of GI Joe* and *A Bell for Adano*—focused on the positive side of America's defaulted ally. In both pictures Italian villagers befriended advancing GIs, aided in their comfort, and swore allegiance to Jeffersonian democracy.

While most of the propaganda films hammered away at the Axis Pact, other screenplays reminded moviegoers that both China and Russia, two important allies, were in the fight, routing America's foes in different parts of the world. On the Chinese mainland—where a large army thwarted Japanese advances—the nationalists slowly began their offensive. Topical motion pictures, such as *Flying Tigers*, *God Is My Co-Pilot*, *China Girl*, and *China Sky*, praised this faraway land and acclaimed its leader, Chiang Kai-shek, a soft-spoken hero. Likewise, two other titles, *Thirty Seconds Over Tokyo* and *The Purple Heart*, acknowledged this country's role in rescuing some Doolittle Raiders, those airmen who crash-landed after their April 1942 Tokyo bombing run. Still other photodramas—*Night Plane from Chungking*, *China's Little Devils*, and *Dragon Seed*—bonded the strong loyalty between America and China, a friendship that would soon drive the Japanese army into the ocean. After all, a wounded Army Corps pilot (Van Johnson) thanked his Chinese physician for skillful, makeshift surgery, saying, "You saved my life, Doc."

As for the Russians, other problems abounded. For over twenty years, ever since the Bolshevik Revolution, Hollywood motion pictures depicted this Communist nation in unflattering, almost pejorative terms, labeling the population as godless, Leninist, and, of course, anticapitalist. But Pearl Harbor changed everything, and now the Soviet Union—with its large Eastern Front army battling the advancing Germans—stood firmly in the Allied camp. Almost overnight, the American film industry changed its tune, producing one title after another extolling its Slavic friends, those gallant defenders of life, liberty, and happiness. Skewed screenplays, such as *Miss V. from Moscow*, *The Boy from Leningrad*, and *The North Star*, glamorized Russian victories while *Days of Glory*, *Song of Russia*, and *Counter-Attack* documented the similarities between Russian and American people. One title stood out. Warner Bros.' *Mission to Moscow* raised propaganda one step up the ladder with its distorted view of Kremlin politics, anti-Trotsky rhetoric, Purge Trials whitewashing, and unabashed Stalin-worshipping. In one scene the American ambassador (Walter Huston), standing proudly next to the Soviet ruler, prophesied, "History will record you as a great builder for the benefit of mankind."

The Chinese and Russian people were not the only groups receiving high praise from America's filmmakers. Back on the home front, millions of civilians kept the factories, steel mills, and shipyards rolling, producing equipment for the overseas fighting man. This workforce—now augmented with women, employees jocularly called Rosie the Riveter—frequently labored long hours, as manufacturers often ran their plants around the clock. Faced with food and gasoline rationing, an unprecedented housing shortage, and wartime separation, everyone adapted to a different way of life. Hollywood, of course, understood these changes and quickly produced films lauding Uncle Sam's matériel force. Strong photodramas, such as *Joe Smith, American*, *Pittsburgh*, and *Gangway for Tomorrow*, praised the assembly worker, exhorting this group to even higher levels of production, while similar stories— *Saboteur*, *Swing Shift Maisie*, *They Got Me Covered*, and *Keeper of the Flame* warned about Axis subversives plotting to undermine factories or social institutions.

Other home-front problems emerged. Wartime family separation appeared in such multilayered dramas as *Since You Went Away*, *Tender Comrade*, and *I'll Be Seeing You*, while the frustrating housing shortage—especially for transplanted workers—provided some levity in lighthearted romps such as *The More the Merrier*, *In the Meantime, Darling*, and *Johnny Doesn't Live Here Any More*. For sheer pathos no wartime title ever attained the heartbreaking poignancy of *The Fighting Sullivans*, the true story of the five apple-pie, Iowan-bred brothers who perished on the USS *Juneau* during the 1942 Guadalcanal offensive. Certain unsavory practices such as black marketeering and stockpiling were decried in *Rubber Racketeers*, *Rationing*, and *The Racket Man*, three titles that explained how daily hoarding and unscrupulous purchasing aided the Axis. Warnings about Nazi agents inside America's borders highlighted *Watch on the Rhine*, *Secret Enemies*, and *Busses Roar*, while Japanese spy rings operated in *Little Tokyo, U.S.A.*, *Betrayal from the East*, and *Texas to Bataan.*

Out on the high plains, fast-galloping cowboys lassoed Axis saboteurs in *Riders of the Northland*, *Wild Horse Rustlers*, and *Cowboy Commandos*, insuring that America's beef and mineral supplies would reach their armed

With his hands gripping the newly crowned Miss America (Amelita Ward), a smooth-talking publicity agent (Wally Brown) explains to her boyfriend (William Terry) that the beauty queen must give up her social life for the next twelve months in John Auer's Gangway for Tomorrow. *Courtesy of RKO Radio Pictures.*

forces. On city streets, quick-thinking detectives uncovered fifth columnists in *Secrets of the Underground, Eyes in the Night,* and *Quiet Please, Murder* while a few independent sleuths—Sherlock Holmes, Bulldog Drummond, Ellery Queen, and Charlie Chan—found time to ferret out Third Reich operatives before these spies could blow up defense plants or poison city water supplies. And, finally, popular songsters, comedians, and dancers provided rousing entertainment in such rip-roaring wartime musicals as *Yankee Doodle Dandy, Reveille with Beverly, This Is the Army, Stage Door Canteen,* and *Here Come the Waves,* foot-stomping screenplays that reminded audiences to keep an upbeat attitude, put their faith in President Roosevelt, and always "Ac-Cen-Tchu-Ate the Positive."

In all, approximately four hundred Hollywood motion pictures bore the propaganda imprint, and these screenplays, in one form or another, provided viewers with a biased interpretation of the global war. When Randolph Scott and his Marine Raiders charged up Makin Island's beach in *Gung Ho,* audiences knew these tough leathernecks would overrun their enemy. After Humphrey Bogart dug those trenches around an abandoned water well in *Sahara,* moviegoers understood an approaching German squad would never breach these makeshift fortifications. How could they? With Bogart barking orders, checking and double-checking the ammunition supply, and, finally, drawing a line in the sand, what hope did the *Wehrmacht* have? And how about Errol Flynn? He parachuted into the uncharted jungle, trekked his squad miles inland, and—after some minor setbacks—routed the Japanese in *Objective Burma*.

Other Hollywood stars fought gallantly. Two tough Marines, William Bendix and Lloyd Nolan, leaped out of their assault boats, dashed across the beach, and eventually pushed the Japanese into the ocean in *Guadalcanal Diary*, while on another South Pacific island, Pat O'Brien moved inland and fought hand to hand against Nipponese defenders in *Marine Raiders*. Over on Norwegian soil, Paul Muni led his attack team through a precarious fjord, climbed a hill, and rescued his countrymen in *Commandos Strike at Dawn*, while in another village, a local fisherman, Errol Flynn, organized the townspeople in an armed rebellion against their German captors in *Edge of Darkness*. For airborne adventure, two photodramas highlighted the Doolittle Tokyo bombing raid. In *Thirty Seconds Over Tokyo*, Spencer Tracy portrayed the flamboyant leader who took his men from a dusty Florida training field to the enemy's major city, while in *The Purple Heart*, another pilot, Dana Andrews, dropped his bombs right on target. But some bad weather forced his crew to crash-land in China, where—after some hit-and-miss adventures—they were captured by the Japanese, dragged before a kangaroo court, and subsequently executed. Even though this mission ended tragically, American audiences took pride in their martyrdom. After all, these airmen refused to divulge military information and accepted death rather then betray their cause.

With their many victories, strong homilies, and patriotic exhortations, these propaganda films defined the war for most Americans even though many of the storylines were distorted or even untrue. So what? Doesn't a little prevarication offer more reassurance? While U.S. Marines and civilian workers fought to the last man in *Wake Island*, historically this closing scene was a fabrication since the Japanese captured many survivors. But what a perfect Alamo ending! Refusing to surrender, the nation's famous leathernecks—machine guns blazing—killed hundreds of their Oriental enemies before capitulation. Have no doubt, the storyline blared, just wait until we return.

And look at the famous Doolittle Raid. While, factually, a few bombs fell on Tokyo, only miniscule damage occurred, but Hollywood went one step further. In *Behind the Rising Sun*, a Japanese national, J. Carroll Naish, walked ruefully through a city reduced to rubble, lamenting that the Greater East Asia Co-Prosperity Sphere brought this destruction upon itself. But what destruction? Not this April 1942 air raid. Maybe it was that nighttime B-17 raid in *Bombardier*, a motion picture glamorizing the men who dropped explosives on enemy targets. This fiction-as-fact mission, likewise, left the capital city in ruins.

SPENCER TRACY
VAN JOHNSON
ROBERT MITCHUM

Thirty Seconds Over Tokyo

Col. Jimmy Doolittle leads his B-52s to Japan to repay the treachery of Pearl Harbor.

6 PM Sunday

WNEW-TV
Metromedia
The choice **5**

A-48 TV GUIDE | New York Metropolitan Edition

Colonel Jimmy Doolittle (Spencer Tracy) ponders the upcoming April 14, 1942, bombing raid in MGM's Thirty Seconds Over Tokyo. *Courtesy of* TV Guide. *If the Doolittle Raiders had actually flown B-52s on that spring morning, the results would have been much different.*

Similar problems existed in these V-for-Victory titles. During the closing scenes of *Air Force*—a screenplay glamorizing a B-17 crew—U.S. aircraft wrecked a large Japanese flotilla in the South Pacific a few days after Pearl Harbor, glossing over the reality that the Army Air Corps lacked a bomber fleet in December 1941 so, of course, no battle took place. What difference did it make? Audiences understood one thing: American airmen destroyed Japanese ships. Why wouldn't they? According to Hollywood, U.S. servicemen possessed remarkable skills. In *Flying Fortress*, a pilot walked on his starboard wing at 10,000 feet; in *Call Out the Marines*, two impecunious leathernecks spent their off-duty hours in expensive nightclubs, wooing pretty women; and in *The Fighting Seabees*, a construction worker clobbered Japanese soldiers with his bulldozer. Even the supernatural helped out. A dead pilot's ghost roamed around an air base, helping an inexperienced flyer hone his volant skills in *A Guy Named Joe*.

As a motion-picture genre, the Hollywood World War II propaganda film—with its red-white-and-blue storyline—reassured the nation that victory was right around the corner. After all, Humphrey Bogart broke up an

Axis plot to demolish the Panama Canal. And Van Johnson positioned his B-25 right over Tokyo and bombed that city. Bow your heads for Vladimir Sokoloff, who defied his Japanese captors, refusing to lower the American flag. Do not overlook Wallace Beery. This overage sergeant snagged some saboteurs outside his base. Do not forget Randolph Scott. He guided his corvette safely to the Irish coast. And tip your hat to Tyrone Power. He and his submarine crew blew up a strategic Nazi oil depot. Clap your hands for the Andrews Sisters and their wonderful songs about Old Glory. Show appreciation to George Montgomery and his flying skills. How many Japanese Zeroes were destroyed over China? Wave a flag for Errol Flynn, who trekked many Canadian miles to capture a stealthy fifth columnist. Say a prayer for Comrade Dana Andrews. He crashed his Russian aircraft into a row of Nazi tanks to halt their offensive. Give Captain Don Ameche some credit for his fancy aircraft carrier maneuvering. And what about Robert Taylor, who sank a Japanese vessel? And stand up and cheer for Blondie, Dagwood, Mr. Dithers, and Daisy. Collectively, their home-front work brought their nation one step closer to victory.

By early 1945—as the Allies pushed eastward toward Berlin, and Japanese cities smoldered in ruins from U.S. bombing raids—the motion-picture industry toned down its propaganda-film production and, instead, returned to traditional entertainment. Why not? the moguls asserted. The war was basically over, and audiences no longer needed reassurances their side would win. Besides, a good comedy or musical feature brought in greater revenue. Months later, the announcement finally came. A beaming President Truman proclaimed that after four years of sacrifice, the Second World War had ended. As the country celebrated, Hollywood also took its bow. During the conflict, their photodramas—an important component of the victory effort—galvanized the nation. These propaganda films, for better or worse, offered hope during the darkest hours and jubilation in days of triumph. And now these motion pictures were no longer needed. Their work was completed.

For Hollywood, the Second World War was far from over, because moviegoers—still interested in a subject that for the most part contained death, destruction, and brutality—wanted more frontal assaults, European bombing raids, and hand-to-hand combat. Why was this? Why did audiences enjoy World War II films? Did they create a chauvinistic, self-congratulatory mood? Or was it something more basic? A primordial function? An atavistic need? Does anybody know? For the motion-picture entrepreneurs, this subject, the pivotal event in twentieth-century history, became money in the bank. Hollywood returned to this war on a monthly basis, churning out one show after another catering to current public tastes and changing ideologies.

Some of these pictures waved Old Glory, others denounced U.S. officers, goldbrickers, 4-Fs, and opportunists. A few dramas poked fun—either in burlesque or black comedy format—at historical events, citing the conflict's absurd nature, while a handful of revisionist screenwriters penned the Axis foes as kindhearted and gentle people. Some blockbuster titles won cinematic awards, while lesser B-stories vanished into oblivion. Many pictures offered explanations for battles, campaigns, and mistakes, while a handful focused on larger-than-life commanders, generals, and presidents. For budgetary reasons, screenplays were made in overseas locations, utilizing unknown foreign actors, anachronistic equipment, and unsynchronized dubbing. Some photodramas were blatantly antiwar, even accusatory, depicting American servicemen in pejorative terms.

What prompted such an abrupt change? For Hollywood, one event explained everything: the World War II propaganda film ended—not with a bang, but with a whimper—on a large battleship, moored in Tokyo Bay, on a historical September 1945 morning. In that fateful hour, America no longer needed its motion-picture heroes. Now these remarkable men could leave quietly, echoing Walt Whitman's sentiments, "The ship has weather'd every rack, the prize we sought is won."

Chapter Two

Victory and Memory

1946–1949

"You've been watching too many war movies."—Colonel Vince Johnson (Powers Boothe) badmouthing his oversexed wife, Jessica Lange, in Tony Richardson's 1994 exposé of army nuclear testing shenanigans, *Blue Sky*

"I hate war movies."—Mrs. Johnson's surly reply

On September 2, 1945, a group of diffident, high-ranking Japanese officials—many of them incongruously decked out in formal attire, including top hats and walking sticks—stood demurely in the hot morning sun on the U.S. battleship *Missouri*'s starboard side anchored in Tokyo Bay. Here, these worried delegates listened nervously as the American war hero and newly appointed occupation director, five-star general Douglas MacArthur, still puffing on his worn-out corncob pipe, dictated the surrender terms and peace conditions. A few minutes later, these Japanese dignitaries affixed their signatures on the surrender document. At that moment, witnessed by hundreds of stern-faced American GIs jammed into the backdrop, the Second World War was finally over.

Back on the home front, the elaborate celebration that started on August 15 was winding down. For two weeks, merriment became the chief order of the day. Strangers danced together in the streets, motorists honked their horns, church bells rang out, and in Times Square a jubilant sailor, wearing winter blues with his hat tilted at a rakish angle, smooched an unsuspecting nurse while a few feet away, Alfred Eisenstaedt snapped their picture.

For Hollywood, the surrender meant a quick return to normalcy. Now the studios could shelve those propaganda films and concentrate on new material. How about more romance with fancy clothing and stylish prancing or some musical comedies with plenty of laughs? As entrepreneurs, the production heads knew that American audiences were tired of war movies. Entertainment, not combat, was the ticket for financial success. Give the public some fun and happiness.

True, a few war pictures were still in production, but their release in late 1945 or early 1946 merely brought closure to the global conflict. MGM's *They Were Expendable* placed Robert Montgomery in the thick of the South Pacific fighting, while over in the Italian theater, RKO's *Step by Step* paired Lawrence Tierney and Anne Jeffreys as two innocents who grabbed some California fifth columnists. Fox's *A Walk in the Sun* downplayed an army squad's routing of a Nazi stronghold a few miles from the Salerno invasion. Back in New York, the FBI, always vigilant and led by Lloyd Nolan, broke up an Axis spy ring working out of the Yorkville section in Fox's *The House on Ninety-Second Street*. MGM's *The Courage of Lassie* pitted America's favorite collie against Japanese soldiers, while RKO's B-meller, *The Bamboo Blonde*, showed off a B-29 crew's fighting skills, and Columbia's *Out of the Depths* extolled the fast-moving naval officers who prevented a Japanese suicide attack against the USS *Missouri*, moored in Tokyo Bay, minutes before the surrender document was signed. Similarly, three titles heaped praise on the Allied espionage network—Warner Bros.' *Cloak and Dagger*, Paramount's *O.S.S.*, and Fox's *13 Rue Madeleine*. Finally, one screenplay put the matter to rest: United Artists' *A Night in Casablanca*, the Marx Brothers' zany war-picture spoof. Clearly, the laudatory days of World War II filmmaking, as personified in more than four hundred propaganda movies that glorified Allied intransigence, were over. Now, after fighting in Uncle Sam's armed forces these four years, Marion Morrison could put his khakis in mothballs and, without missing a step, mount his horse—with guns blazing and eyes hell-bent for leather—and gallop back to the range.

Why not? By now, American audiences wanted enjoyment on their night out, and a good shoot-'em-from-the-hip Western always provided vicarious thrills when the man in white rescued some comely widow from the clutches of a greedy, mustachioed cattle baron. How about some music and romance? Bring out Jack Carson and Dennis Morgan for *A Song, a Dance, and a Girl*. Rather watch some bill-and-cooing? How about Cary Grant and Alexis Smith in *Night and Day*?

But not everyone seemed satisfied with escapist movies. After all, the events of World War II—the greatest political, social, and economic upheaval of the twentieth century—simply would not go away. Thousands of returning veterans, wearing their Ruptured Duck decorations, flooded the workforce, causing unemployment in certain sectors. Racial violence, especially in the South, flared up as Jim Crow laws forced black GIs into direct confrontation with local officials bent on keeping their segregated lifestyle. Other problems included marital infidelity, war profiteering, and short memories. And, of course, there were the wounded veterans who returned to their hometowns with permanent injuries. These disabled servicemen frequently were unable to walk, see, or hold someone's hand.

Soon a few titles emerged that took a hard look at the readjustment many veterans suffered as they entered mainstream U.S. life. Warner Bros. led the way with *Pride of the Marines*, a combat story that featured John Garfield in the real-life role of Al Schmid, a marine sergeant who lost his eyesight at Guadalcanal. Laden with examples of social consciousness, the film—directed by Edward Dmytryk—forged a few swipes at America's three-tier system, pointing out the war was fought both at home and abroad, and it was generally the men from working-class origins, such as Al Schmid, who bore the casualty brunt.

Another photoplay—RKO's *Till the End of Time*—focused on three marines as they reentered California's mainstream middle-class life. Starring Robert Mitchum, Guy Madison, and Bill Williams as close friends, who, like Al Schmid, fought at Guadalcanal, the threesome confronted their own postwar dilemmas. Mitchum, recovering from a head trauma, suffered nightmares, while Bill Williams, unable to walk because of spinal injuries, could not adjust to wheelchair life. Only good-looking Guy Madison, with a modicum of stability, offered some comfort to his pals while romancing a pretty widow. Eventually, the three ex-jarheads confronted some war profiteers and, in an elaborate barroom-fight scene, showed off their Marine Corps stuff. As social commentary, the film fired some lukewarm salvos at stateside opportunism, but its tepid treatment of this ongoing situation seemed mute. That would soon change. Just five weeks after *Till the End of Time* premiered, RKO released a motion picture that defined the World War II experience better than any other movie ever made, either before or after. Finally, an elaborate three-hour film epic detailed—in the simplest of human terms—the high cost, both tangible and intangible, of the Second World War.

Strictly speaking, *The Best Years of Our Lives* was not a combat picture but, instead, an elaborate human document pointing out the frustrations that most returning veterans experienced firsthand as they slowly uncovered the many unsavory practices that abounded on the home front while they were overseas. With an all-star, Academy Award cast that included Dana Andrews, Fredric March, Myrna Loy, and Hoagy Carmichael, the photodrama, like *Till the End of Time*, followed three veterans—now back in their hometown—and their gradual perception about the war itself and its aftermath on family and friends.

Directed by William Wyler, it was no coincidence that *Best Years'* opening scene took place in a large stateside airport terminal where an anxious Air Corps captain, Fred Derry (Dana Andrews)—a recently discharged, decorated B-17 bombardier—pleaded with a ticket clerk about a flight for Boone City, his hometown. No chance at all, she answered sympathetically. It was summer 1946, the fledgling airline industry catered to a civilian clientele, and business was booming. Because the war had ended almost a year ago, servicemen no longer received priority and, like any cash-paying customer, must wait their turn. Why should they have first choice, the scene implied? What do we owe the armed forces? Haven't we said thank you enough times?

Now what? As a well-heeled businessman curtly stepped in front of him to check his golf clubs, Derry's frustration level moved up another notch. Why all those European bombing runs over enemy territory with his life and limb in peril? And what about the numerous deaths of friends and squadron members? What was that all about? To ensure this overage civilian—who stayed behind reaping huge profits from the matériel industry—an airline seat, always at his beck and call, clean and comfortable.

In this opening sequence—less then one minute of script time—William Wyler's taut direction established the confrontational theme that continued for three more hours. Simply put, the war, now over, no longer prevented most Americans from pursuing the good life. Normalcy prevailed: no more rationing, blackout shades, food points, and gasoline stickers. And what about returning veterans? Give them a hearty pat on the pack, a few governmental handouts, and a victory parade. No more special privileges. Here, in this municipal airport—surrounded by well-dressed, well-fed civilians—came the moment of truth for Derry. Stranded, pushed aside by some golf clubs, what was next? How would he get home?

If the civilian world would not help, how about the military? "You might try the ATC, Captain," the ticket agent proffered, "off the terminal, to the right, across the field." Minutes later Derry—his name on a makeshift boarding list, his B-4 bag nearby—was standing in the modest operational room of the Air Transport Command, surrounded by dozens of GIs, sailors, and marines milling around, grabbing seats on space-available military aircraft. While Derry waited for the call, a quiet seaman, Homer Wermels (Harold Russell), stared pensively at the wall, mulling over the future. Already, the tar had balked when some GIs, lifting a skid, called for help. "What's the matter sailor, tired or something?" an Air Corps private sneered.

What was wrong? Why didn't the sailor pitch in and help the GIs move the skid? Was he a goldbricker? A slouch? Derry, eyeing this small interservice rivalry, couldn't care less. Chair tilted, head back on the wall, feet up, he was through with that. Let the army and navy bicker all they want. Finally—after dozens of bombing runs, dodging hundreds of ack-ack blasts, and witnessing untold carnage—he was going home.

Hours later came the good news: "Got a call from Base Ops. There's a B-17 taking off in a few minutes for Boone City." Quickly, Derry—followed by an enthusiastic Wermels—stood at the counter. "Probably have a long ride cause she's making a lot of stops," the NCO explained. "OK, sign here!" At last, the words every serviceman waited to hear. "Boy, it sure is great to be going home," the bombardier retorted. After signing the manifest, Derry handed the pen to the bluejacket. Here, in a quiet, unassuming, and polite manner, Wermels—the navy man, who demurely sat off to the side, lost in his own thoughts—grasped the pen between the two hooks on his right prosthetic arm and wrote his name. Stunned, both officer and NCO quietly sized up the situation. "What's the matter, " the sailor voiced, "think I can't spell my own name?"

Using the hooks on his left prosthetic arm, the double-amputee sailor hoisted his duffel bag, and the two Boone City residents scooted toward the aircraft, a modified B-17. Here, they picked up a third GI, Sergeant Al Stephenson (Fredric March), a tired combat infantryman, who, like any veteran, just wanted to go home. Soon, the threesome—now airborne, sequestered in the snug quarters of this converted bomber plane—recounted their wartime stories. Derry, a former soda jerk in the town's simple drugstore, saw plenty of action in the German skies, while Stephenson, a respected

Smiling from ear to ear, two discharged servicemen (Harold Russell and Dana Andrews) head toward a military aircraft boarding area for their long flight home in William Wyler's story of lost time and short memories, The Best Years of Our Lives. *Courtesy of MGM.*

banker turned ground-pounder, fought on Pacific islands, finally reaching Hiroshima. But Wermels, a shy, ordinary flattop seaman, worked belowdeck. "When we were sunk, all I know there was a lot of fire," he recalled. "When I came to, I was on a cruiser. My hands were off."

What about their families back home, who waited these four long years? Derry, married only ten days before shipping overseas, hardly knew his bride, a Texas beauty he met while in flight training. Stephenson, a husband for twenty years, felt confident about his wife and two children. Only Wermels seemed apprehensive. "Well, you see, I got a girl," he started. "Wilma's only a kid, she's never seen anything like these hooks." Eventually, the all-night talk shut down, and soon all three men, secure in the womb of this B-17, fell asleep.

Using less than twenty minutes of exposition time, William Wyler, a former World War II military cameraman, reaffirmed the uncertainty every veteran knew when the fighting ended and peace was restored. Many, of course, remembered vividly their friends who died during this global conflict. Others, like Wermel, suffered horrendous injuries that impeded any type of normalcy. For the rest, everything was unclear, ambiguous. What awaited them? Could they ever pick up where they left off? Would these veterans—the men who gave their country the best years of their lives—reap the benefits of the postwar society?

Finally, after interminable hours in the air, the new friends reached their hometown airport, and now, sitting in their taxi, each man felt uneasy. As the car pulled into Wermel's street—a pretty, lawned neighborhood dotted with clean single-family houses—the nervous sailor balked. "Say, how 'bout the three of us going back to Butch's place? We'll have a couple of drinks and then we can go home," he suggested. No dice, the sergeant gestured, "You're home now, Kid." After the taxi stopped, the young seaman, shaky and insecure, lumbered out. Wermels, a double amputee, the clean-cut boy next door, the youth who joined the navy to fight for his country, was home.

Probably no motion-picture scene has ever captured the pathos, warmth, nuance, and happiness associated with a veteran's return as these brief cinematic moments when Wermels emerged from the taxi and stared at his boyhood house, recalling the joyous, idyllic moments of growing up on this block. Immediately, his eleven-year-old sister, followed by their parents, dashed out and greeted him. Then Wilma—his fiancée, the sweet girl-of-his-dreams—rushed over. Now what? How could she not see those prosthetics? Looking past the two sets of hooks, she hugged and kissed him. "I'm so glad you're back."

Watching from the taxi window, Derry and Stephenson eyed this wholesome scene with quiet approval, hoping for a similar happy homecoming. A few minutes later, Stephenson, the battle-weary, middle-aged former GI who once dodged Japanese bullets on a South Pacific island, stepped into a swank apartment building only to confront a surly doorman, who obviously was not a veteran: "Just a minute," the man brayed, "I'll have to announce you first." Here was another moment of truth. All those months in the combat zone—for what? Some ill-tempered lip from a mealy-mouth draft dodger? "Put that phone down," Stephenson interjected, "I'm her husband."

Ignoring the man's confusion, Stephenson rode the elevator to his floor and rang his doorbell. What a reception! A teenage son could not believe his eyes while a twenty-year-old daughter beamed. From the kitchen emerged his comely, dignified, and faithful wife (Myrna Loy) who stared ecstatically at her returning husband. Finally, after months of uncertainty, Stephenson—like his newfound navy friend on the other side of town—was home. But unlike the young sailor, Stephenson could wrap his arms around his smiling Milly.

As for Derry, his welcome-home party proved less satisfying. Standing in his father's run-down kitchen, while a few feet from the building, a steam-engine-locomotive train chugged by, the former Air Corps bombardier, the man from the wrong side of the railroad tracks, received his dad's gratitude for a job well done. Only, where was his wife? What happened to the pretty girl he married after a ten-day, whirlwind Texas courtship? "She took an apartment downtown," his stepmother hesitated, while his father added it was near her job. "Some nightclub," he whispered, "I don't know which one."

Nightclub? What nightclub? What did her absence mean? Was she another Allotment Annie, a gold digger? Was he a chump? Had he, like so many other GIs who hastily married before going overseas, been screwed, blued, and tattooed? For Derry, here was another realization. Now that the war was over, what did the future hold? Could he ever pick up where he left off with his sexy wife? Was there a place in this booming economy for an ex-bombardier? Now for a few answers. Leaving his father's tenement district, Derry pondered his fate. This much he knew: nothing would ever be the same.

Here, in less than one hour of screen time, William Wyler's storyline emerged as a caustic social criticism of America's shaky values during the postwar period. Using these three men as his fulcrum, Wyler's cameras followed their ups and downs as each man tried to find a niche in the Boone City prosperity. Wermels, after much soul-searching, eventually married his high school sweetheart while Stephenson, now a bank loan officer, fidgeted uncomfortably with applicants as he pondered their financial woes. As for Derry, his readjustment was more complex. Eventually he located his wife, and, as her unsavory, adulterous past spilled out, he had no choice but to leave. Later, a new romantic interest—with Stephenson's grown-up daughter—would blossom, but first another indignity pushed him against the wall.

Derry's first order of business was finding a job. Before enlisting in the Army Air Corps, while working as a soda jerk at a busy drugstore, scooping ice cream sundaes and malts for local teenagers, Derry seemed content in small-town America. But like thousands of other uprooted fellows—who joined the service and traveled overseas—that provincial way of life, with all its innocence and charm, was inextricably lost forever. No more banana splits or cherry cokes, Derry vowed. After flying all those combat missions, he was ready for something better. But what?

One afternoon, Derry strolled into the old drugstore but was dumbfounded by its upscale appearance. A big chain had bought the owner out and remodeled its interior, transforming this quaint turn-of-the-century shop into a slick departmental emporium. Everything was changed, including the personnel. At first the manager appeared pleasant, but soon his haughty, patronizing mood took over. "We're under no legal obligation to give you your old job back," he cautioned. "Old job," Derry retorted, "I'm looking for a better one." Soon this informal interview soured as Derry's military experiences unfolded. "But, unfortunately," the manager sneered, "we've no opportunities for that [Air Corps bombardier] in Midway Drugs." For Derry, those bitter comments said it all: the young men who fought in the war and were lucky enough to come home, were now at the mercy of the overage 4-Fs and draft-dodgers who stayed behind. Here, in their safe, capitalist, civilian world, opportunism flourished. While he spent three years behind the Norton bombsite—the best years of his life—these stateside civilians gobbled up everything. "I think I'll look around," Derry concluded, "thank you."

A few weeks later, Derry, wearing the familiar white jacket and apron of a soda jerk, stood behind the counter serving customers. What choice did he have? Where could an ex-bombardier find work in postwar America? With his mustering-out pay almost gone and his marriage in shambles, he swallowed his pride and grabbed his old job. As a combat officer, he reflected, the pay was over $400.00 a month. Now he earned $32.50 a week. To exacerbate matters, his boss was a former teenage assistant. At least he knew the ropes: no one needed to show him how to dish out a hot fudge sundae or a bacon, lettuce, and tomato sandwich. What difference did it make? Everybody parroted the same bromide: the war was over.

However, this employment was short-lived. One morning at the counter, Derry listened idly as his friend Wermels and a customer bantered about the war. At first, the stranger seemed sympathetic to Homer's plight—even appreciative—but soon the talk turned nasty. "We let ourselves get sold down the river," the man jeered, "by a bunch of radicals in Washington." One word led to another, and soon a loud argument developed. A shoving match ensued, and Wermels teetered. That was enough for the former bombardier turned soda jerk. Leaping over the counter, eyes riveted, Derry sucker-punched the agitator, sending him crashing into a perfume display. As scented bottles rolled around the floor, Derry knew his time was up. "I'll meet you outside in a minute, Kid." Turning to the manager, he discharged both barrels. "Don't say it chum, I know, the customer is always right, so I'm fired—but this customer wasn't right."

Now what? For Derry, the answer was obvious: leave town and start fresh somewhere else. Next stop: the Air Traffic Command. Here, the former officer stood in the local airport bumming another military ride. No problem with that. A plane, leaving in a few hours, would take him eastward. Killing time, Derry strolled over to the runway's edge where hundreds of obsolete, discarded Air Corps bombers—the cream of America's offensive attacks—were parked ignominiously in the afternoon sun, awaiting demolition. Armament and engine parts, strewed all over the place, transformed this airplane graveyard into an eerie memory of their formidable power, a ghostly recollection of past victories. Pausing in front of a dusty B-17, the *Round Trip?*, Derry could feel those volant days when he was jammed into a turret, carefully aligning a target, and then yelling "bombs away."

Without hesitating, he quickly slid into the *Round Trip?*'s escape hatch and wiggled into the bombardier's pit. Finally, after all these months of readjustment, he was back in the saddle. No more unfaithful wife, loudmouth store manager, or draft-dodging opportunists giving him grief. No more lost dreams or right-wing pamphleteers. Absorbed in his memories, recalling the dangerous European flying missions, Derry seemed stupefied as recessed events slowly emerged. Enclosed in this earth-mother womb, with his eyes shut, throat parched, and body taut, Derry's thoughts meandered back to the ethereal world of air combat. Oblivious to any stimuli, the young man—who left rural America to fight for his country—had, perhaps unknowingly, drifted off to another dimension.

"Hey, bud, what are you doing up there?" Hearing these words, Derry quickly snapped back to reality. Standing in front of the fuselage, a burly man yelled, "Hey, you, what are doing in that plane?" Flustered, he left the plane and backpedaled his daydreaming. "I used to work in one of those," he told this construction boss. "Getting some of them [memory demons] out of my system." The men sized each other up, then, after some introductory banter, compared war stories. Out of the blue, Derry saw an opportunity: "You don't need any help, do you?" The former tank sergeant, who battled his way across Europe, squeezed his brow. "Hey, Gus," he barked down the line, "see if you think this guy can be of any use to us."

What a perfect Hollywood ending: one veteran helping another. Both men eyed each other, and their facial expressions said it all: military bonding—that was the ticket—always help your buddy. Now Derry could stay in town, his readjustment completed. True, many problems loomed ahead, but with both feet on the ground he was ready. Like his two pals, Wermels and Stephenson, he was back in mainstream America. As for the war, forget it, that counted for nothing. Whether he liked it or not, 1946 began a new era. Don't ponder the past, move on.

As a social document, *Best Years* combed through the myriad of problems veterans faced, indicting the different modes of home-front opportunism. While many of the young men went into the service, those who stayed behind reaped countless benefits. Derry's teenage assistant (known as "Sticky") worked in the drugstore and, by war's end, became a manager in the new conglomerate. When Derry capitulated and returned to soda jerking, he endured added humiliation because this floor supervisor—an obvious 4-F—crowed with new authority. Likewise, during the three-year marriage, Derry's wife squandered her monthly allotment check, lavishly entertaining various boyfriends. While her husband constantly endured harm's way, she spent her evening hours as a nightclub hostess, making eyes at anyone wearing pants.

What did America owe its veterans? Everything, according to *Best Years*, and Wyler's storyline, sometimes subtle, occasionally blatant, reiterated that point. Certainly, there was not a dry eye in any theater when homespun Wilma removed the prosthetics from Wermels and was confronted by the reality of his wartime injury. Over in a fancy banquet hall, a few capitalists did not appreciate Stephenson's diatribe blasting the U.S. economic system. While back in shantytown, Derry's simple father, a quiet man from the lower class, glowed with amazement while reading his son's Distinguished Flying Cross citation: "Despite intense pain, shock, and loss of blood, with complete disregard of his personal safety" he told his wife, "signed by Lt. General Doolittle."

After *Best Years*, where could Hollywood go? This Academy Award picture said it all and closed the book on the Second World War. Why not? It was time for the moguls to churn out traditional entertainment or escapist titles. No more war pictures; instead of watching American GIs mounting barbed steeds, postwar audiences applauded when hoofers like Donald O'Connor clicked his heels or when crooner Bing Crosby wowed some pretty lass with his mellifluous melodies. How about Tommy Dorsey's throbbing trombone or Benny Goodman's wailing clarinet? Bring on the dancing, singing, or music. Who needed to be reminded of the war?

So for a brief period—1947 and 1948—only a handful of photodramas used the war as backdrop. MGM's *The Beginning or the End* declassified some of the secrets associated with the Manhattan Project, while Paramount's *Golden Earrings* allowed British officer Ray Milland, now disguised as a *Mitteleuropa* gypsy—with Marlene Dietrich's help—to elude Gestapo agents. On a lighter side, jokester Danny Kaye fantasized heroics in RKO's screen adaptation of James Thurber's classic short story *The Secret Life of Walter*

Mitty. A few titles—MGM's *Homecoming*, Universal's *All My Sons*, Warner Bros.' *To the Victor*, MGM's *Gallant Bess*, United Artists' *Arch of Triumph*, and MGM's *High Barbaree*—reminded moviegoers that infidelity, opportunism, equine loyalty, collaboration, and lost love were universal themes, found both in peace and war, while two B-potboilers—Fox's *Jungle Patrol* and Southern California Pictures' *Women in the Night*—retold the Australian and China fighting in their simple, budget formats.

But the motion picture industry—never known for consistency—soon realized that while most moviegoers enjoyed song-and-dance entertainment, they also needed tangible reminders of their nation's prowess. After all, didn't the United States just win a war? Why keep World War II films on the back burner? Why not celebrate America's victories? After this brief two-year hiatus, Hollywood reloaded its cameras, and soon moviegoers watched Edmund O'Brien climb into his pursuit aircraft's cockpit and, with his fellow pilots, blast the *Messerschmitts* out of the crowded European skies in Warner Bros.' *Fighter Squadron*. Once more, the floodgates opened, and now the World War II photodrama—with all its glories and tragedies, its triumphs and mistakes—became a prominent fixture in theaters everywhere.

Every aspect of the war flickered on the screen. In MGM's B-meller *Act of Violence*, an embittered army veteran (Robert Ryan), now stateside, tracked down his former officer (Van Heflin), seeking revenge for some misdeeds in a German prisoner-of-war camp. Told in flashback, the storyline ignored heroism and, instead, emphasized that under duress, any soldier became vulnerable. After a suspenseful cat-and-mouse chase back in Southern California, the two men confronted each other, and in an ironic twist, Van Heflin's accidental death atoned for his POW actions. As a dark melodrama, *Act of Violence* proved that self-interest, a basic human instinct, overshadowed everything else in wartime. A similar MGM title, *Desire Me*, paired Robert Mitchum and Greer Garson as a Brittany married couple separated by the June 1940 call-up. When the pretty wife learned her POW husband died in an escape attempt, a quiet despondency eventually turned into a reclusive lifestyle. Later, a smooth-talking stranger appeared at her oceanside cottage, detailed her spouse's death, offered comfort and solace, and finally suggested marriage. Unaware of this man's duplicity, the lonely woman reluctantly acquiesced but—in a typical sudsy ending—her husband returned home, assaulted the opportunist, and reclaimed his bride—proving once more the Shakespearean maxim that "love is not love that alters when alteration finds." As a World War II moving picture sharing the problems of a French couple, it defied imagination to insinuate that Robert Mitchum, a well-known, rough-around-the-edges, Hollywood tough guy and the London-born Greer Garson, an actress with a distinct British accent, could convince moviegoers they were two simple Brittany villagers. Likewise, Paramount's *Beyond Glory* told the difficult story of a West Point cadet (Alan Ladd), whose tormented memories of his enlisted-man's North African combat experiences interfered with the academy's rigid discipline system. With the help of pretty Donna Reed, these problems dissolved, and as an added bonus, General Eisenhower delivered the graduation address. Paramount's *Sealed Verdict* recounted the complexities of assigning guilt, as a U.S. major (Ray Milland), examining a Nazi general's role in some wartime atrocities, found ambiguous evidence that suggested exoneration.

In the Air Corps, other problems abounded. MGM's elaborate *Command Decision* took a hard look at the high casualty rate caused by the daylight bombing raids over Germany. While the British tacticians ordered nighttime attacks—a calculated operation with fewer losses—U.S. strategists demanded accuracy. In this highly charged, all-male photodrama, an American general fought not only the Nazis but also fellow officers and a buttinsky congressman.

Loosely structured on *The Dawn Patrol*, Warner Bros.' 1938 World War I drama *Command Decision* updated a standard Hollywood theme: the difficulty of sending men into risky aerial-combat situations. Each day—from his British countryside air base—General Casey Dennis (Clark Gable) ordered another maximum effort against the German factories that were assembling a jet fighter—an aircraft that, if mass-produced, would blow any Allied plane out of the sky. For General Dennis, these raids represented the difference between victory and defeat. Unless these war matériel sites were obliterated, the European theater, at best, would bog down into an agonizing stalemate. At worst, the Nazis could emerge victorious.

In human terms, the cost was astronomical: forty-eight crews lost the first day, fifty-two on the second, on a target, a staff officer bemoaned, the American people couldn't find on a map. Now what? Should the bombing continue? After a heated discussion, everyone balked. An up-for-election congressman—fearing public outcry and a possible November defeat—appeared penitent, while a senior general—his eye on another star—also demurred. However, off to the side, General Dennis understood the military necessity for the next day's mission. "It's on," he instructed his operational chief, "There's a mission tomorrow, maximum effort."

As a major Hollywood production, *Command Decision* took numerous potshots at World War II politics, blasting the many opportunists who placed their self-interests above the important task of maintaining low casualties. While American airmen routinely risked their lives, their senior officers—basking comfortably in field headquarters—seemed oblivious to the moral question of death in warfare. Instead, they pondered the efficacies of each day's mission,

Two grim-looking Air Corps officers (Clark Gable and John Hodiak) mull over a recent strategic offensive against a German munitions factory in Sam Wood's airborne saga Command Decision. *Courtesy of MGM.*

examining such personal dilemmas as career advancement, interservice rivalry, military appropriations, adverse public reaction to high fatalities, inaccurate bombing runs, and the oft-repeated frustration that—unlike the military troops—the weather could not be controlled. True, this motion picture sanitized aerial combat—no scenes depicted airmen being blown apart from a direct ack-ack blast—but it still pointed the *j'accuse* finger at numerous noncombatants, especially high-ranking personnel, who for one reason or another reaped lavish benefits from their authoritative positions.

Another screenplay that continued Hollywood's examination of the controversial Allied precision daytime-bombing program, Fox's *Twelve O'Clock High* reaffirmed the daily dangers each Eighth Air Force airman experienced when his B-17 left the comfort of the English landscape and headed east toward Axis targets during the fall 1942 offensive. In this screenplay, Gregory Peck portrayed General Frank Savage, a hard-nosed disciplinarian assigned to a jinxed bomber group that no longer functioned efficiently. Here, he observed that military protocol and regulations were lax, pilots were drinking heavily, and morale seemed nonexistent. Soon, Savage implemented changes that gradually transformed this hard-luck company into a well-honed fighting unit. Along the way, he encountered rejection, animosity, antagonism, and, finally, appreciation from the crewmembers, who, stereotypically, learned the difficulties of command. However, Savage's hard work vanished one early morning on the runway, prior to an important bombing mission. In full view of his officer staff, he suffered a complete mental collapse, requiring restraint and observation. His overpowering sense of mission had, in fact, destroyed him.

Released only twelve months after *Command Decision* and directed by aviation expert Henry King, *Twelve O'Clock High* confirmed that the daily daylight attacks—waged by human blood—extracted a high cost from American airmen. At his first briefing, General Savage's draconian instructions, "Write yourself off, tell yourself you're already dead; once you accept that fact, it will be easier to fly," set the tone for the many casualties that followed. Almost devoid of flag-waving antics, this film weighed those myriad personal relationships and psychological profiles found in combat, including self-aggrandizement, elaborate glorification, and overblown egos. Clearly, this motion picture, along with *Command Decision*, exposed a darker side of the European air war.

On a more positive note, Warner Bros.' *Task Force* heaped dollops of praise on the U.S. Navy's airpower, asserting that aircraft carriers won the Pacific war and now, in 1949, would protect the nation against any foreign (specifically, Russian) aggression. Starring Gary Cooper in the role of the indefatigable Admiral Jonathan Scott, the part-fictional, part-documentary storyline traced this officer's twenty-seven-year career beginning with his first carrier takeoff in the early 1920s, then into the congressional appropriations battle where isolationists opposed military funding, and finally, World War II, where the navy warships proved a major component of the armed service. Unlike *Command Decision* or *Twelve O'Clock High*, this motion picture downplayed the heavy combat losses. Instead, it glamorized all facets of seagoing victories, as America's powerful Pacific fleet, spearheaded by its flattop warships, pulverized the Japanese into ignominious defeat.

Still other titles appeared in 1949 that recounted different aspects of the War. Fox's *I Was a Male War Bride* poked fun at the marriages between American GIs and their foreign spouses, spoofing the bureaucratic difficulty of arranging stateside passage. Here, Cary Grant, a French army captain, married an American officer, and the twosome faced a red-tape dilemma: how to enter the United States as man and wife. Actually a male war "bride," Grant donned women's clothing, hoping this distaff disguise would bring him to America's shores because military regulations did not cover his unusual conjugal situation. In Columbia's *Jolson Sings Again*, Larry Parks portrayed the popular songster Al Jolson as he entertained the troops in various combat zones. Now, a new generation of fans applauded the singer who—back in the thirties—made "Sewanee" a household word. Warner Bros.' *My Foolish Heart* recounted the anguish a young woman endured after her GI sweetheart died in a training accident. Starring Susan Hayward and Dana Andrews, this soap opera ignored combat heroics and, instead, concentrated on the heartache associated with lost love. RKO's sixty-three-minute meller *The Clay Pigeon* put an American seaman into first gear after he spotted a former Japanese prison guard hiding out in a California town. Once again, the Hawaiian-born actor Richard Loo—famous for his fanatical roles—portrayed another Japanese villain brought to justice by a fast-moving bluejacket.

A few more photodramas returned the war to American audiences, but in different formats. MGM's *Malaya* heated up the Southeast Asian peninsula, where two American mercenaries, Jimmy Stewart and Spencer Tracy—in a series of make-believe adventures—hoodwinked their Japanese occupiers by smuggling huge quantities of unprocessed rubber to a nearby U.S. Navy ship. Basically devoid of any realism, *Malaya* contained many flimsy situations, suggesting that the Japanese military commanders were nothing more than overblown bags of wind. However, United Artists' *Home of the Brave* was a different matter. Here a black GI (James Edwards), fighting on a South Pacific island, experienced racial gibes from his fellow soldiers, causing hospitalization for paralysis hysteria. With the help of a psychiatrist, the root of his physical breakdown—he could not move his legs—was traced to an inferiority complex about being a black man in a white world. For a 1949 movie, *Home of the Brave* opened new doors by attacking America's two-tier racial-segregation system and blatantly criticized the military for maintaining this policy. Who were the real enemies in the South Pacific, the film asked, the Japanese hiding in the jungle or the southern GIs loathing most black people?

Still the European fighting continued. MGM's *Battleground* replayed the 1944 Christmas defensive at Bastogne, where thousands of American troops dug in as the German war machine, now with its back to the wall, launched its last hurrah. Hampered by the coldest Belgian winter in recent memory, the U.S. front lines, caught completely off guard, resembled a fragile protuberance on the military map as the *Wehrmacht* pushed forward, hoping to press the Allies back into the sea. Eventually, the GIs reassembled and—with a lucky break in the weather—repelled the German attack. In retelling this famous Battle of the Bulge saga, director William Wyler followed the adventures of one airborne platoon, highlighting each man's fears, aspirations, and anguish in this forest battleground.

Starring Van Johnson, John Hodiak, and James Whitmore as hardened members of the 101st Screaming Eagles, an outfit known for its esprit de corps, *Battleground* bared the frustrations every combat GI knew as supplies dwindled, rumors replaced information, casualties mounted, and cold weather prevented uninterrupted sleep or cooked meals. For over two cinematic hours, this squad—a microcosm of faraway American life—shared its laughter, joys, and sorrows as each man mused the same question: would he live through this battle, this war? As Private Van Johnson bantered, "I'm just a PFC—praying-for-civilian."

With the platoon as motif, *Battleground* downplayed heroics and emphasized each man's introspection as they pondered their fate. One GI fiddled with dentures, wondering if their loss would constitute reassignment out of the combat zone, another trooper waited anxiously for an official letter approving a hardship discharge, while happy-go-lucky Johnson just needed a few minutes to scramble some peculated eggs. Another dogface pooh-poohed the *Stars and Stripes*, mocking this newspaper's sanitized reporting, while a young replacement, the Kid, searched for an old buddy. Amid the occasional death and misery, *Battleground* eschewed any blame or incompetence but, instead, focused on quiet virtues and American values. In one scene, Johnson casually reminded an officer—who stumbled over some Texas-leaguer password information—of the national pastime's importance: "May I suggest, Sir, that you study up on baseball." Later, this same levity appeared in command headquarters when a German major, confused by General McAuliffe's laconic, one-word no-surrender dictum, inquired, "Das ist negativ or positiv?" With a wry smile, an American colonel sneered, "'Nuts'—is strictly negative."

While *Battleground* low-keyed its characterization of heroes by portraying most GIs as nonbelligerent, Republic's *Sands of Iwo Jima* showed viewers the other side of the coin by glorifying the U.S. Marine Corps' many Pacific island victories. Starring the indomitable John Wayne as Sergeant John Stryker, *Sands* followed a rifle squad from their early fighting at Guadalcanal, then on to Tarawa, and, finally, to the lava beachheads of Iwo Jima, where they watched in awe as six marines raised the American flag on Mount Suribachi in a scene that can only be described as breast-pounding. Probably no Hollywood picture made since V-J Day inspired such patriotism, pride, and loyalty as this 1949 production. Has any movie ever equaled it? Probably not. Was this film—released during the Cold War—a strong warning to the Soviets? Without question.

Directed by Allan Dwan, *Iwo Jima* began in elaborate Hollywood fanfare. First, Republic Pictures' logo—the outstretched eagle—stood defiantly as the Marine Corps hymn blared, followed by the semper fidelis emblem, superimposed by the screen credits that included a dedication for valor that "left a lasting impression on the world and in the hearts of their countrymen." Also listed were the three surviving flag raisers—Rene Gagnon, Ira Hayes, and John Bradley—captured in the photo taken by Joe Rosenthal, who played cameo roles. Then, the omniscient voice-over introduced the photoplay. "This is the story of marines," the narrator intoned, "a rifle squad." What a rip-roaring opening. Where was this picture heading? Only one place—victory.

Why not? With America's best fighting man, John Wayne, riding roughshod over his charges, his familiar cry, "Saddle up," echoed the Marine Corps' credo for tough training. "You joined the Marines because you wanted to fight," he bellowed, "well, you're going to get your chance and I'm here to see that you know how." In the end, of course, his martinet policies paid off. Each man, now ready for combat, owed part of his survival to the sergeant's persistence. But for Wayne/Stryker, it was a different matter. Basically a fatalist, he understood his father-figure/tragic-hero role and seemed ready for the inevitable. Charging up a volcanic hill, at the exact moment the Mount Suribachi flag was raised, a sniper's bullet pierced his heart. Stunned, his squad balked in disbelief. After a few reflective moments—while an unfinished letter, written by Stryker to his son, was read—the marines stood tall. "Saddle up," a private mimicked, "let's get back into the war."

As a 1949 Hollywood Film, *Sands of Iwo Jima* glorified every facet of World War II, recalling such previous propaganda titles as *The Purple Heart*, *Gung Ho*, *Wake Island*, and *Thirty Seconds Over Tokyo*. Standing alone, John Wayne, the leader of a finely tuned Marine squad, personified the best of America's military. Here was a film character that refused to take no for an answer, a rough-and-ready fighter willing to stand up for his beliefs. Without question, John Wayne, this former B-actor and stunt cowboy—who, after many trials and errors on Poverty Row, metamorphosed into an indelible, blast-'em-from-the skies, hard-drinking, fist-flying, anti-Communist image—articulated a mythic adventure that kneaded a nation's psyche during this foreign war. Unknowingly, *Sands of Iwo Jima* became Wayne, and Wayne became America. Then what happened? Did America become Wayne?

Probably. How far does an icon's mystique travel? In 1976 Vietnam veteran Ron Kovic wrote in his best-selling indictment, *Born on the Fourth of July*, that watching John Wayne in *Sands of Iwo Jima* inspired him to join the Marine Corps and volunteer for combat. For Kovic, the ineffaceable John Wayne image in Iwo Jima—the unrelenting sergeant who charged a Japanese pillbox, pulled the safety from his explosives, tossed the pack into the enemy's lair, and then somersaulted away—said it all. Why hold your manhood cheap? Next stop: the dotted line.

As the prototype recruitment film, *Iwo Jima* rammed heavy doses of patriotism down American moviegoers' throats with its many red-white-and-blue scenes proving, once again, the Marine Corps would fight their battles in the air, on land, and sea. True, it took John Wayne four years to kick off his cowboy spurs, change into khakis, grab a rifle, and blast away at enemy snipers, but his return brought new meaning to Old Glory. As the decade came to an end, America's World War II memories really boiled down to one man and one movie. What was World War II all about, a youngster might have asked back in 1949? How did we win the war? Who were our heroes? Easy answer. Go watch John Wayne—the marine with steely eyes, taut muscles, and poised fingers—charge up the ashen hill in *Sands of Iwo Jima*. On that hot February day, America won the Second World War.

Chapter Three

The Cold War Turns Hot
1950–1953

"I didn't see you at our movie tonight. I thought Errol Flynn was your kind of guy."—Navy doctor Scott (Richard Thomas) poking fun at a fellow officer in Robert Iscove's 1990 harrowing tale of shipwreck survival, *Mission of the Shark*

"Actually, I don't find motion pictures about the war all that informative."—Marine captain Wilkes (David Caruso) explaining his absence.

"No, well, they're meant for the civilian population, I imagine."—Dr. Scott's rationalization.

During the final week of January 1950, president Harry S. Truman, at a dramatic news conference, promised the nation that—unlike many Eastern European countries now trapped behind what Winston Churchill had recently labeled the Iron Curtain—the United States would never capitulate to Communist expansion. To ensure our safety, the chief executive stressed, a new retaliatory weapon, the hydrogen bomb, was basically operational. For many Americans, the White House's strong words evoked a ten-year-old rhetoric, reminiscent of President Roosevelt's fireside chats. What did this announcement mean? Was war with the Soviet Union inevitable? Would young servicemen fight another global conflict? Could atomic weapons fall on American cities? Certainly, it wasn't easy—as the popular songster, Evelyn Knight, warbled—to powder your face with sunshine.

While the question of a future war loomed ominously, many Americans—looking for the elusive better life—turned their attention to a novel entertainment format, the television set that by 1950 was quickly becoming a permanent home fixture. Each night millions of viewers plopped down in front of their twelve-inch black-and-white screens to catch the Paul Whiteman, Fred Waring, or Aldrich Family shows. In the afternoon only test patterns were available. As most demographers prophesied, this electronic medium, now in mass production, would transform the nation's social, economic, and political life.

Hollywood, of course, could read the handwriting on the wall. As more people purchased these sets—a Philco cost $199, a TeleKing was $159, and for the well-heeled, a DuMont Rumson was $329—motion-picture attendance edged downward. Now people could watch their favorite movies from the convenience of their home. No more nightly walks to the neighborhood shows and, for the practical-minded, no admission charges. However, one drawback offered the moguls some optimism. Television networks could not air current films. Instead, they reached back to the many photodramas from the thirties and early forties. So the movie industry had this one advantage. If audiences wanted to see a recent title, they still needed theaters.

As for the Second World War, many viewpoints prevailed. For ex-servicemen—especially combat veterans—that four-year event evoked painful recollections that, realistically, would never go away. In many households, Gold Star mothers still agonized on Memorial Day as elaborate civic parades and religious services remembered the many deaths required for victory. Still others saw the war in distant terms, stating it was time to move on and forget the past. One large group, however—the young men called into military duty by the selective service system—heard about the war on a daily basis as their drill sergeants reminded the draftees about the lessons learned from the recent conflict and their possible application against a new enemy, the Soviet Union.

As expected, Hollywood continued to churn out World War II feature films that—in one way or another—still glorified America's dominance. In early February, Fox released *When Willie Comes Marching Home*, an offbeat tale that starred song-and-dance-man Dan Dailey as a West Virginia GI who, despite his best persuasive efforts, remained stationed near his home. After some wheeling and dealing, this happy-go-lucky lug convinced his superiors to send him behind enemy lines, where he procured strategic information. His homecoming, however, downplayed this secret mission, much to the townspeople's chagrin. Modeled after the Preston Sturges 1944 madcap comedy, *Hail the Conquering Hero*, this updated version likewise lampooned unbridled patriotism. On a more somber note, Fox's *Three Came Home* dramatized the harrowing events in a Japanese prisoner-of-war camp. Here Claudette Colbert and her four-year-old son suffered many indignities in a Borneo compound, under their captors' draconian rule. Based on the novel by Agnes Newton Keith, *Three Came Home* indicted the Japanese for their hatred of all Caucasians.

Over in the European theater, Paramount's *Captain Carey, U.S.A.* placed a former army officer (Alan Ladd) in Italy months after the war to hunt down a renegade foe. After a few setbacks involving some stolen art treasures, he found the traitor and, as a bonus, an old girlfriend. Up in northern Germany, Fox's *The Big Lift* highlighted every aspect of the 1949 Berlin Blockade, depicting the air force's herculean effort to supply the old capital after the Russians imposed their cordon. One afternoon a former POW (Paul Douglas) bumped into the *Wehrmacht* soldier who had abused him six years earlier, and now with the tables turned, the confrontation offered retribution. As with *Three Came Home*, this screenplay reiterated the cruelty inflicted upon American captives.

However, on June 25, 1950, stateside television viewers stared incredulously as news commentators interrupted their Sunday-night programs to announce the North Korean army had crossed the demarcation line—formed by the thirty-eighth parallel—pushing toward Seoul. Vowing to stop this Communist aggression, Truman ordered combat troops into this faraway peninsula. Within hours, U.S. soldiers stationed in Japan were hastily dispatched into the fighting zone and told by their commander, World War II conqueror General MacArthur, to halt the advancement. Euphemistically dubbed a police action, the Korean struggle would seesaw for three years, resulting in approximately fifty-four thousand American deaths until a July 1953 armistice agreement was signed.

Within the first weeks of this unexpected conflict, the Hollywood machine reloaded its cameras and after a shaky start released its first Korean conflict screenplays. Titles such as Eagle Lion's *Korea Patrol*, Lippert's *The Steel Helmet*, RKO's *Tokyo File 212*, and Fox's *Fixed Bayonets* glorified fast-moving GIs blowing up a bridge, surviving a POW massacre, knocking off a Communist spy ring, and attacking from a cave hideout. While these motion pictures exalted American prowess and promised victory, the newspaper accounts of the hostilities told a different story. After winning an important battle at Inchon in September 1950, U.S. forces ran into stiff opposition as thousands of Chinese "volunteers"—now part of the North Korean military—curtailed further advancement. To exacerbate matters, Truman, in a sudden volte-face, relieved America's popular hero Douglas MacArthur of his command when the general, hoping for a quick triumph, threatened to bomb China.

What happened? How could the nation's greatest champion—the larger-than-life officer who kept his I-Shall-Return promise to the Philippines—fall from grace? Did this mean that the United States, the indisputable victor of the Second World War, would suffer its first defeat? Against an Oriental foe? At least in the movie houses, Americans found comfort with past glories as their popular male stars continued to blast their Axis foes at every turn, reminding audiences that no matter who the adversaries were, the republic would prevail.

While Hollywood slowly fine-tuned its Korean battle stories, the stable World War II photoplay—also in full production—offered tangible proof of the nation's military strength. Early in the police action, titles such as Columbia's *Okinawa*, Fox's *An American Guerrilla in the Philippines*, RKO's *Flying Leathernecks*, Warner Bros.' *The Tanks Are Coming*, MGM's *Go for Broke*, and Universal's *Target Unknown* were released. These recapped Japan's kamikaze defeats, navy steadfastness behind enemy jungle lines, marine airpower, a tank sergeant's heroism, the nisei's role in routing Hitlerism, and fast-moving GIs battling in Nazi-occupied France. Other screenplays—Warner Bros.' *Operation Secret*, Columbia's *Eight Iron Men*, Universal's *Red Ball Express*, Allied Artists' *I Was an American Spy*, and Republic's *Fighting Coast Guard*—re-created a traitor's perfidy in an Allied division, a squad's perseverance to thrash the Germans, the pertinacity of an integrated outfit that drove trucks supplying the Normandy breakout, a Manila chanteuse's bravery against the Japanese, and the Coast Guard's skill in pounding the Axis.

Still other motion pictures idolized past victories: Universal's *Mystery Submarine* heralded a U.S. officer's role in destroying a German *Unterseeboot* operating furtively off the South American coast; Republic's *The Wild Blue Yonder* saluted the B-29 crews' many Pacific triumphs and allowed two fliers, in their spare time, to woo the same nurse. Another Republic B-formula, *Thunderbirds*, also venerated Air Corps pilots and their wartime role in Italy. Again, two airmen, during their idle moments, chased the same girl. Allied Artists' *Flat Top* exalted the training and combat record of aircraft carrier aviators while Paramount's *Submarine Command* traced a naval officer's role in both World War II and Korea and the heavy burden involved with life-and-death decisions. Warner Bros.' *Breakthrough* told the rousing story of an American infantry unit from its basic training to the Normandy invasion, where an eager platoon fought diehard Nazis. As one GI bragged, "Nobody breaks through those stinking hedgerows—you got to fight for each one, sixty, seventy yards at a time."

Occasionally a few titles departed from the God-is-on-our-side storylines established years earlier by the propaganda films. Two Fox releases, *The Desert Fox* and *The Desert Rats*, heaped praise on the military skill of Field Marshal Rommel, downplaying his role as an adversary, while Columbia's *El Alamein* applauded the English troops for North African victories. Fox's *Decision before Dawn* glorified a German POW (Oskar Werner), who returned to the Fatherland as an agent, hoping to glean information that would end hostilities and spare his birth land further destruction. For the young idealist, his mission seemed noble: "I did it because I wanted to help my country and, now, more then ever, I am sure what I did was right." Another Fox production, *Five Fingers*, conversely, glamorized the exploits of a Nazi spy, who surreptitiously photographed strategic British operational orders in wartime Turkey. RKO's *Sealed Cargo* heralded a Newfoundland fishing-boat captain who exposed an intricate Nazi plot to supply their submarines—hidden off the Canadian coast—with fuel and torpedoes. Here, Dana Andrews realized that a derelict sailing vessel was really "a mother ship for the U-boats." With a nod to science fiction, Briskin-Smith's *The Magic Face*, a B-meller, depicted the unlikely story of a German actor who became Hitler's valet, quietly murdered the führer, assumed his identity, and then, without missing a beat, canceled a scheduled British invasion by asserting, "We should deal with the Bolsheviks first."

American casualties were not forgotten. United Artists' *The Men* told the sobering story of some paralyzed veterans and their arduous road to recovery. With Jack Webb and Marlon Brando portraying disabled servicemen, the screenplay emphasized the high cost of the recent victory. Likewise, Universal's *Bright Victory* explained a blind soldier's gradual adaptation to his postwar life. Here, the soldier (Arthur Kennedy), with the help of a sympathetic caretaker, slowly adapted to his sightless world. A similar storyline, Columbia's *Purple Heart Diary*, allowed a mutilated GI to find comfort with a caring nurse. Another Columbia entry, *The Juggler*, offered a somber look at a concentration-camp survivor (Kirk Douglas) and his difficult adjustment, without his wife and family, in the new nation of Israel.

In a different mood, some high jinks lightened up military drudgery. Fox's *You're in the Navy Now* starred Gary Cooper as a ninety-day wonder, working hard to make a decrepit destroyer seaworthy. Inadvertently, he rammed this vessel into a flagship carrier, much to the chagrin of some top-heavy brass. Warner Bros.' *South Sea Woman* highlighted the unauthorized comings and goings of a marine sergeant (Burt Lancaster), who broke up a friend's marriage, fled to a South Sea island, posed as a deserter, joined the French Resistance, seized a Nazi supply ship, and sank a Japanese destroyer, even though he was technically AWOL. Universal's *Up Front*, based on Bill Mauldin's cartoon book, turned the European war into a series of laid-back, breezy moments for two ground pounders, Willie and his sidekick Joe, a streetwise dogface, who crawled through mud and rain exclaiming, "I can't get no lower, my buttons is in the way." On the soap opera circuit, MGM's *Teresa* confronted the problems a returning GI (John Ericson) endured when he brought home an Italian bride, a situation that angered his domineering mother.

Other photodramas, however, explained the war more realistically. The Marine Corps, with its reputation as the first to fight, charged the beaches in Fox's CinemaScope production, *Halls of Montezuma*. Directed by Lewis Milestone and released in 1950, this combat picture followed Republic's *Sands of Iwo Jima* by a few months, and the two titles seemed cast from the same mold. Naturally, no Corps film would ever outdo John Wayne's performance as Sergeant John Stryker, the hard-boiled NCO who blasted Japanese pillboxes, but *Halls of Montezuma*, featuring Richard Widmark as a push-pull squad lieutenant, proved, as always, that the quick-moving jarheads, standing behind their semper fidelis credo, would keep their honor clean.

With the stirring martial refrains of the Marine Corps' hymn blaring in the background and the distinctive anchor, eagle, and globe emblem superimposed over the opening credits, this motion picture glamorized the all-volunteer outfit's go-get-'em daring. Here, in 1944, America's seafaring fighters stood ready to disembark from the safety of their transport ship into a vulnerable, flat-bottomed landing craft that would bring them to the hostile shores of another Japanese-held Pacific island. But this time, a senior officer adjured, the strategy was different. "We used to say," the colonel barked, "that the only good Jap was a dead Jap. That's changed! From here on in, the only good Jap is a Jap prisoner who tells us things."

Now what? How do you capture a crazed enemy that prefers death to surrender? For one company the rules were simple, "Keep your eyes on your squad leaders and platoon leaders." Soon the men applied these principles as they slowly moved away from the beachhead into jungle warfare's terra incognita. Using many of the classical propaganda film tenets, *Halls of Montezuma* focused on the marines' diversity: The lieutenant was a high school chemistry teacher, his medic a South Dakota farmer. Other riflemen—including a boxer, a stutterer, a petty hoodlum, a writer manqué, a brewer, and a Japanese-speaking aesthete—were Guadalcanal and Tarawa veterans. As always, this 1950 motion picture restated that the leathernecks represented all facets of American society, and this eclectic background, a reiteration of national pride, honored the Corps.

Since John Wayne had already seized Iwo Jima, director Lewis Milestone (whose World War II film credits included *The Purple Heart*) realized that a similar victory was needed to establish *Montezuma* as a significant screenplay rather than another humdrum. Instead of assaulting Mount Suribachi, the marines—now embarked on a risky search-and-destroy mission to wipe out a hidden Japanese rocket-launching pad before H-Hour—cautiously moved forward. After a circuitous trek, this tightly knit squad reached the Japanese stronghold and—in an obvious nod to Lewis Seiler's 1943 red-white-and-blue extravaganza *Guadalcanal Diary*—wrecked their Oriental foes, diehard fanatics burrowed in-

A Marine translator (Reginald Gardiner) explains the contents of a Japanese message to his squad lieutenant (Richard Widmark) while another gyrene (Jack Webb) listens in Lewis Milestone's Pacific victory adventure Halls of Montezuma. *Courtesy of Twentieth Century–Fox*

side hilltop caves. With this threat eliminated, hundreds of leathernecks, waiting patiently behind their front lines, moved ahead and quickly secured the island.

Certainly, this hard-driving Marine victory, coming months after John Wayne's flag-waving triumph, reassured moviegoers that the same fate awaited those North Korean invaders now fighting on that faraway peninsula. Why not? If John Wayne and Richard Widmark, the best of America's prowess, could push the Japanese off an island, the new enemy was next. After all, in the closing moments of *Montezuma*, didn't Richard Widmark stand up, hand-signal his squad, and order them frontward, barking, "Give 'em hell!"?

Other themes mirrored the war's consequences. Warner Bros.' *Operation Pacific* allowed submarine commander John Wayne many trial-and-error opportunities to unravel a defective torpedo problem and then blow up some Japanese ships while, on the Italian front lines, another Warner Bros.' story, *Force of Arms*, showcased William Holden routing the *Wehrmacht*. During his spare time the good-looking army officer courted pretty Nancy Olson, proving once again Virgil's maxim that true love conquers all, while an army

Romeo (Kirk Douglas) learned, in United Artists' *Act of Love*, that military life was not a bed of roses. Here, the decorated soldier, fresh from combat, found that his Paris command assignment offered unexpected problems when a loudmouthed officer, unsympathetic to any enlisted-man's situation, quashed a romance with a fragile French woman. In another area, tough-talking Richard Widmark—basking in *Halls of Montezuma* triumph—led his underwater demolition team into hostile South Pacific waters in Fox's *The Frogmen*, destroying enemy targets whenever they found them. In Allied Artists' *Torpedo Alley* a former World War II pilot (Mark Stevens), unable to adjust to civilian life, joined the submarine service as a tribute to the men who rescued him years earlier after a failed aerial mission.

Probably the best Hollywood screenplay to explain the Korean conflict era was MGM's *Above and Beyond*, a docudrama depicting the top-secret training of the men assigned to fly the *Enola Gay*, a high-powered, modified B-29 that on August 6, 1945, dropped the first atomic bomb on Hiroshima. With matinee idol Robert Taylor portraying the fly-by-the-book flight commander, Colonel Paul Tibbets, this 122-minute part-history, part-soap-opera drama detailed the intricate crew selection process, the daily, repetitive stateside training flights, the surreptitious trek to the Mariana Islands, and, finally, the early morning westward deployment to the Japanese mainland. Directed by Melvin Frank, this glorification-of-airpower adventure tale reassured anxious moviegoers that the military machine responsible for a swift and decisive end to the Pacific War—by using two nuclear bombs—would defend the nation again, if necessary, by the same means.

With its January 1953 opening date—a time when many Americans feared the Korean War could escalate into a deadly conflagration with the Soviet Union—*Above and Beyond* reaffirmed the popular 1941 propaganda song's slogan, "We Did It Before and We Can Do It Again." Why not? With Robert Taylor in the cockpit bellowing orders to specific crew members, checking and double-checking various control settings, and then pulling back the throttle and screaming off into the wild blue yonder, audiences knew their nation's defense was inviolable. After all, Taylor rode roughshod over his staff, demanding impeccable performance, firing or demoting anyone who sullied their training's secretive mission, constantly reminding his men, "Each of you has a job that could shorten the war." Even his wife— unaware of the reasons for his late night hours, unexplained absences, and vague dinner conversations—patiently endured one frustration after another until that fateful August afternoon when radio commentators interrupted all scheduled programs and told the nation about this historical mission, explaining that for all practical purposes, the atomic-bomb attack meant the end of World War II.

Still other low-budget screenplays showed the diversity of global fighting. Deep in the African desert, a GI mechanic (Rod Cameron) tinkered with an abandoned, run-down Panzer tank and turned it against the Axis in *The Steel Lady*, while over in the Asian theater, Edmond O'Brien's marine patrol captured an important Japanese naval commander needed for interrogation in Columbia's *China Venture*. In Allied Artists' *Fighter Attack*, Sterling Hayden recalled his last combat flying mission over Italy, and Dan Duryea dealt with leadership responsibility in Columbia's *Sky Commando*. Helmut Dantine frustrated the Nazis on his native Greek soil in Lippert's *Guerrilla Girl*, while Alan Ladd, a former U.S. officer turned British enlisted man, fought the Germans in Columbia's *Paratrooper*. Another Fox title, *Destination Gobi*, placed naval meteorologist Richard Widmark deep in the isolated Central Asian desert sending weather reports to various command posts. In United's part-comedy, part-melodrama *Stalag 17*, William Holden, an American POW wheeler and dealer, shuffled in and out of lighthearted situations with his captors in a manner that sugarcoated Nazi cruelty in these prison compounds. As with any motion picture that portrayed the war as one laugh after another, many scenes lacked any reality about the ongoing conflict.

But one photodrama took a hard look at military life and pointed the finger at the U.S. Army, denouncing this organization for its officer-caste elitism, unfettered brutality in the ranks, and harsh regulations. Based on James Jones's acclaimed novel, Columbia's Academy Award–winner *From Here to Eternity* opened the floodgates with its unforgiving, microcosmic portrayal of barracks life on a sunny Hawaiian base, weeks before the December 7 attack. With an all-star cast that included Burt Lancaster, Frank Sinatra, Montgomery Clift, Deborah Kerr, and Ernest Borgnine, this 118-minute moving picture downplayed those John Wayne mock heroics found in most World War II screenplays. Instead, it excoriated the armed forces for a variety of unpleasant practices. Clearly, screenwriter Daniel Taradash crossed the Rubicon with *Eternity*, indicting the military as an undemocratic institution precariously sinking from the weight of its quasi-fascist policies.

In telling the story of the rise and fall of army private Robert E. Lee Prewitt (Montgomery Clift), stationed at the Schofield Barracks Field near Honolulu, director Fred Zinnemann slowly limned every nuance of 1941 military life as most enlisted men—often victims of loneliness, alienation, and insecurity— sought camaraderie through hard soldiering, payday drinking, and weekend catting. But Private Prewitt, with his slow-talking, quiet behavior and tattered postbellum mannerisms, kept away from this crowd and, instead, derived satisfaction from his intrinsic claims about honor and integrity. For this simple Kentucky-born soldier, orphaned at seventeen, the army meant everything. "I'm a thirty-year man," he once reflected, "I'm in for the full ride."

On a bright November morning Private Prewitt, wearing a freshly starched, gig line-perfect, Class-A khaki uniform, explained to his new top sergeant (Burt Lancaster) and commanding officer (Philip Ober) why, as a corporal, he left an easy-living bugle assignment to join a no-nonsense rifle company, a voluntary transfer that, along with other disadvantages, mandated a reduction in rank. Shifting his weight from one foot to another, the spit-and-polish private's explanation seemed hollow. "I was first bugler for two years," Prewitt asserted, "the topkick had a friend who transferred in from another outfit. The next day, he was made first bugler over me. I was a better bugle player." Unimpressed by this answer the captain offered a remedy. "I'm the regimental boxing coach, you know," he boasted, alluding to the numerous photographs on his office wall, "all I need is a top middleweight."

But Prewitt, a one-time contender, quickly demurred, "I'm sorry, sir, I quit boxing." He apologized, detailing an unfortunate event months earlier that resulted in blinding a friend in a military sparring match. "That's why I decided I would quit, sir." Aloof to his subordinate's predicament, Captain Holmes pushed his authoritative button. "Looks to me like you're trying to establish a reputation as a lone wolf, Prewitt," he barked. "You should know that in the army, it's not the individual that counts." Minutes later, the slick-sleeved private, walking across the quadrant with the first sergeant, explained his refusal: "A man [that] don't go his own way, he's nothing." Smiling sardonically, Sergeant Warden retorted, "You'll fight because Captain Holmes wants to be Major Holmes."

Clearly, in less than ten minutes of screen time, the plot of *From Here to Eternity*, unlike any previous World War II photodrama, ignored patriotic themes but instead became a vehicle for social criticism with its inflammatory messages. As an impersonal institution, the U.S. Army, with its low pay, meager facilities, and dubious enlisted-man recruitment standards sharply contrasted the well-paid, pleasant accommodations and elitist selection found in the commissioned ranks. Here, in balmy Hawaii, a lone infantry private, unwilling to join a boxing squad, soon felt the brunt of sadistic field sergeants and unpleasant work details, while his commanding officer, standing in the background, encouraged this treatment.

Other problems emerged. In an unusual turn of events, Captain Holmes's love-starved wife (Deborah Kerr) seduced her husband's first sergeant, and soon the twosome sneaked around the island looking for seclusion. Likewise, Private Prewitt fell for a club hostess, a friendly Oregon girl (Donna Reed), while his new barracks friend Private Angelo Maggio (Frank Sinatra), waving his whisky bottle, smiled approvingly. For Prewitt, this unexpected romance, coupled with Maggio's congeniality, offered brief solace from the miserable treatment on the training field. Finally, after weeks of harsh military discipline, the former bugler, lacking any family ties, became warm and affectionate now that he found both a girlfriend and an army buddy.

Checking out the Hickman Field parade ground, Private Angelo Maggio (Frank Sinatra) envisions a respite from soldiering with a Saturday-night foray into the Honolulu bar scene in Fred Zinnemann's indictment of military authority, From Here to Eternity. *Courtesy of Columbia Pictures.*

But *Eternity* was not a soap opera. Mrs. Holmes, angry that her lover would not apply for a commission and marry her, broke off the affair. For the ramrod sergeant, the whole idea seemed implausible. "I'm no officer, I'm an enlisted man," he bragged. "If I try to be an officer, I'll be putting on an act." As for Private Maggio, another difficulty arose. Caught on a drinking binge that involved guard-post dereliction, he received a six-month stockade sentence, placing him under the heel of a sadistic guard, Fatso Judson (Ernest Borgnine). Finally, following weeks of physical torture, Maggio escaped only to die hours later from blunt trauma. Enraged, Prewitt swore revenge and, in few days, lured Fatso into an alley and after a short scuffle, killed this tormentor. Knifed in this fight, Prewitt squirreled away in his girlfriend's Honolulu apartment to recuperate. For Private Prewitt, the southern idealist who only wanted to soldier, the future seemed ominous.

What future? On Sunday morning, December 7, Japanese planes strafed Schofield Barracks, and immediately the soldiers ran to their posts, firing at the low-flying aircraft. Spearheaded by Sergeant Warden, the troops shot down a few Zeroes and then regrouped at water's edge, ready to repel an amphibious invasion. That evening, everyone's nerves were taut. When a guard spotted a lone figure zigzagging furtively on the beach, he first warned the intruder and then fired. Immediately other sentries pulled their triggers, and moments later they stood over the lifeless Private Robert E. Lee Prewitt, the loner returning to his squad. Sergeant Warden, summoned to identify the body, looked pensively at Prewitt's anguished face and uttered a makeshift eulogy, "He loved the army more than any soldier I've ever known."

As a naturalistic tract, *From Here to Eternity* offered moviegoers their first glimpse of the unsavory elements found in military life. Unlike any previous World War II story, this photodrama raised serious questions about basic rights and rigid authority. Really, how many young men would rush out to enlist in the armed services after eyeing Fatso Judson bludgeon a helpless GI? What mother, with a son in the army, would feel comfortable after watching Private Prewitt spend hours digging an elaborate five-foot hole so a smart-aleck noncom could bury a newspaper? But in 1953, with the selective service pulling men into the army, recruitment was not an issue. The real problem was the Korean conflict. On a monthly quota, thousands of draftees routinely shipped out to stateside basic-training bases and each man pondered the same thoughts: How long would this war last? When would they go home? Or, would they suffer the same fate as Private Robert E. Lee Prewitt, an unknown cipher looking for a modicum of comfort, a fallen victim to a harsh, impersonal system?

Chapter Four

Public Attitudes and Revisionism
1954–1967

"We can tell lies about the good old days in the war."—Detective James Doyle (Wendell Corey) reminiscing with his World War II pal, photographer-turned-voyeur L. B. Jefferies (James Stewart), in Alfred Hitchcock's 1954 thriller, *Rear Window*

"Hollywood just never caught on. In their casting they looked in the wrong places. Well, that's how old Georgie Patton wanted it. He wanted a very couth looking soldier. Sanitized killers."—Former World War II infantryman, Bill Mauldin, creator of the popular cartoon series *Up Front*, featuring Willie and Joe, two dogfaces hoping to make it home, bemoaning that combat offered the GIs little chance for clean clothes, hot showers, and regular meals, unlike the handsome, tidy, and well-fed soldiers portrayed on Hollywood screens

By early 1954 Americans seemed divided about the recent Korean police action. For some, the high death toll—over fifty-four thousand servicemen—was excessive, especially for a seesaw war that, basically, ended the same way it began, at the thirty-eighth parallel. For others, serious questions remained unanswered. What happened? Why didn't Uncle Sam roll up his sleeves and push these Orientals into the ocean? Why did the strongest military force in the world, the nation that eight years earlier brought the Axis scourge to its knees, agree to a stalemate with its Communist enemy? And what about General MacArthur? Why was America's World War II hero removed from command?

The most challenging question involved nuclear weapons. While numerous voices advocated dropping the atomic bomb on Red China, saner minds realized that such a dramatic act would only bring a retaliatory attack from their puppeteer, the Soviet Union. Clearly, this three-year conflict altered the rules of warfare. No longer would a frontal assault guarantee success. As for airpower, what good are destructive weapons if they cannot be used? What choices did the United States have? According to the wags, only one: Hobson's choice.

As public interest in this faraway war waned, the Hollywood moguls—realizing this conflict lacked the visceral qualities of the rousing World War II titles—quietly phased out this genre, and in 1954 only a handful of Korean conflict photodramas opened in American theaters. For the producers, the bottom line prevailed. Audiences were not interested in lost causes, they averred, because ticket buyers wanted clear-cut victories and red-blooded heroes to cheer when the Stars and Stripes, a tangible symbol of the republic's strength, flew defiantly over the enemy's stronghold.

So in 1954, Hollywood—staring at the handwriting on the wall—quickly returned to previous glories, heaping more adulation on World War II victories. United Artists' *Beachhead* praised the U.S. Marines for their tough stance in the Philippines, a feat that allowed MacArthur's invasion fleet untroubled access. Starring Frank Lovejoy and Tony Curtis, this eighty-nine-minute testimony glamorized many aspects of the dangerous, behind-enemy-lines strife. Similarly, MGM's *Betrayed* placed Clark Gable and Lana Turner in the Dutch underground movement, thwarting the Nazis at every turn and allowing the King to utter sweet nothings to the sweater girl: "You're beautiful when you're angry." On a lighter note, Universal's *The Glenn Miller Story* told the quiet narrative of the musician whose snappy rendition of "Little Brown Jug" became a household song, and his combat-related death reiterated the high cost associated with V-E Day. With the venerable Jimmy Stewart in the leading role, this heartwarming movie received accolades from everyone. Another musical, Fox's *Carmen Jones*, offered a GI version of the famous Bizet opera. As predicted, an army corporal, Harry Belafonte—stationed in an all-black unit training for overseas duty—fell victim to the sensuous wiles of an off-base Circe, Dorothy Dandridge.

Another title, Columbia's *The Caine Mutiny*, projected a moral dilemma encountered during wartime service. Based on Herman Wouk's best-selling novel, this screenplay depicted the not-so-glamorous adventures of a minesweeper's captain, Philip Queeg (Humphrey Bogart). Queeg's many shipboard failures, coupled with ongoing irrational behavior, resulted in an unprecedented mutiny as junior officers—fearful of capsizing—seized control of the vessel during a raging storm. Eventually, a court-martial exonerated the accused when a persuasive navy lawyer (José Ferrer) pushed the commander over his edge with rapid, no-nonsense questions, causing an obvious nervous breakdown in the witness chair. But for the victors, their joy fizzled out after their slightly bibulous defense counsel, now on the high ground, berated his charges, "Queeg was sick, he couldn't help himself. But you—you're real healthy. Only you didn't have one-tenth the guts that he had."

As a major World War II feature film, *The Caine Mutiny* posed several ambiguous questions: how many neurotic officers still commanded naval vessels, and at what point can military directives—those regulations responsible for maintaining authority—be overridden? Certainly, Wouk's novel sided with Queeg, with his discernible shortcomings, and, for the most part, the movie echoed those sentiments. Even with Queeg's emotional entropy, the defense lawyer rationalized, this officer deserved respect. "When I was studying law and Mr. Keefer here was writing his stories," he blurted out, "and you, Willie were tearing up the playing fields of dear old Princeton, who was standing guard over this fat, dumb, happy country of ours? Not us!" he screamed. "Oh, no, we knew you couldn't make any money in the service. So, who did the dirty work for us? Queeg did! And a lot of other guys. Tough, sharp guys who didn't crack up like Queeg."

Another screenplay offering similar equivocation was Warner Bros.' *The Sea Chase*, an oversimplified revisionist tract expostulating that not all Germans were rabid, goose-stepping Hitlerites but instead intelligent, sympathetic nationals snared in a vicious system that, by 1939, was out of control. In his most atypical role, John Wayne portrayed a German hero, a sea captain, whose freighter—moored in an Australian port—awaited shipping orders. Then, news of the Poland invasion changed everything. Considered an outcast, Wayne quickly took to the high seas, setting his compass toward the other side of the world hoping to reach his birth land. After much travail and months of perilous adventures—including an elaborate pursuit by the British navy—he abandoned this course and, in a misty, surreal ending, disappeared into a Norwegian fjord.

Was this the John Wayne who dashed between Japanese bullets to blast his foes from their pillboxes? The man who constantly barked, "Saddle up!" to his marine squad? Would audiences accept their red-blooded, anti-Axis fighter in a new role as a good German, a type of spiritual exile, an ironic hero, a citizen who can love his nation but not its politics? Who knows? For all its symbolism, *The Sea Chase* wasn't really a World War II motion picture but, instead, a Cold War metaphor. Here in 1955, as the USSR menaced NATO forces with their saber-rattling choreography, it was time to reinstate Germany—not the Nazis—into the Allied fold against a contemporary threat. Who was the best man for this job? Who could convince American moviegoers that most Germans were oblivious to Hitler's lebensraum? Who could wear a German naval uniform with the same authenticity as any rough-and-tumble leatherneck? Only one person, the plain-talking, in-your-face, flag-waving, Iowa-bred Marion Morrison.

For the next thirteen years, Hollywood continued to turn out an array of photodramas that in one shape or another recalled the World War II glory days when American forces rammed their enemies at every turn. Warner Bros.' *Battle Cry* heaped dollops of praise on the Marine Corps and their many South Pacific victories, as the young men in this all-volunteer unit—led by competent, father-figure officers—leaped out of LSDs, slammed the beaches, pushed inland, and obliterated the Japanese menace. Likewise, Universal's *To Hell and Back* offered quiet admiration for an average soldier, Audie Murphy, a bashful, gee-whiz, Texas GI whose exploits in the European theater culminated with the coveted Medal of Honor. Similarly, in Warner Bros.' *The McConnell Story*, Alan Ladd portrayed the American air ace, Joseph McConnell, expounding his World War II career, his Korean conflict experiences, and his accidental death testing an experimental jet aircraft.

Other titles continued the fight against the Axis in different formats. Columbia's *The Cockleshell Heroes* extolled the surreptitious adventures of some British kayakers as they paddled up a Bordeaux inlet to destroy Nazi warships moored in this strategic waterway. Starring José Ferrer, this photodrama embellished the daring exploits of an exclusive commando unit. Likewise, Fox's *The Man Who Never Was* unraveled a complex espionage tale involving a British cadaver—set afloat in the Iberian Peninsula—which lulled the German high command into false security. With Clifton Webb in the starring role, this unusual story offered some insight about the English intelligence operations. Universal's *Away All Boats* was another Pacific naval tale about an attack transport commander (Jeff Chandler), who, after much trial and error, fine-tuned an inexperienced crew into a precision team that repelled the kamikazes. One anachronistic scene—depicting a black sailor firing at incoming enemy Zeroes—offered a special nod to Dorie Miller, the real-life mess gob who received the Navy Cross for manning a machine gun at Pearl Harbor, probably destroying a Japanese aircraft. Another navy tale, Columbia's *Battle Stations*, highlighted the hard work involved in saving a carrier after a Japanese bomber blow. Here, Richard Boone bellowed many orders to keep his ship from sinking and, finally, after some Yankee intransigence, brought this damaged flat-top back to its Brooklyn port. In Lippert Pictures' B-potboiler *Silent Raiders*, two U.S. commandos (Earle Lyon and Richard Bartlett) knocked out a Nazi communications center hours before D-Day.

In RKO's *The Bold and the Brave*, Wendell Corey and Mickey Rooney routed the *Wehrmacht* in the 1944 Italian hills, while over in England, Tom Tryon, in Columbia's seventy-nine-minute B-meller *Screaming Eagles*, dropped behind enemy lines hours before the D-Day invasion, disrupting enemy fortifications. Paramount's *The Proud and the Profane* placed William Holden in the South Pacific jungle, fighting the Japanese. As in most of his photodramas, the good-looking colonel found a love interest. Another Paramount title, *When Hell Broke Loose*, a low-cost B-quickie, showed off the efforts of a smooth-talking GI sharpie (Charles Bronson) as he broke up an assassination attempt on General Eisenhower, days before the Normandy invasion. Fox's B-picture *Under Fire* put Henry Morgan and three lost GIs in a tight spot when Nazi soldiers donned American uniforms. Eventually, these Axis infiltrators were dispelled. Warwick's *Tank Force* placed an American sergeant (Victor Mature), a GI who tried to assassinate Josef Goebbels, in North Africa leading an escape from a Nazi prison compound. After some desert adventures that included a spy in their group and a flight from a German-sympathizer sheikh, the men seized a Tiger tank and reached Allied lines.

A few soap operas offered personal insights into everyday life. Fox's *D-Day—The Sixth of June* revealed the complexities of wartime separation when a married American intelligence captain (Robert Taylor) could not keep his romantic hands off a pretty English social worker (Dana Wynter), whose husband was fighting in the North African campaign. Eventually, wounded during the Omaha Beach assault, the captain, now older and wiser, proffered a sudsy farewell to his British girlfriend and headed back to his wife. Similar unhappiness abounded in MGM's *Gaby* (a remake of MGM's World War I tearjerker, *Waterloo Bridge*) in which a French ballerina (Leslie Caron), unable to cope with the battle death of her American fiancé (John Kerr), reverted to promiscuity, believing that such unbridled behavior would purge all tormenting memories. When the "dead" sweetheart returned to London, their reconciliation proved that true love never faltered. A similar situation existed in Columbia's *The Key*. Here, a disillusioned woman (Sophia Loren) gave numerous naval men her room key, hoping such romantic trysts would alleviate seagoing dangers, even though one officer (William Holden) exclaimed he didn't want to become "another jacket on the hanger." In Fox's *The Man in the Gray Flannel Suit*, a former airborne captain (Gregory Peck)—ensconced in the New York City corporate world—belatedly learned that his cozy liaison with a lovely signorina during the 1945 Italian Campaign had produced a son. Now married to his American dream girl, some difficult decisions were made to rectify this problem. Down in New Zealand, a marine major (Paul Newman) wooed a steadfast woman (Jean Simmons) in MGM's *Until They Sail*, despite the many frustrations found in wartime separation when American servicemen, away from home for the first time, courted local females.

Similar issues moved forward. For many years Hollywood's portrayal of U.S. armed services officers—those men selected to lead others into combat—was exemplary. No one questioned the skill of Colonel Van Heflin in *Battle Cry*, Commander Jeff Chandler in *Away All Boats*, General Clark Gable in *Twelve O'Clock High*, or Admiral Gary Cooper in *Task Force*. Who

could fault them? Fair-minded, down-to-earth, and perspicacious, these officers, according to filmdom's interpretation, fostered victories through wis-
dom, inspiration, and fortitude even though a frontline captain (Brian Fox in
Breakthrough) could use a grammar lesson after bellowing, "I ain't gonna let
no second guesser foul them up." True, occasional problems surfaced: Captain Humphrey Bogart in *The Caine Mutiny* or Captain Philip Ober, the inef-
fectual company commander in *From Here to Eternity* who allowed his boxing squad to ride roughshod over Montgomery Clift. By their malfeasance,
both men violated their leadership roles and, subsequently, were drummed
out of the service, allowing the officer corps' system to remain intact.

Other officers likewise did not fare well. In Warner Bros.' *Mister Roberts*,
a Napoleonic supply-vessel captain, James Cagney, stood on his bridge bellowing one inconsistent directive after another, in a manner that was both
comical and irrational. Clearly, the crew—infused with loneliness, uncertainty, and boredom—realized that their commander had lost his marbles. In
turn, they looked to a junior lieutenant, Mister Roberts (Henry Fonda), and a
kindly naval doctor (William Powell) for advice and assistance. After many
shipboard mishaps, including the obsessive cultivation of a palm tree, the
captain begrudgingly approved a transfer for his lieutenant, much to the chagrin of the enlisted sailors. But worse news followed. Months later, Mister
Roberts, now on a combat destroyer, perished in action.

As a comedy turned tragedy, *Mister Roberts* depicted a naval captain who
was both loony and paranoid—an officer who had slipped through the cracks
and was given command of a supply vessel—while his foil, the always smiling Henry Fonda, worked unsuccessfully to restore civility in a hostile work-
place. Frequently kibitzing with the crew, the easygoing ensign represented
the best of the commissioned corps while his nemesis spouted one contradic-
tion after another. In many ways, audiences could laugh at James Cagney's
foolery because he posed no danger—his ship was on a logistical mission,
safely ensconced from harm. More of a clown than a villain, his behavior
elicited belly laughs rather then anger or protest. Here was an officer who was
a fool, not an opportunist.

This was the exception to the out-of-control command leaders. Putting
aside the portrayal of high-strung, easily duped commissioned bumpkins in
such lighthearted comic-book stories as *Francis* (a lieutenant and a talking
mule held discourse) or *Don't Go Near the Water* (junior naval officers ran
amok in a public relations section), the irresponsible, incompetent combat officer presented a deadly threat. In Fox's *Between Heaven and Hell*, a psychopathic army captain (Broderick Crawford) ran his frontline Pacific island
stronghold in a manner reminiscent of a medieval fiefdom. Surrounded by ob-
sequious but degenerate goons who addressed him as "Waco," he arbitrarily

punished any soldier who did not kowtow while he heaped rewards on his many sycophants. Almost frothing at the mouth, this officer encouraged brutality and sadism on a regular basis. When challenged by a liberal-minded National Guard private (Robert Wagner), "Waco" exploded with rage, sending the soldier on a dangerous scouting mission.

Would this film play in Peoria? Probably. Released eleven years after V-J Day, *Between Heaven and Hell* provided a replay for many veterans who knew firsthand about those unstable combat officers whose judgments were mired by their numerous mental problems. Clearly, these ex-GIs remembered screwballs like Waco and the misery associated with their command. For these viewers, this motion picture downplayed heroics and, instead, told a realistic story about military life's seamy side. Finally, Hollywood—after years of tap dancing around this sacred cow—broke new ground with this unconventional screenplay. Now, the die was cast; the days of the sanitized officer corps were over. No longer would this privileged caste system's misdeeds go unnoticed.

Why should they? Why should the officers eat fresh meat while the ground pounders gulped down K-rations? Why should the commissioned ranks enjoy showers while the enlisted men remained unwashed? How do you effectively control a rigid separatist system—allowing pleasing accommodations to one segment while denying basic comforts to another—during wartime? These annoying questions formed the backdrop of Warner Bros.' scathing antiofficer, antiauthority photodrama *The Naked and the Dead*, another screenplay that purported the armed services contained a good percentage of unstable individuals. Based on Norman Mailer's naturalist novel, this 131-minute indictment portrayed military regulations and contemporary fascism as two elements cut from the same cloth.

In some ways *The Naked and the Dead* followed a conventional plotline. U.S. Army troops, controlled by a megalomaniac commander, invaded a fictional Japanese-held island, moved inland, attacked their enemy, and, finally, secured every objective. Along the way, one squad, headed by a misogynistic, rabid sergeant, killed Japanese prisoners and—with an eye toward his financial future—extracted their gold-plated teeth, while other GIs either smiled approvingly or displayed disinterest. For the foot soldiers, only one concern mattered—survival.

For the high command, stronger issues prevailed. Standing in his commodious tent and reaching into his well-stocked refrigerator for a cold beer, General Cummings (Raymond Massey), a steely-eyed patrician, offered his young aide (Cliff Robertson) a beverage, explaining that such niceties were inherent with rank. "Every time an enlisted man sees an officer getting an extra privilege," he bragged, "it makes him fight harder." For the Ivy-league-schooled lieutenant, his superior's callous viewpoints jarred his liberal upbringing, and soon a polite, but formal, downward-thrust discussion ensued. "I don't care what kind of man you give me," the commander pontificated, "if I have him long enough, I'll make him afraid." As a concluding taunt he accused his charge, "Under that mask of humanism," he sneered, "you're a reactionary, just as I am."

Clearly, General Cummings's crypto-fascist ideas rattled his aide, but every lieutenant knew the imprudence of contradicting a commander. A few days later, a conversation proved more difficult. In a show of absolutism, General Cummings, his face livid with rage, ordered his subordinate to pick up a crushed cigarette butt or face many years in a military prison. After an unhealthy pause, Lieutenant Hearn, the idealist who espoused humanism, bent over, picked up the butt, and tossed it into an ashtray.

As a reformist film with strong leftist ideals, *The Naked and the Dead*'s weak ending did not spawn much optimism. Lieutenant Hearn, wounded behind enemy lines, recovered and in a syrupy homily, argued that love, not fear, motivated the fighting man (even though in the novel, a Japanese sniper killed him). The misfit sergeant's death seemed ample punishment for his unsociable behavior, and General Cummings, with his autocratic ideas still in tow, remained in power, while off to the side, the foot soldiers grubbed along,

In a rage, a one-star general (Raymond Massey) rebukes his orderly (Edward McNally) for bringing flowers into the command tent in Raoul Walsh's scalding condemnation of autocratic rule, The Naked and the Dead. *Courtesy of Warner Bros.*

realizing another island invasion loomed. Clearly, at the next battle site, General Cummings would enjoy more alcoholic beverages while the enlisted men—those GIs who bore the brunt of combat—sipped their powdered milk.

Another title that hammered away at the self-serving officer was United Artists' *Attack*, a strongly worded indictment that blasted command figures for a variety of opportunistic offenses. Here, Eddie Albert portrayed a sniveling National Guard captain, Erskine Cooney, leading an infantry company during the 1944 French offensive. Completely unfit for a combat assignment and displaying blatant psychotic tendencies, his bad judgments, flagrant blunders, and high casualties frustrated his battalion superior, a fellow southern-hometown politician manqué, Colonel Clyde Bartlett (Lee Marvin). The colonel needed the support of this subordinate's father—an influential county judge—to tout him for public office when the war was over; "Tippecanoe and Bartlett too," he envisioned. At the same time, the platoon's popular lieutenant, Joe Costa (Jack Palance), vowed to protect his men from the irrational behavior of their misfit captain: "If I ever lose another man on account of you, just one, you'll never see the States again," he threatened.

As a 1956 photodrama, *Attack* took American audiences into the officer caste system's terra incognita with all its quid pro quo shortcomings, double-dealings, elitism, cover-ups, privileges, and watch-my-back protection, while off to the side the enlisted men endured poor food, hard work, and constant danger as they wondered what dopey plan their captain would concoct. Even Colonel Bartlett, the man who fantasized about postwar political glories, knew the judge's son was unfit for command but did not want to relinquish that old-boy network so important in determining a stateside election. Rather, he admonished his subordinate, "You're commanding this company for one reason, as a favor to the judge. He always wanted a son, now I'm trying to give him one." But that suggestion was wishful thinking. Within hours, Cooney ordered an attack on a small village. Minutes later a handful of GIs lay dead, the squad lieutenant badly wounded, while huddled in a cramped cellar, an out-of-control Captain Cooney, yelling incoherently, opted for capitulation to the rampaging Nazi forces: "The way I see it, we're trapped! There's only one thing to do—surrender."

Now what? Would this out-of-it officer hand over his squad to an enemy that would probably shoot the GIs on the spot? Could anyone stop him? As the enlisted men watched in disbelief, Lieutenant Costa, bleeding profusely, aimed a pistol at his captain but collapsed and expired before he could pull the trigger. Moments later, Captain Cooney, shaking his rifle toward the GIs, sneered, "I'm still in command here! And the first wisecracker that gets out of line is going to get it right in the head. How about it? Any takers?" Seconds later, a lone shot resounded in the cellar. Captain Cooney—the man responsible for numerous casualties—dropped to the ground, killed by a junior officer, Lieutenant Harold Woodruff (William Smithers). Stunned, the GIs eyed him cautiously. "Good shot," a private uttered, "from the hip." Minutes later, the enlisted men, anxious to protect their lieutenant, took their weapons and, in a solidarity gesture, fired into the corpse. "The Krauts got the captain," a private scoffed, "they got him coming through the door," while another soldier argued, "Look Lieutenant, if ever a man needed killing it's that no-good putrid piece of trash laying there."

Certainly this motion picture pulled no punches with its depiction of those deranged individuals assigned to the U.S. Army's command positions, and this soldier's words clearly emphasized the anger every GI knew when their superiors simply lost it. While Colonel Bartlett and Captain Cooney—two men cut from the same cloth—oozed opportunism in every frame, the junior officer, Lieutenant Woodruff, represented their antithesis. Clear-minded, agile, and resourceful, he understood the dangers the squad faced following Cooney's orders. But was his killing justified? Would two wrongs make a right? Apparently not. In typical Hollywood fade-out, Lieutenant Woodruff—the young officer who witnessed so much military corruption—began the redemptive process by notifying the general staff.

In this Pollyanna ending, director Robert Aldrich abruptly shifted the storyline from hard-boiled realism to Hollywood mush by insinuating that Lieutenant Woodruff would get a fair shake from his superiors. What happened? After blasting the officer caste system for over a hundred minutes, could Aldrich suggest that—according to basic American ideals—the truth would set Lieutenant Woodruff free? Perhaps he forgot the admonition of the PFC down in the cellar, scoffing at Captain Cooney's bullet-ridden body, "Some sharp operator, bucking for his majority, will make you look like a blood-thirsting maniac." Apparently, Aldrich wanted to end *Attack* on a positive note, so he downplayed the private's warning and, instead, waved the flag during the final sixty seconds.

Without question, no other World War II moving picture depicted the officer corps in such derogatory terms as *Attack*. Years later, of course, titles such as *M*A*S*H*, *Apocalypse Now*, *Dr. Strangelove*, and *Seven Days in May* ran these men into the ground with their nasty depictions of command life, while similar screenplays—*Catch-22*, *What Did You Do in the War, Daddy?*, *Fail-Safe*, and *In Harm's Way*—also took potshots. Another picture, the Academy Award–winner *The Bridge on the River Kwai*, portrayed Colonel Nicholson (Alec Guinness) in a slightly ambiguous role. Released at the same time as *Attack*, David Lean's *Kwai* re-created the ordeal of British and American prisoners of war who were forced to build a railroad bridge in Japanese-occupied French Indo-China. Here a senior officer became obsessed with this project, and cooperating with his captors was either an act of treason or the ultimate

Unable to contain his anger toward an unfit company commander, an infantry lieutenant (Jack Palance) swears retribution for any future mishaps in Robert Aldrich's denunciation of frontline incompetency, Attack. *Courtesy of United Artists*

insanity. Finally, the structure was completed, but the following day, British commandos wired the bridge. In a controversial ending, Nicholson fell on a detonator, destroying his creation. But a bigger question remained unanswered: did Nicholson blow up the bridge as an expiatory gesture, or was his fall merely an accident, caused by his stupefaction and imbalance?

In the late fifties, most Hollywood producers—eager to reap large returns on World War II photodramas—kept the old red, white, and blue at high mast. United Artists' *The Sharkfighters* placed a navy officer (Victor Mature) in the warm Cuban waters until his research team perfected a repellent that would protect downed flyers from the marauding sharks found in both oceans. Determined to protect U.S. servicemen, the no-nonsense commander argued, "There's only one way to prove what we're doing, we must try it with a man in the water." Another seagoing man, submarine commander Ronald Reagan, attacked many Japanese warships in Columbia's *Hellcats of the Navy*, as his girlfriend, Nancy Davis, smiled enthusiastically.

Tough-talking Robert Mitchum kept the enemy at bay in two combat zones: first, as a naval officer chasing a lone Nazi U-boat in Fox's *The Enemy Below*; then, as a stranded marine corporal, protecting a Roman Catholic nun from the Japanese in Fox's *Heaven Knows Mr. Allison*. Another hard-drinking, chain-smoking hero, John Wayne, portrayed the real-life aviation pioneer Frank "Spig" Wead in MGM's *The Wings of Eagles*. Here, Commander Wayne explained his "jeep carrier" idea, an innovative plan to supply depleted flattops: "That's it—jeep carriers, that's what we've been needing."

Other films that glamorized America's past victories included Warner Bros.' *Darby's Rangers*, a salute to the unorthodox volunteer battalion that advanced in North Africa and Italy. Starring James Garner, this spit-and-polish homage cheered every aspect of his maverick fighting unit. Fox's go-get-'em title, *In Love and War*, verified the Marine Corps' prowess as the leathernecks seized another Japanese island. Conversely, Warner Bros.' *The Deep Six* downplayed the quiet conversion of a Quaker naval officer (Alan Ladd), who modified his pacifist views while fighting Nazi forces. A similar moral issue occurred in MGM's *Torpedo Run*. Here, a submarine commander (Glenn Ford) unknowingly sank a Japanese transporter carrying fourteen hundred civilians, including his wife and son. Over in the Philippines, AIP's *Suicide Battalion* highlighted the exploits of two GIs who sneaked into a Japanese-occupied building and destroyed coded documents. Mike Connors starred in this seventy-nine-minute B-potboiler. In southern France, a lieutenant (Frank Sinatra) halted German forces in United Artists' *Kings Go Forth*, unaware that an enlisted man (Tony Curtis), annoyed by the junior officer's authority, sneered sardonically. In another AIP contribution, *Warrior's Five*, an American soldier (Jack Palance), along with five Italians, destroyed a strategic bridge, aided by a pretty national (Giovanna Ralli).

Action pictures always waved the flag. In MGM's *Underwater Warrior*, song-and-dance man Dan Dailey, now wearing khakis, developed the principles of below-the-waves demolition proving, "A man underwater could sink a battleship, foul up an enemy landing, or neutralize a minefield," while Columbia's B-tale, *Tarawa Beachhead*, showed Kerwin Matthews spearheading his squad during this important Pacific island invasion. Back in London, an American agent (Jeffrey Hunter) duped the Axis intelligence service about the upcoming Normandy invasion in Fox's *Count Five and Die*, while a surreptitious second-story man (Ray Milland) was recruited to steal German documents in MGM's *The Safecracker*. A similar storyline appeared in Allied Artists' seventy-two-minute caper, *The Secret Door*. Here, two likable yeggs (Robert Hutton and Peter Illing), expediently released from prison, traveled to neutral Lisbon, where after some cloak-and-dagger episodes they stole a Japanese codebook. Columbia's *The Two-Headed Spy* fictionalized the exploits of Alexander P. Scotland, a Berlin sleeper spy who worked with Hitler. With Jack Hawkins in the leading role, the British Empire remained intact even though the führer (Kenneth Griffith) claimed, "The defeatists! They are the enemy." Another Columbia drama, *Ghost of the China Sea*, placed a seaman (David Brian) in the midst of another Philippine skirmish aboard a dilapidated ship, facetiously dubbed the USS *Frankenstein*. Moving fast, the quick-thinking bluejacket lured an enemy cruiser into an ironclad trap. On another issue, Fox's *The Inn of the Sixth Happiness* told the simple story of an English missionary (Ingrid Bergman) and her many experiences in China under the Greater East Asia Co-Prosperity Sphere.

Not every movie was about combat. Eventually, a few titles surfaced that accented the frivolous side of the World War II experience, motion pictures that downplayed the horror and mayhem and, instead, looked at human nature's droll side. For starters, Danny Kaye and Curt Jurgens romped together in Columbia's *Me and the Colonel*, a screenplay based on Franz Werfel's *Jacobowsky and the Colonel*. Here an anti-Semitic Polish officer and a Jewish refugee, scheming an escape to England, frolicked in a foolish, lighthearted manner. Over in France, Glenn Ford and Red Buttons pushed the comedy button in MGM's *Imitation General*, an easygoing farce about a master sergeant who inadvertently impersonated a one-star general in the countryside during the 1944 fall offensive. Under the waves, Commander Cary Grant enjoyed many laughs harassing the Japanese in Universal's *Operation Petticoat* even though he worked from a pink submarine. On the other side of the ocean, Jack Lemmon and Mickey Rooney schemed to host a madcap, off-base party in a small Normandy town in Columbia's *Operation Mad Ball* while Rossano Brazzi and Mitzi Gaynor rhapsodized about an upcoming enchanted Solomon Island evening in Fox's elaborate musical, *South Pacific*. Universal's *The Secret War of Harry Frigg* offered many laughs as a recalcitrant army private (Paul Newman), sent to rescue five Allied officers from an Italian fortress, outwitted Nazi officials.

Naval lieutenant Jack Lemmon took to the Bismarck Sea aboard a broken-down scow used as a decoy in Columbia's *The Wackiest Ship in the Army*, while over in the Far East, Don Knotts and Ernie Kovacs used their ingenuity to build a fancy hotel from army supplies in Fox's *Wake Me When It's Over*. Later, ABC capitalized on this whimsical theme in a made-for-television yarn, *Wake Me When the War Is Over*. In this comedy a German baroness (Eva Gabor) convinced a bumbling American officer hiding in her chateau—five years after V-E Day—that the conflict was still raging. A similar idea appeared in Paramount's *Situation Hopeless—but Not Serious*, in which Alec Guinness creaked along as a lonesome German national who kept an American airman (Robert Redford) prisoner in his cellar long after the war ended. United Artists' *The Last Time I Saw Archie* starred Robert Mitchum and Jack Webb as two leftovers from a stateside training program for overage pilots, while an army intelligence officer (Jim Hutton) slid from one escapade to another in MGM's *The Horizontal Lieutenant* as he searched for a Japanese soldier still hiding on a South Sea Island. Over in sunny Italy, two smoothies (Charlton Heston and Harry Guardino) spoofed army regulations with their numerous shenanigans in Paramount's *The Pigeon That Took Rome*, while in the North African desert two romps offered more laughs: in Columbia's *The Best of Enemies* a British officer (David Niven) crisscrossed paths with an Italian adversary (Alberto Sordo) as the two armies tried to outwit each other, and AIG's *War Italian Style* paired two American GIs sparring with a high-ranking Nazi general (Buster Keaton) about some phony invasion plans.

Other lighthearted screenplays included Universal's *Captain Newman, M.D.*, in which a stateside army psychiatrist (Gregory Peck) encountered daily bureaucratic mishaps, exclaiming that his office was "short of beds, doctors, orderlies, nurses—everything except patients," while over in the Pacific, Warner Bros.' *Ensign Pulver* continued the *Mr. Roberts* saga as Robert Walker pulled numerous pranks on his dour-faced captain (Burl Ives). Another South Pacific romp, Universal's *Father Goose*, placed an easygoing beachcomber (Cary Grant) in unusual circumstances when he hid a gaggle of schoolgirls from the Japanese forces. Universal's *McHale's Navy* and *McHale's Navy Joins the Air Force* highlighted the oddball antics of a PT crew stranded on an unmarked Pacific island, while United Artists' *What Did You Do in the War, Daddy?* was a madcap spoof of military regulations. In this screwball story, James Coburn and Dick Shawn lampooned the 1943 Sicilian campaign, deriding every aspect of the armed services and prompting an exasperated company officer to exclaim, "The village is in an uproar and I'm queen of the May." Likewise, Paramount's *On the Double* contained laughs aplenty when mild-mannered Danny Kaye impersonated an English general, a ruse that fooled the gullible Germans, while Warner Bros.' harmless frolic,

Onionhead, placed Andy Griffith as a likeable Coast Guard cook aboard a combat vessel that attacked an Axis submarine. Another hide-and-seek romp, Fox's *Kiss Them for Me* gave three navy aces a few days' shore leave in happy San Francisco before returning to Pacific combat duty. Here, Cary Grant chased pretty girls, spoofed military regulations, and enjoyed—as the title suggested—many osculations in the City by the Bay.

Most of these breezy shows seem mute when compared to MGM's dead serious, antiwar, black comedy, 1964 masterpiece *The Americanization of Emily*. Directed by Arthur Hiller and adapted from the novel by William Bradford Huie, *Emily* vacillated between slapstick, satire, exposé, and serious drama in telling the high-jinks story of an admiral's aide, Charlie Madison (James Garner)—stationed in London during the volatile, pre-D-Day invasion—whose main assignment was to provide high-ranking officers with plush hotel accommodations, unlimited alcoholic beverages, succulent food, and friendly women. A natural at this job, the good-looking lieutenant commander weaved in and out of pleasant situations, enjoying the many advantages available to a smooth-talking officer well connected to the general staff. Soon, he courted a comely English war widow, Emily (Julie Andrews), a woman who originally resented his privileged status but, subsequently, capitulated to his boyish charms with one request: "Don't show me how profitable it will be fall to love with you Charlie—don't Americanize me." Frequently at odds with her glib lover, she listened to Charlie's many rationalizations about the goldbricking life. "I'm yellow, honey, clear through," he bragged, "I'm a practicing coward."

His lackadaisical life fell apart when an eccentric senior admiral, William Jessup (Melvyn Douglas)—anxious to create a public relations coup—concocted the perfect plan: "A lot of brave men are going to die on D-Day," he gloated. "The first brave man to die on those beaches must be a sailor." Unavoidably caught up in this cockamamie, steamrolling scheme, Charlie was drawn into the logistical planning and ordered ashore on D-Day with an advance photography team to record this auspicious event. Now, in the early hours of June 6, Charlie Madison, the self-avowed dodger, after weeks of unsuccessful finagling, crouched on a French beachhead, movie camera in hand, as hundreds of bullets whizzed by. "What's the matter with you?" he yelled at another officer, "They're shooting at us." Suddenly, he fell. Minutes later, the news reached London: D-Day's first fatality was a sailor.

Elated by this news, Admiral Jessup ordered an elaborate testimony, complete with medals and a statue, for his fallen aide, while Emily quietly withdrew into her private world of pain. "What was admirable about Charlie was his sensation of life, his cowardly, selfish, greedy appreciation of life," she recalled. Finally, after days of preparation, the tribute was in place. Only one thing went wrong.

Living high on the navy's hog, two smooth-talking officers (James Coburn and James Garner) contemplate their next move as they scheme to fulfill their superiors' every whim in Arthur Hiller's runaway spoof of military shenanigans, The Americanization of Emily. *Courtesy of MGM.*

The first casualties from Normandy were returning to England. In this group, one man limped unobtrusively: Charlie Madison—a well-known opportunist famous for milking the system—had returned. Now what? The first man to die on Omaha Beach was, in fact, very much alive. Without missing a beat Admiral Jessup beamed, "We're going to make a brass-band hero out of Charlie."

As an unruly satire, *The Americanization of Emily* fired off both barrels deriding military authority, unbridled opportunism, male lasciviousness, and mock heroics while giving the thumbs-up signal to men like Charlie Madison. Certainly, in 1958, no U.S. service base would allow *Emily*, a wide-eyed picture that mocked every echelon, in their PX movie houses. Who could blame them? In scene after scene, director Arthur Hiller reduced World War II from a global conflagration to the youthful silliness found at most university fraternity parties: drinking, sex, jealousy, bragging, affectation, role-playing, and gibberish. No wonder this screenplay was taboo. What commander in his right mind wanted his servicemen to watch a film that lampooned regulations, caricatured senior officers, praised goldbricking, and championed unlicensed behavior?

Certainly, most Hollywood productions from 1958 to 1966 contained enough fast action and visceral thrills to fulfill those vicarious experiences enjoyed by many moviegoers. MGM's *Up Periscope* praised the Silent Service for its good work by having a navy commando (James Garner, fresh from his successful *Americanization* role) stealthily infiltrate a Japanese headquarters and remove vital secrets. Nearby, Admiral William "Bull" Halsey routed the Japanese seagoing forces in United Artists' *The Gallant Hours*. With James Cagney in the starring role, this 115-minute hagiography detailed the minute planning necessary for his Pacific Ocean victories and his wartime philosophy, "There are no great men, only great challenges that ordinary men are forced by circumstances to meet." A few miles away, a submarine captain (John Bentley) torpedoed many Japanese vessels in AIG's B-quickie, *Submarine Seahawk*, while another underwater-vessel captain (Cliff Robertson), stranded on an enemy island, relayed important messages to American commanders in Columbia's *Battle of the Coral Sea*. Later, the good-looking Robertson portrayed Lieutenant John F. Kennedy's South Pacific combat experiences in Warner Bros.' *PT 109*. Here the future president used skill and ingenuity to save his crew from encroaching enemy troops. On the Japanese-occupied island of Guam, a young bluejacket (Jeffrey Hunter) avoided capture for three years in Universal's *No Man Is an Island*, while another Universal title, *The Outsider*, replayed the life story of a Pima Indian, Ira Hayes—one of the leathernecks who raised the Mount Suribachi flag—his unaccustomed fame, and subsequent postwar death. With Tony Curtis in the leading role, this motion picture glamorized every facet of the Marine Corps Pacific island victories. In AIP's B-story *Operation Bikini*, a trio of U.S. soldiers destroyed a submarine containing secret information, even though one of the GIs (teen idol Frankie Avalon) paused to sing a few anachronistic rock-and-roll songs. Over in China, the Allies routed their Oriental nemesis in Columbia's B-potboiler, *The Mountain Road*. Here, Major James Stewart, an army engineer, braved both Japanese soldiers and rebel bandits before destroying a strategic roadway.

For Tinseltown producers, the war in the Philippines—against the Japanese invaders—provided plenty of excitement in thirteen motion pictures. Associated Producers' *Blood and Steel* was another B-quickie in which some rough-and-tumble Seabees, led by John Lupton, rescued island villagers, while down on the beach, Michael Parsons battled encroaching enemy soldiers in Hemisphere's *Raiders of Leyte Gulf*. Over in a nearby valley, Keith Andes rallied native soldiers from their hideouts in Allied Artists' *Surrender—Hell*, while Van Heflin deployed ground forces in Allied Artists' *Cry of Battle*, determined, for mercenary reasons, to protect his young charge (James MacArthur), boasting, "No Jap is going to get their hands on this kid."

Myriad's *W.I.A. Wounded in Action* dwelled on developing love interests between wounded soldiers and their nurses in a Philippine infirmary. With Steve Marlo and Maura McGiveney in leading roles, this wartime B–soap opera offered few resolutions. John Saxon eluded the encroaching Japanese army in Hemisphere's *The Ravagers*, while in Warner Bros.' *The Steel Claw*, a Marine captain turned guerrilla and minus his right hand (George Montgomery) routed the Japanese forces during a rescue attempt of a one-star general. In AIG's *Lost Battalion* Diane Jenkins and Leopoldo Salcedo kept one step ahead of enemy troops. Likewise, Hugh O'Brien trekked through this archipelago, disrupting enemy forces in United Artists' *Ambush Bay* even though his private (James Mitchum) wore a bright red hat, visible for many miles. Jack Mahoney attacked Japanese troops holed up in Manila's Intramuros (the Walled city) in Hemisphere Pictures' *The Walls of Hell* while Jimmy Rodgers and Jack Nicholson, two Intelrecon rangers, undertook a dangerous reconnaissance mission in Fox's *Back Door to Hell*. There, another GI (John Hackett) took a fatalistic approach: "Yeah, we're all gonna die anyway tomorrow, next week, thirty years from now. Did that little thought ever penetrate your thick skull?" Another Fox production, *Battle of Bloody Beach*, saw Audie Murphy, a civilian working for the navy, help the insurgents defeat their invaders, while in F-8 Productions' *Once Before I Die*, Major John Derek encountered many close calls in the dense, mountainous terrain.

Four more films took American forces into the Burmese hinterland: General Jeff Chandler led his machete-wielding fighters in Warner Bros.' *Merrill's Marauders* to attack a Japanese stronghold at Myitkyina but privately admitted, "Sneaking 3,000 men through this damn jungle is gonna drive me nuts." Likewise, Ron Foster eluded Japanese forces, saved some Oriental girls, and blew up a strategic supply line in United Artists' B-quickie, *Operation Bottleneck*. Squadron leader Gregory Peck, haunted by memories of his deceased wife, endured both emotional and flying problems in United Artists' *The Purple Plain*, and Captain Frank Sinatra chased the Japanese in MGM's *Never So Few* while his girlfriend (Gina Lollobrigida) waited patiently for his return. Later, Sinatra—now demoted to a chief navy corpsman—aided the wounded during the Solomon Islands fighting in Warner Bros.' *None But the Brave*. Back on Guadalcanal, two leathernecks (Keir Dullea and Jack Warden) fought their Oriental enemies in Allied Artists' adaptation of James Jones's novel *The Thin Red Line*, while George Segal, James Fox, and other Allied POWs struggled in Columbia's *King Rat*. In Filmgroup's sixty-four-minute B-travesty, *Battle of Blood Island*, two GIs (Richard Devon and Ron Kennedy) stranded on a Pacific island put aside their religious differences to avoid capture. Another B-meller, Fox's *Seven*

Women from Hell, depicted the horrors of Japanese prison camp. Here, Patricia Owens spearheaded an escape from a sadistic guard (Richard Loo) in their New Guinea compound. Rank's *A Town Like Alice* likewise depicted the misery of internment on the Malaysian Peninsula, where a spirited English woman (Virginia McKenna) fell for an Australian outbacker (Peter Finch), a man who helped her during this ordeal. In a different tempo, an American C-47 pilot (Victor Mature), making daily runs across the Hump, married a local beauty in United Artists' *China Doll*. One year later both perished in a Japanese attack while their infant daughter, only a few months old, survived. Rescued by friends, the baby drifted from orphanage to orphanage until, fourteen years later, the airman's pals located the teenager and brought her to America.

On the European front, the battle continued. In MGM's *The Angry Hills*, an agile war correspondent (Robert Mitchum) escaped from Athens with important data for the Allied command, while on a nearby Greek island, Gregory Peck trekked many kilometers and experienced numerous close calls before his undercover team destroyed two monster cannons in Columbia's *The Guns of Navarone*—even though his British explosive expert complained, "I prefer to leave the killing to someone like you, an officer and a gentleman, a leader of men."

Nearby, on the island of Crete, a British national (Shirley Eaton) joined a band of female guerrillas disrupting Third Reich advances in Universal's B-drama *The Naked Brigade*, while miles away in neutral Stockholm, William Holden personified the quiet heroism of an American-born businessman, Eric Erickson, who infiltrated the Nazi war machine, gleaned intricate secrets, and sent this information to British agents in Paramount's *The Counterfeit Traitor*. Another spy meller, Fox's *I Deal in Danger*, highlighted Robert Goulet in the tricky role of an Allied operative posing as a fervent Hitlerite, gleaning needed logistical information while gloating to his Berlin superiors that he would, "Convince the American people they can't possibly win the War." Likewise, Glenn Ford, a Parisian bon vivant, obtained critical war news from high-ranking *Wehrmacht* officers in MGM's remake of the 1921 Rudolf Valentino silent classic, *The Four Horsemen of the Apocalypse*, a grim story of brothers who fought on opposite sides. Also in France, an SNCF (national railway) Resistance fighter (Burt Lancaster) derailed a locomotive loaded with priceless stolen art treasures in United Artists' fast-moving cat-and-mouse cliffhanger, *The Train*, even though an effete Nazi colonel (Paul Scofield) claimed, "A painting means as much to you as a string of pearls to an ape." A similar screenplay involving an Italian high-speed rail chase was Fox's *Von Ryan's Express*. Here, an American colonel (Frank Sinatra) seized a POW freight train, and after many close calls the escapees reached Switzerland. But in an atypical Hollywood ending, Frank Sinatra perished, another victim of Axis brutality.

Other themes continued the fight against Hitler's forces. United Artists' *The Secret Invasion* paired Stewart Granger and Mickey Rooney as two criminals recruited to liberate an Italian general imprisoned by the Axis, while an OSS officer (Van Johnson) and a French Resistance fighter (Jean Pierre Aumont) rescued a high-ranking German officer who wanted to defect in Columbia's *The Enemy General*. Over in Ireland, Robert Mitchum, an IRA member, battled a comrade who worked for the Third Reich in United Artists' *The Night Fighters*. Not to be outdone, Marlon Brando, now an anti-Nazi, helped the Allies capture a German cargo ship in Fox's spy thriller *Morituri*, while Cliff Robertson, flying for the British, attacked a strategic Norwegian fuel factory in United Artists' *633 Squadron*. Still in Scandinavia, Kirk Douglas and Richard Harris traversed many miles to destroy an enemy heavy-water plant in Columbia's *The Heroes of Telemark*, while deep inside the Fatherland George Peppard obliterated an underground V-2 factory in MGM's double-agent thriller, *Operation Crossbow*. Alexandra Film's *Then There Were Three* told the B-story of six GIs (including Frank Latimore and Barry Cahill) searching for lost soldiers, unaware that a friendly stranger offering aid was a Nazi spy gathering logistical information. Similarly, in Filmgroup's wintry B-for-budget *Ski Troop Attack*, five GIs became stranded behind German lines, and in Universal's *Tobruk* some Jewish commandos fighting for the British destroyed critical oil reserves stored at this heavily guarded North African port. With a Canadian major (Rock Hudson) overseeing this unorthodox squad, everyone understood Captain George Peppard's warning, "If those tanks reach El Alamein, the Germans have Egypt."

Fox's *Up from the Beach* matched Cliff Robertson and Red Buttons as two GIs moving inland after the D-Day invasion. Along the way they encountered retreating Germans and pretty French women. Allied Artists' *Armored Command* assigned Howard Keel and Burt Reynolds as two U.S. Army men who thwarted the efforts of a charming Axis spy (Tina Louise). In another venue, equestrian master Lilli Palmer worked hard to protect her prized Lipizzans from German and American troops in Disney's *The Miracle of the White Stallion*. In Paramount's *Five Branded Women*, a group of unwanted Yugoslavian peasants (Jeanne Moreau, Carla Gravina, Barbara Bel Geddes, Silvana Mangano, and Vera Miles) fled their small village and joined the Resistance, where they fought their tormentors. Another B-production, Warner Bros.' *Hitler*, starred Richard Basehart as the führer in a role that portrayed the National Socialist leader as a demented, lovesick schoolboy bemoaning, "Compulsion turns me away from every woman."

A few blockbusters examined the European conflict with more detail. Fox's *The Longest Day* documented the planning and implementation of Operation Overlord, the multifaceted Normandy invasion. Here, the storyline weaved in and out of various command posts, asserting each side's strengths, weaknesses, joys, and failures even though the German defense commander Erwin Rommel (Werner Hinz) prophesized, "Not a single Allied soldier shall reach the shore." Another elaborate production, Paramount's *Is Paris Burning?* traced the numerous quid pro quo arrangements responsible for countermanding Hitler's draconian order and saving the French capital from destruction after the military commandant declared, "We're soldiers, not tourists." Using many famous movie stars, this screenplay spotlighted Gaullist determination to preserve its City of Lights. Warner Bros.' *Battle of the Bulge* fictionalized the details of this 1944 Belgian confrontation. With Henry Fonda, Robert Ryan, and Dana Andrews in leading roles, this 165-minute screenplay offered new problems associated with the Allied victory. One accurate scene, however, the German massacre at Malmedy, reiterated the *Wehrmacht*'s unbridled cruelty toward captured Americans.

Sometimes a motion picture looked philosophically at the European war. Columbia's *The Victors* contained poignant vignettes as U.S. servicemen moved cautiously from Sicily toward the Fatherland, experiencing pleasures, hardships, defeats, even romance. One episode, a thinly disguised version of Private Eddie Slovak's death, spooked moviegoers because an incongruous holiday song—Frank Sinatra's warmhearted version of "I'll Be Home for Christmas"—accompanied this controversial execution by a firing squad. United Artists' *Judgment at Nuremberg* explained the international court trials that brought Nazis to justice, even though a German lawyer (Maximilian Schell) waggishly suggested to a senior American judge (Spencer Tracy), "In five years, the men you sentenced to life imprisonment will be free." Another title concerned with punishment for Nazi leaders was Allied Artists' *Operation Eichmann*. Here, Israeli agents traced this prized fugitive to a South American hideaway and returned him to trial.

But Hollywood never strayed far from the real foes. Columbia's *The Last Blitzkrieg* highlighted the *Wehrmacht*'s destructive efforts during the Battle of the Bulge, where German soldiers, dressed in American uniforms and speaking excellent English, infiltrated Allied lines, disrupting their communication network. This time, Van Johnson—in an atypical role—played the leader of this Axis spy force. Another Columbia title, *Night of the Generals*, depicted the perverse killings of some French prostitutes during the Nazi occupation and the subsequent capture, some twenty years later, of the murderer. Starring Peter O'Toole, this revisionist screenplay suggested that the German judicial system was fair, honest, and unrelenting. Universal's *In Enemy Country* placed a French Resistance colonel (Anthony Franciosa) in a cat-and-mouse espionage plan near the Normandy coastline. After many close calls, he destroyed a German torpedo plant.

A few screenplays focused on the prolonged Italian campaign. AIG's *Tank Commandos* found two demolition specialists (Wally Campo and Robert Barron) thwarting some advancing Germans before they could fortify an Italian city, while Parade Releasing Organizations' eighty-four-minute B-clunker *Shell Shock* emphasized the comings and goings of a frontline army squad whose sergeant (Beach Dickerson), fearful that one of his men was faking battle fatigue, set out to expose him. Another B-quickie, AIG's *Paratroop Command*, placed U.S. airborne troops in the thick of battle during the 1943 offensive. Here a corporal (Richard Bakalyan) performed heroically in the grape-growing countryside. Beckman's low-budget filler *The Quick and the Dead* placed B-actor Larry Mann as a stealthy GI working with Italian partisans to rout the Nazis during the northern offensive, while in Fox's B-yarn *The Cavern*, five Allied soldiers and a German sergeant were trapped in a cave with a pretty woman (Rosanna Schiaffino). As expected, everyone survived. Nearby, an American spy (Rory Calhoun) moved quickly to avoid capture by the Gestapo in Embassy's eighty-one-minute thriller, *A Face in the Rain*. In Columbia's *Verboten*, an American sergeant (James Best) fought his way across the Rhine and after VE-Day took a fast discharge, married a German national, worked as a civilian adviser, and, using his army training, broke up a neo-Nazi group.

Near the Siegfried line a recalcitrant private (Steve McQueen), harboring a death wish, clashed with army regulations and Nazi soldiers in Paramount's *Hell Is for Heroes*, a blatant photodrama acknowledging that American forces contained a good percentage of sadistic and mentally unbalanced foot soldiers. A similar storyline about the unstable fighting man, Columbia's *The War Lover*, again showcased Steve McQueen as a monomaniacal B-17 pilot obsessed with dropping bombs on German targets regardless of the danger. In United Artists' *The Great Escape*, McQueen's portrayal became more mainstream. As a captured American pilot—rotting away in a POW camp—he joined other officers in an elaborate tunnel escape from their stalag. After a long countryside motorcycle chase, the hard-driving McQueen, just meters from the Swiss border, could not clear the fence. Nabbed by the *Wehrmacht*, the never-say-die Captain McQueen, undaunted by this setback, planned his next breakout attempt. In another vein, MGM's *36 Hours* offered a *Twilight Zone* D-Day scenario. Here, an American intelligence officer (James Garner)—after being drugged and taken to a German base disguised as an U.S. hospital—slowly emerged from a deep sleep. For the next day and a half, German officers posing as American doctors explained away his amnesia, concocting a wild, hocus-pocus story, hoping the disorientated major would fall for their ruse and reveal Operation Overlord information. Using bogus newspapers, magazines, and radio programs, an elaborate tale purported that World War II ended five years earlier. Ever vigilant, the quick-thinking major picked up on their scheme, and in one deft moment, turned the tables on his captors.

Even though many World War II titles depicted combat adventures, a few screenplays put aside flag-waving heroics and, instead, examined the emotional vicissitudes and psychological disorders the global conflict produced. AIP's *The Pawnbroker* told the poignant story of a concentration-camp survivor (Rod Steiger) living in suburban Long Island, tormented by horrific memories of the Nazi prison camp where his family perished. As one flashback after another emerged, the film accentuated the hopelessness this moneylender faced each morning—anger, poverty, and deprivation—as locals, cast-offs looking for a few dollars, stumbled into his Spanish Harlem shop. For the pawnbroker, the Holocaust reduced his worldview to simple nihilism: "I do not believe in God, or art, or science, or newspapers, or politics, or philosophy." Another motion picture about a concentration-camp survivor, Paramount's *Judith*, added to the despondency theme. Here, Sophia Loren—after many hardships—reached Israel, looking for her husband, the opportunist who betrayed her to the Gestapo. Likewise, Fox's *The Diary of Anne Frank* recounted the tragic story of a Dutch household, hiding from the Nazis in a makeshift Amsterdam attic. With Millie Perkins in the leading role, the photodrama recalled the daily frustrations an unassuming Jewish family endured in such cramped quarters. Two similar storylines, told in low-budget format, Hammer Film's *The Camp On Blood Island* and its sequel, *The Secret of Blood Island*, offered gruesome scenes of Japanese atrocities against British and American prisoners of war, portraying their Oriental captors as uncompromisingly vicious and arrogant.

MGM's *A Bridge to the Sun* examined the unusual circumstances of Gwen Terasaki (Carroll Baker), a Tennessee belle who married a Japanese diplomat stationed in Washington, D.C., but was reassigned to Tokyo just before the war started. After Pearl Harbor, her world turned upside down, resulting in one problem after another for a blue-eyed American blonde living in Japan. Paramount's *Another Time, Another Place* told the age-old story of lost love. Here, a woman (Lana Turner) working in London enjoyed an extramarital affair with a BBC correspondent (Sean Connery) until his combat death. In a strange, remorseful mood, she befriended her dead lover's wife, offering the widow many consolations. Another screenplay depicting problems of the heart, Warner Bros.' *Miracle in the Rain*, recounted the poignant story of two lovers (Van Johnson and Jane Wyman) brought together in New York City

only to experience sorrow by a combat death. In a different format, Warner
Bros.' *The Incredible Mr. Limpet* provided some levity, as a mild-mannered
Brooklyn bookkeeper (Don Knotts) held discourse with a porpoise and, using
his special skills, trained this mammal to destroy Nazi submarines operating
in the North Atlantic. Fox's *The Rookie* added a few more chuckles after two
GIs (Peter Marshall and Tommy Noonan)—stranded on a deserted island
with a gorgeous model—bump into two inept Japanese soldiers. On a har-
monious level, Fox's *The Sound of Music* offered wonderful melodies as the
von Trapp family moved quickly to elude encroaching Nazis in their native
Austria.

Columbia's *Bitter Victory* paired Richard Burton and Curt Jurgens as two
British officers—with antithetical viewpoints—fighting both the Axis and
each other during the difficult North African campaign. Schooled in the romantic tradition, the Welsh captain often berated his superior, pontificating,
"War is inhuman." In nearby Tunisia a wounded GI (Wally Campo), separated from his unit, employed old-fashioned American know-how to escape
from a German officer in AIP's sixty-four-minute *Hell Squad*, while over in
the Pacific, a hard-minded fighter pilot (Sterling Hayden) who lost a leg in a
combat crash, inspired his men to defeat the enemy in Republic's *The Eternal Sea*. Many miles away in an Indian courtroom, Fox's *Man in the Middle*
focused on a controversial court-martial of an American officer (Kenneth
Wynn) charged with murdering a British soldier. The defendant argued that
the dead man's personal life provoked his shooting, while off to the side, his
lawyer (Robert Mitchum) offered a more realistic defense, purporting that his
client—suffering from numerous mental problems—could only be classified
as insane, an argument that infuriated the English prosecutors, tight-lipped
men demanding the death penalty. Another Fox melodrama, *The Revolt of
Mamie Stover*, downplayed heroics when a mismatched couple (Richard
Egan and Jane Russell)—stumbling to resolve their romantic differences—
watched Japanese aircraft attack Pearl Harbor, prompting the buxom nightclub hostess to exclaim, "They're all running scared." As predicted, this incompatible twosome never found happiness.

Sometimes the motion-picture industry drifted off into another dimension.
Science fiction titles, always a popular genre, offered weird interpretations of
postwar activities. Paragon Films' *They Saved Hitler's Brain* told the creepy
story of escaping Nazis, fleeing toward the South American country of Man-
doras, carrying the führer's brain sealed in a vacuum-packed jar. Hoping to
regroup and use a deadly G-Gas weapon, these officers planned to resume the
war against the Allies and promised this preserved head, "You will see a great
victory, mein führer." With Walter Stocker as a federal agent searching for the
cerebral organ, this screenplay—often paired with *Attack of the Killer Toma-*

toes as one of the worst pictures ever made—appealed to many cult-film followers. Three other titles followed this screwball formula. Gold Star's *The
Frozen Dead* permitted a demented scientist to keep the heads of Nazi war
criminals alive until appropriate bodies were located for reattachment.
Screencraft Enterprises' *She Demons* showed a German scientist mutilating
pretty girls, removing their faces, and attempting a reconfiguration with zom-
bielike women. Majestic's *He Lives* chronicled Hitler's bunker escape to an
Argentine castle where in 1967 he roamed around large rooms extrapolating
about the Fourth Reich, while Martin Bormann—his devoted follower—proclaimed, "Yes, the Führer is old but he is still our guiding force." Both died
when Israeli troops attacked their mansion.

Not all motion pictures took potshots at former foes. As the events of the
global conflict slowly receded, old villains and past misdeeds were sugarcoated as revisionist titles appeared. Columbia's *I Aim at the Stars* backpedaled
the career of Werner von Braun, a leading German V-2 rocket scientist, and
his role in creating weapons that attacked London and, instead, highlighted
his work in developing America's postwar missile program. Here Curt Jurgens played another stellar role as a "good" German who did not accept Hitlerism. A similar persona appeared in Paramount's *Under Ten Flags*, in which
a benevolent Nazi captain (Van Heflin) behaved humanely toward the survivors of ships he destroyed. To continue this positive image, United Artists'
Ten Seconds to Hell portrayed Jeff Chandler and Jack Palance as two German
weapons defusers in postwar Berlin, disabling thousand-pound, unexploded
British bombs.

Universal's *A Time to Love and a Time to Die* depicted an ordinary
Wehrmacht private (John Gavin) as a kind and sentimental individual who eschewed Nazism and was himself a victim of an out-of-control system. Based
on the book by Erich Marie Remarque (of *All Quiet on the Western Front*
fame), the screenplay dismissed most of the German brutality and in a closing scene, with an obvious nod toward Cold War politics, indicted the Russians for their cruelty. Another title that portrayed kindly German nationals,
Fox's *Fräulein* told the romantic story of an American officer (Mel Ferrer)
who escaped from a POW camp, received help from a university professor,
and, at war's end, discovered happiness with his daughter (Dana Wynter). As
another Cold War tract, this motion picture accused the Nazis, not the German people, for the recent conflagration.

Now what? Was the tide turning? Why were old enemies becoming new
friends? For American filmgoers the answer seemed simple. The nation's current enemy was the Soviet Union, and the postwar German Federal Republic,
headed by members of the pro-Western Christian Democratic Union—Kon-
rad Adenauer, Ludwig Erhard, and Kurt Kiesinger—stood firmly as a partner

against this Communist threat. After all, was every German bad? Didn't some of them resist Hitlerism? What about Marlon Brando? As a German national, didn't he abhor Nazism and help the British destroy a ship in *Morituri?* And how about *The Young Lions?* Didn't Brando, that handsome, blond-haired Nazi officer, behave charitably?

As an elaborate 167-minute, black-and-white CinemaScope production, Fox's *The Young Lions* traced the joys and sorrows of two American draftees, Michael Whiteacre (Dean Martin) and Noah Ackerman (Montgomery Clift), and a *Wehrmacht* officer, Christian Diestl (Marlon Brando) from their prewar civilian lives, induction into military service, their combat experiences, and finally, a serendipitous April 1945 meeting on an isolated German hilltop. Directed by Edward Dmytryk, this screen adaptation of Irwin Shaw's leftist novel—with its synchronistic storyline—juxtaposed the comings and goings of these three individuals as each man searched for his own niche in the global conflict.

On New Year's Eve 1938, a high-spirited Diestl, working as a ski instructor in a cozy Bavarian resort, flirted openly with an American tourist, Margaret Freemantle (Barbara Rush). For the German lothario, this pretty foreigner, easily charmed by his Teutonic smile, represented another possible sexual conquest. However, at midnight—as the happy Germans raised their glasses, sang patriotic songs, and praised their führer—Margaret, upset by this annoying chauvinism, ran from the restaurant. Moments later, Diestl, standing on the porch, explained his country's lebensraum policies. "Hitler will bring us a better life," he bragged, referring to the nation's lopsided caste system. "He has promised to change all of this." Unimpressed, the young American abruptly walked away, leaving Diestl alone to ponder his *Nationalsozialist* slogans.

Two years later, at a fancy New York City cocktail party, Margaret and her boyfriend, Michael Whiteacre, chat amiably with Noah Ackerman about social and political inequities. Both men, recently classified as 1-A, realized their carefree civilian days were numbered. But Ackerman, a department store salesclerk, seemed more philosophical about the impending induction and later told his future father-in-law, "I make $35 a week and am 1-A in the draft." But Whiteacre, a successful Broadway showman, expressed disdainfully, "I've read all the books. I know that in ten years we'll be bosom friends with the Germans and the Japanese." For both men, however, their personal views meant nothing. A few months later, on a southern basic training base, they listened to sergeants bellow orders, regularly cleaned their weapons, scrubbed the barracks floor, and marched on the parade grounds.

After an arduous training period—that included some AWOL punishment for Ackerman—the two friends parted. Whiteacre's connections landed him a cushy Washington, D.C., assignment and then, after Pearl Harbor, another soft London public relations job. Ackerman remained with his rifle squad and eventually landed at Normandy in June 1944. Weeks after this D-Day invasion, Private Whiteacre, reassigned to his old outfit, joined his New York pal, and for the next ten months, their unit advanced eastward. Finally, in April 1945, as part of a forward operation, this group liberated a German concentration camp. For a few days, the two friends remained here, helping the Nazi victims. One afternoon, these GIs, hoping to clear their minds, took a few hours off and strolled around the countryside.

Back in France, Diestl, now a dashing *Wehrmacht* lieutenant, found many of his 1940 Paris occupation duties distasteful. Assigned to a martinet captain, he routinely arrested Frenchmen for minor violations and complained, "I am not a soldier, I'm a policeman." Later, he was transferred to a North Afrika Korps fighting unit and watched in disbelief when his attack team routed a British patrol, killing everyone including the wounded. A few months later, when the tide changed, he escaped from the advancing Allied offensive and, after some good luck, returned to Berlin. Here in the Third Reich's bombed-out showcase city, he confronted the utter futility of war: children were orphans, wonderful homes destroyed, churches burned to the ground, and food nonexistent. For Diestl—the idealist German who envisioned Adolf Hitler as the New Order's messianic savior—Nazi horrors loomed everywhere.

For the German army, everything was in disarray, and Captain Diestl became part of a retreating horde. After U.S. fighter planes strafed his ragtag unit, everyone dispersed into the forest. Alone and without resources, Diestl traveled for days until he finally reached a concentration camp. Standing in a dilapidated office, he watched the commandant destroy military documents until another sight caught his eyes: the remnants of Hitler's Final Solution. For the one-time believer in National Socialism, here was the moment of truth. Quickly, he left this killing site and, after scrutinizing the timberline, chose a hilltop hiding place. A few days later, secretly watching American troops liberating the camp, Christian spotted two GIs walking nearby. Slowly, he began a cautious descent toward these two soldiers, struggling to maintain his balance on the steep terrain.

When Private Whiteacre spotted a German soldier noisily stumbling down the hilltop, he impulsively aimed his rifle and fired off some rounds. Seconds later the two GIs stared at the lifeless body of a *Wehrmacht* officer, Christian Diestl, the former Bavarian ski instructor who, six years earlier, attempted to seduce Whiteacre's fiancée. Here in a rain-filled ditch lay a one-time Hitler devotee who blindly accepted the Master Race's doctrine of purity, loyalty, and strength but, after witnessing his nation's collapse, renounced all these ideas. Standing over another dead German, the two Americans shrugged their

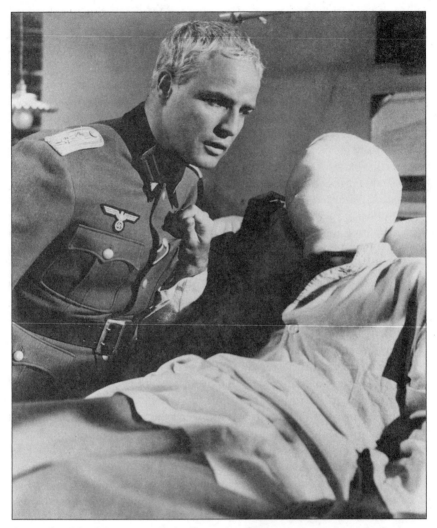

Demoralized by his commanding officer's horrific injuries, a Wehrmacht *lieutenant (Marlon Brando) realizes that total capitulation is close at hand in Edward Dmytryk's three-tier saga of love and war,* The Young Lions. *Courtesy of Twentieth Century–Fox.*

shoulders and continued down the road. For these victors, men who had witnessed hundreds of combat deaths, this Axis soldier was just another fallen cipher of the European carnage.

Certainly this Hollywood ending exulted the fighting prowess of the common GI, but on a spiritual level Captain Diestl's accidental (or sacrificial) death symbolically atoned for Germany's misdeeds. Was it coincidental that this *Wehrmacht* officer's first name was Christian? What about his untimely end? Was it an act of redemption? A modern-day crucifixion? An expiation? Clearly, his sinuous path—from a rabid Hitlerite to pious humanist—offered some consolation for a former enemy, especially a nation aligned with the Western bloc.

By 1967, while many Americans watched (and enjoyed) World War II motion pictures, these moviegoers realized that larger issues—emanating nightly from the television news—seemed ominous. Every evening the popular commentator Walter Cronkite reminded the nation that a civil war was raging in a former French colony, Vietnam, pitting the Communist forces from the north against the Western-aligned government of the south. Routinely, President Johnson shipped thousands of servicemen into this red-hot combat zone. For the second time since V-J Day, American casualties from a foreign battlefield appeared in daily newspapers. Once more, the United States, the perennial arsenal of democracy, ordered its young men into harm's way. Now what? How would Hollywood handle this new crisis? Was it time to load up the cameras, call up the special effects department, and send John Wayne, complete with rifle, ammunition clips, and hand grenades, back into combat?

Chapter Five

Vietnam Boils Over

1968–1976

"The Japanese were right to do it. From their point of view, we were their mortal enemy. As long as we existed, we were a deadly threat to them. Their only mistake was that they failed to finish us at the start."—Finger-snapping, Brylcreem-laden, right-wing political science professor and U.S. presidential adviser Dr. Walter Groeteschele (Walter Matthau) justifying the Japanese Pearl Harbor attack in Sidney Lumet's 1964 Cold War tract *Fail-Safe*

By January 1968, the red-hot Southeast Asian cauldron—fueled by repeated American B-52 high-altitude bombing strikes around Hanoi—finally boiled over after Communist leader Ho Chi Minh, hoping for a decisive win, launched his Tet Offensive. Soon, Vietcong forces, confident of a quick victory, attacked more than thirty South Vietnamese cities, including Hue and Saigon. For many stateside undergraduates watching this elaborate winter assault on nightly television, the news painted a grim picture. This ongoing war—a conflict that by now had polarized the nation—was far from over. Where does this leave us, the male students, who were always nervous-for-the-service, pondered, who will the draft board grab next? What time does the next bus leave for Canada?

For Hollywood, it was business as usual. The motion-picture industry, keeping its eye on the bottom line, wanted profitable screenplays, not liabilities. The facts of capitalist life were clear. Any movie glamorizing the Vietnam fighting would collapse at the box office. No producer in his right mind would touch this political hot potato with the proverbial ten-foot pole. But World War II films—with their uplifting, red-white-and-blue endings—were a different story. After all, didn't last year's audiences flock to watch MGM's *The Dirty Dozen*, an action drama that showed hard-boiled GIs annihilating a

Nazi command center? Who could forget former football star Jim Brown's dash across an Axis courtyard, zapping hand grenades into air vents as bullets and explosives went off everywhere after Major Lee Marvin barked, "Blow it!"?

As the fighting escalated in Vietnam with no end in sight, new World War II photoplays recalling past glories and achievements kept popping up in stateside theaters. Controversy was everywhere. The protest movement viewed these pictures askance, claiming they were nothing more than right-wing propaganda, while the let's-go-in-and-win-the-war crowd argued that here was America at its rough-and-tumble best. Just look at United Artists' *The Devil's Brigade* (a *Dirty Dozen* copycat), they argued. Watch tough-talking William Holden hone those recruits into a deft commando unit that eventually routed the *Wehrmacht*. How about Richard Burton and Clint Eastwood, two behind-the-lines experts, who rescued a U.S. general from an Alpine Gestapo fortress in MGM's *Where Eagles Dare*? Don't forget Major Lloyd Bridges's assault team fighting on the Normandy shoreline. These Allied soldiers destroyed an enemy naval base in United Artists' *Attack on the Iron Coast*. Why wouldn't they? Didn't Major Bridges, urging his men forward and (with a nod to the Vietnam conflict), exclaim, "This is a war we have to win!"?

Certainly, the American people needed a Vietnam victory, but by 1969 that goal seemed far away as casualties climbed to fifty thousand, threatening to eclipse the Korean conflict's grand total. For many stateside viewers, the same questions dominated every discussion: when will this war end? Who will lead us out of this quagmire? While President Nixon and his supporters proposed numerous offensive policies, his opponents argued, conversely, for a quick withdrawal. Back and forth the debates resounded off the congressional walls with no resolution in sight. Then, in 1970 a Hollywood motion picture appeared that suggested the United States could win the war. An elaborate 171-minute, Academy Award screenplay recalled the let's-go-get-'em demeanor of a modern-day warrior, detailing his numerous World War II exploits that resulted in solid European victories and earned him the sobriquet, "Blood-and-Guts."

As a monumental cinematic production, Fox's *Patton* told a straightforward story of the controversial general, beginning with his North African and Sicilian campaigns, then the French eastward advances, until, finally, his triumphant Berlin entry. Patton was noted for his salty language and frequent expletives—he told the foot soldiers, "We are advancing constantly," and reminded them when encountering a German "to kick the hell out of him all the time." As a flag-waving photodrama, *Patton* emphasized the many World War II triumphs and (with George C. Scott in the leading role) articulated that victory comes from strong leadership and a determined will to win. "No bastard ever won a war by dying for his country," he exhorted. "He won it by making the other poor dumb bastard die for his country!"

Without question, American moviegoers understood Patton's bellicose words and their obvious analogy to the Vietnam problem, "We're gonna keep fighting. Is that clear? We're gonna attack all night, we're gonna attack the next morning." Certainly this motion picture pleased the chief executive. Why wouldn't it? George C. Patton was a no-nonsense soldier, the three-star general who bragged, "Americans have never lost and never will lose a war, because the very thought of losing is hateful to Americans." He personified the best of U.S. military determinism. When he prophesized, "We're going to have to fight the Russians eventually anyway. It might as well be now while we've already got the army here to do it," it was no wonder that Nixon gave private White House screenings to numerous subordinates, hoping this film, or at least George C. Scott's persuasive oratory, would inspire them.

Patton was not the only World War II photodrama to remind audiences that U.S. military forces were invincible. Over in the Pacific theater, Paramount exalted the navy's determination to turn the tide by starring the quintessential icon, John Wayne, in a role that gave stronger meaning to Old Glory. Directed by Otto Preminger, *In Harm's Way*—a 180-minute extravaganza glorifying the intricate planning and logistical support needed for victory—glamorized every facet of America's seafaring, fighting manpower. Without question, when Admiral John Wayne stood on his flagship bridge,

A tough-talking navy commander (Kirk Douglas) blasts a spoiled-brat ensign (Brandon De Wilde) for his double-dealing, backstabbing behavior in Otto Preminger's three-hour epic about seafaring prowess, In Harm's Way. *Courtesy of Paramount Pictures.*

peered at maps, discussed underwater currents, and, finally, gave the go-ahead order, moviegoers knew that the Japanese vessels, navigating through a narrow strait, would end up at the bottom of the ocean.

As a major Hollywood production, *In Harm's Way* gathered many established stars, including Dana Andrews, Henry Fonda, Kirk Douglas, Patricia Neal, and Burgess Meredith. It wove one subplot after another, detailing the uncertainties associated with the Pearl Harbor bombing, the U.S. Navy's slow recovery, some opportunistic backstabbing, a father-and-son reconciliation, the perils of alcoholic consumption, the joys of new love, a suicidal redemption, the importance of fast-moving PT boats, the impeccable high-command planning, and, finally, the routing of Japanese forces. Certainly, this film echoed America's unremitting prowess, and only Admiral John Wayne could raise his glass, turn to his fellow sailors, and express these sentiments: "To our country, our Navy, and all the best things they stand for."

While *In Harm's Way* depicted a fictional South Pacific naval battle, another major screenplay, Universal's *Midway*, told the high-powered story of the June 1942 clash in which the Japanese lost four aircraft carriers and over two hundred aircraft—destruction so great that it ended any future threat of a Hawaiian invasion. *Midway* was saturated with famous movie personalities, including Henry Fonda, Charlton Heston, Glenn Ford, Robert Mitchum, and James Coburn. Replete with juxtaposed subplots involving high-risk planning, code breaking, Japanese pride, an admiral's bout with shingles, intricate air battles, and uneasy miscegenation, this 132-minute screenplay highlighted this important American victory even though U.S. casualties included one aircraft carrier and approximately 150 planes.

In embellishing this decisive win, director Jack Smight re-created both sides of the story by interweaving American and Japanese commands as stony-faced officers, unsure of the other side's strategy, peered ominously at oceanic maps, hoping to find a vulnerable spot. For the U.S. Navy, under the control of Admiral Bull Halsey, his succinct words said it all: "Don't worry about what I would do. Your only job is to go to sea, find Yamamoto, and chew his ass." A Japanese officer, Tamon Yamaguchi (John Fuioka), realizing his precarious situation, seemed more realistic: "Once, we filled the sky with our aircraft, we win or lose with six fighters and ten torpedo planes."

While both *In Harm's Way* and *Midway* provided moviegoers with overwhelming U.S. military victories, everyone seated in the audience already knew the dire outcome of Fox's Pearl Harbor saga, *Tora! Tora! Tora!* This 144-minute production detailed the December 7 attack, an event whose impact was prophesized in the cinematic (and no doubt, apocryphal) words of Admiral Isoroku Yamamoto (Sô Yamamura), "I fear all we have done is to awaken a sleeping giant and fill him with a terrible resolve." In retelling this often-discussed, frequently argued day of infamy, three directors pooled their talents for a standard historical interpretation. They elaborated on America's lackadaisical, "we-are-protected-by-two-oceans" philosophy while the Japanese nationalists, intent on continuing their expansionist policy, felt threatened by the Roosevelt embargo—even though Yamamoto advocated, "There is no last word in diplomacy."

As a major Hollywood screenplay, *Tora! Tora! Tora!* unfolded in sequential order between the American military command in Hawaii, the Japanese officers aboard their aircraft carriers streaming eastward, and various Washington, D.C., departments, where high-ranking officials examined incomplete logistical information, argued about Tojo's Greater East Asian policies, and scheduled meetings with Japanese diplomats. For the U.S. forces stationed on this mid-Pacific island, everything seemed to work against military logic. The Hawaiian Park Service, concerned with maintaining a mountaintop's natural beauty, prohibited a radar screen installation, while a junior officer, staring at the fighter aircraft tightly aligned on the runway, warned, "We got 183 combat planes on this base. The way they're parked right now, a one-eyed monkey, hanging from a ten-cent balloon, could scatter them all to hell with just one hand grenade."

Other problems highlighted these ambiguous days. A senior intelligence colonel (E. G. Marshall) spent hours deciphering intercepted communiqués and concluded from his Washington office, "Japan is going to attack us. We're going to be attacked on Sunday, the 30th of November," while back at Pearl Harbor, General Walter Short (Jason Robards) listened attentively as his aide read a standing order, "If hostilities cannot be avoided, the United States desires that the Japanese commit the first overt act." With such equivocal information, the Hawaiian command, unaware of the enemy task force heading toward them on December 6, acted indecisively. Back in Washington, in the early hours of December 7, the U.S. cryptologist finally pieced together the last segment of an intercepted message, prompting General Marshall (Keith Andes) to announce, "I am convinced the Japanese intend to attack at or shortly after one o'clock today." However, his warning—stamped highest priority—would not arrive in time. Meanwhile, dozens of Japanese aircraft, using a Honolulu radio station as their beacon, reached their target, dropped bombs and torpedoes on the unsuspecting ships, blew up parked aircraft, machine-gunned scores of servicemen, and triumphantly returned to their carriers.

In its own investigatory way, *Tora! Tora! Tora!* sustained cinematic interest by projecting a few hypotheses. What if, the photodrama suggested, the radar sighting, issued minutes before the Japanese planes arrived, was sounded instead of frivolously dismissed by a young officer, whose smart-aleck remark, "Don't worry about it," reflected the slapdash nature of prewar life? And how about General Marshall's directive? Would a four-hour warning have made a difference? And, do not forget the Japanese ambassador! If he was a better typist, would the ultimatum have reached the White House, as planned, before H-Hour? And what about the numerous American officers and diplomats who foresaw the handwriting on the wall? Why were they ignored? In all, the screenplay asked, was this attack preventable?

While *Tora! Tora! Tora!* allowed moviegoers to speculate about history, other Hollywood titles continued to pulverize the Nazi war machine. In United Artists' low-budget production, *Submarine X-1*, a Canadian naval officer (James Caan), after losing his first battle to a Nazi predator, utilized a midget submarine to foil his enemy. Back on land, Allied soldiers, led by Tony Franciosa, infiltrated the Fatherland, wrecking a secret torpedo factory in Universal's *In Enemy Country*. Down in Italy, army troops, after many setbacks, finally advanced inland in Columbia's *Anzio*. Here, an American war journalist (Robert Mitchum) chronicled the intricacies of this hard-fought campaign.

In United Artists' *Hornet's Nest*, an American GI (Rock Hudson) received help from some spirited children when he blew up a heavily guarded Nazi dam in southern Italy, reminding the youngsters, "If we do it right the Germans will never know we were here." Closer to Berlin, George Segal and Ben Gazzara spearheaded their army troops across the Rhine in United Artists' *The Bridge at Remagen*, a screenplay that exalted the fighting man while taking numerous potshots at an opportunist general (E. G. Marshall) who, oblivious to the human cost, ordered, "We're not going to blow that bridge—we're going to take it!" Down in North Africa, a motley crew of British Tommies became pawns in an upper-echelon debate about military deployment tactics in United Artists' *Play Dirty*. With Michael Caine in the starring role, this 117-minute desert tale blasted the British command structure for blatantly sending troops on a suicide mission. Also in North Africa, a U.S. Army sergeant (Lee Van Cleef) and his attack team decimated a fascist oasis, disrupting *Wehrmacht* advances in Heritage Enterprises' *Commandos*. A third North African tale, United Artists' *Massacre Harbor*, recounted the exploits of a four-man team, dubbed the Rat Patrol, who concocted a mass prisoner escape from a German compound using local fishing boats.

A few screenplays examined the Balkan Peninsula hostilities. Continental's *Operation Cross Eagles* paired Lieutenant Richard Conte and Sergeant Rory Calhoun with some Yugoslavian guerillas to free an American general. Another drama in the mountainous region, Bosna Film's *The Fifth Offensive*, depicted the Nazi effort to destroy Marshal Tito and his followers. With Richard Burton portraying the Communist leader, these craggy fighters easily outflanked their Axis foes. Republic's version of the Yugoslavian campaign, *Battle of Neretva*, placed glabrous Yul Brynner as a spirited partisan at odds with Curt Jurgens, a Nazi commandant, in the rugged terrain. Avala Film's *Hell River* pitted two adversaries, a Serbian loyalist (Rod Taylor) and a reluctant Nazi (Adam West) in the hostile countryside. Dubraya Film's *The Ravine* cast David McCallum as a German special agent who chased down a pretty Tito partisan (Nicoletta Machiavelli) in an isolated mountainous region. Stranded by an elaborate snowstorm, the twosome, after a shaky start, put aside their differences, fell in love, and, in an unexpected volte-face, left together.

Other photodramas glamorized the heroics found in combat. United Artists' *The 1,000 Plane Raid* detailed the planning, implementation, and bombing of numerous German factories. With Christopher George and Gary Marshall cramped in the cockpit, this aviation story highlighted the Air Corps' role in halting all Axis matériel production, while another airborne saga, United Artists' *The Battle of Britain*, chronicled the 1940 defense that repelled the *Luftwaffe*, compelling Winston Churchill's words of praise, "Never in the course of human endeavors have so many owed so much to so few." On the espionage front, in Warner Brothers' *Triple Cross*, a light-fingered safecracker (Christopher Plummer), released from a London jail, feigned Axis loyalty but, in reality, served as a British double agent. This screenplay was loosely based on the real-life story of Eddie Chapman, the man who claimed, "I'm a realist. I'm in prison and I want to get out!" In Sagittarius's B-yarn *The Last Day of the War*, a U.S. sergeant (George Maharis) rescued an important scientist secluded in an Austrian hideaway, while an American agent (Stuart Whitman) likewise freed a German rocket maker from a Nazi stronghold in United Artists' *The Last Escape*. Hispamer Films' *When Heroes Die* told the weird story of some commandos assigned to kidnap General Rommel. The plan backfired after the Germans caught these GIs, took their uniforms, and, in a reversal of ideas, planned to kill General Eisenhower. Fast-moving Craig Hill saved the day in this ninety-minute clunker.

Another off-the-wall idea, Silverton Production's ninety-minute *Death Race* clashed a disabled American fighter plane—that could not take off—against a Nazi tank in an African desert duel to the death. Sitting in the cockpit, the lieutenant (Doug McClure) employed Yankee know-how to outmaneuver his Nazi nemesis (Lloyd Bridges) and, eventually, gain the upper hand and obliterate his enemy. A similar high-jinks tale, AIG's sixty-four-minute romp *Hell Squad*, depicted a small American patrol, led by Wally Campo, that spent many days eluding a German intelligence officer (Brandon Carroll) in the uncharted Tunisian desert. In Clover Films' *The Cut-Throats*, an infantry officer (Jay Scott), along with five unsavory volunteers, attacked a secret stronghold, killed every German, retrieved some top-secret Axis battle plans, and—seizing an opportunity—helped themselves to Nazi gold. As an unexpected bonus, a few sexy women living in this enemy compound provided a little prurient diversion. Another behind-enemy-lines drama, American Allied Picture's *Operation Daybreak*, re-created the assassination of Reinhard Heydrich, the infamous Nazi controlling Czechoslovakia. Here, a group of expatriates, led by Timothy Bottoms, parachuted into their native land and, after a series of close calls, assassinated the führer's handpicked man. Based on historical facts, this made-for-television reenactment detailed much of the intricate planning necessary for success. In ABC's *Carter's Army*, a racist army captain (Stephen Boyd), commanding an all-black rearguard outfit, defended a strategic dam from the Nazi army even though his many solecisms—"I've never seen no one stand guard like that"—seemed contradictory. Later, this B-potboiler, with its eye on the African American audience, was renamed *Black Brigade.*

Occasionally, other nations, hoping to capitalize on the American motion-picture market, produced World War II screenplays utilizing one or two Hollywood stars (or former box office draws), in leading roles. Mostly Italian directors—in concert with stateside distributors and financiers—created a novel type of photodrama as European and American actors mingled in rehashed, cost-efficient storylines, usually with unsynchronized dubbing, a process that permitted lips to move in one direction while words went somewhere else. These wartime movies, produced in Italy, borrowed unabashedly from their motion-picture cousin, the spaghetti Western genre. Fast-moving dramas such as *The Battle of El Alamein*, *The Battle of the Last Panzer*, *A Bullet for Rommel*, *Code Name—Red Roses*, *Churchill's Leopards*, *Desert Commandos*, *Desert Battle*, *Dirty Heroes*, *The Dirty Two*, *Eagles Over London*, *The Fifth Day of Peace*, *Hell Commandos*, *Hell in Normandy*, *Heroes in Hell*, *Kill Rommel*, *Probability Zero*, *Suicide Commandos*, and *War Devils* showcased American GIs fighting the Nazis in various locales. One title, *Attack and Retreat*, employed a different approach, sugarcoating the Axis's ill-fated Russian campaign, an invasion where many Italian troops perished.

Occasionally, a few pictures took a prurient look at the European conflict. Another made-in-Italy drama, *The Damned*, chronicled the uneasy relationship between German nobility and the emerging Third Reich. With numerous scenes depicting homosexuality, pedophilia, and incest, this production—a condemnation of Hitler's industrialists—left little to the imagination with its sadomasochistic presentations. Going one step further, an American clunker defied all conventions with male castrations, vicious floggings, onanistic orgasms, and toenail extractions. WIP's *Ilsa: She-Wolf of the SS* pushed the limits of World War II drama with its voyeuristic, perverted, and pornographic images. With Dianne Thorne in the starring role—as a *Schutzstaffel* (SS) dominatrix who tortured, mutilated, or raped anyone in sight—this cult favorite, frequently referred to as disgusting, filthy, and degrading, offered, in its own exploitative fashion, another interpretation of Nazi cruelty. Three mirror copies, Olympic International's *Love Camp 7*, Coralto's *Salon Kitty*, and Italian Stallion's *SS Special Section Women* also titillated viewers with nude prisoners, bootlicking females, suspension bondage, forced lesbianism, brothel madams, and kinky foaming at the mouth.

Frequently, the World War II film examined complexities beyond the rigors of combat. Universal's *Counterpoint* depicted the adventures of a European symphony orchestra, under the baton of Charlton Heston, forced to perform for the Nazis, while MGM's *The 25th Hour* told the existential tale of a Rumanian peasant (Anthony Quinn) and an eight-year separation from his family. Columbia's *Castle Keep* treaded openly into the ontological nature of battle as eight soldiers sought refuge in a baroque castle while the Battle of the Bulge raged nearby. With Burt Lancaster in the starring role, the screenplay deftly pronounced the absurdity of war. United Artists' *The Secret of Santa Vittoria* portrayed Italian nationals as fun loving and antifascist. Here, Anthony Quinn presided as the mayor of a small, hilltop town. When the Germans arrived to confiscate their prized wine collection, the townspeople quickly revolted, preventing the *Wehrmacht* from taking their harvest. Over in Scotland, a tough-talking intelligence officer (Brian Keith) played a cat-and-mouse game with Axis prisoners of war in MGM's *The McKenzie Break*. After some sub rosa planning, the Germans launched a well-coordinated escape with a nearby U-boat, while the British, asleep at the switch, recaptured only one man. Another taut drama, Universal's *The Birdmen*, detailed the planning of an airborne escape from an alpine castle by an American officer (Doug McClure) in a secretly constructed homemade glider. Hemisphere's *The Only Way* heralded the efforts of a few Danish folks, led by Jane Seymour, who saved their Jewish countrymen from the Nazi roundup.

Sometimes productions looked askance at the war, depicting the global conflict in amusing terms. In Universal's *Slaughterhouse-Five*, Michael Sacks portrayed the stumbling Billy Pilgrim, an inept GI who eventually became a prisoner in Dresden. Basically, an antiwar tract (with black comedy overtones), the screenplay—based on Kurt Vonnegut's acclaimed novel—took a science fiction approach to the February 1945 firebombing of this baroque city. Scimitar Films' *Hannibal Brooks* told the peripatetic saga of a British POW (Oliver Reed) working in the Munich zoo, who—after an Allied bombing attack and numerous adventures—walked the town's elephant many kilometers to neutral Switzerland. In an offbeat fashion, ABC's fast-moving *The New, Original Wonder Woman* highlighted this comic-strip heroine's fight against Nazi soldiers and spies. With Lynda Carter twirling her magic lasso, the Axis foes quickly capitulated.

MGM's *The Extraordinary Seaman* told the easygoing story of three American sailors who teamed up with an eccentric Englishman aboard a dilapidated ship on a Pacific island, only to learn the British officer was really a ghost, doomed to roam the high seas until a heroic deed redeemed him. With David Niven as the wraith, this seventy-nine-minute fairy tale, with its supernatural motif, offered many chuckles, especially when the staid Englishman confessed, "I died approximately at 1430 hours, the tenth of October 1914, and that is the real reason why I have no need of food or sleep." Allied Artists' winter tale *Snow Treasure* explained how Norwegian children, living in an occupied village, smuggled gold bullion across the border right under the nose of a Nazi commandant (James Franciscus). Another MGM title, *Kelly's Heroes*, spoofed the war, as four enlisted men with itchy fingers (Clint Eastwood, Telly Savalas, Don Rickles, and Donald Sutherland) planned a bank robbery behind German lines, while perennial jokester Bob Hope entered the fray in United Artists' *The Private Navy of Sgt. O'Farrell*. Here, on a South Pacific island safely ensconced from any combat, the ski-nosed comedian—along with Phyllis Diller—poked fun at military life, including a parody of the famous Deborah Kerr, Burt Lancaster, *From Here to Eternity* beach scene. Warner Bros.' zany *Which Way to the Front* portrayed Jerry Lewis in the unenviable position of the world's richest man. Classified as unfit for military service, this tycoon, determined to help Uncle Sam, recruited other 4-Fs into a private army, traveled to Italy, impersonated a Nazi commander, was introduced by a general to "Von Pabst, Von Heineken, Von Busch, and Von Schlitz," and, after a few mad, comic routines, attempted to assassinate Hitler.

One zany title took the cake with its brooding dark humor and trenchant satire of military life. Based on Joseph Heller's madcap first novel, Paramount's *Catch-22* lampooned every aspect of a B-25 squadron operating from a small Mediterranean island and assigned to bomb strategic Axis targets. With Alan Arkin, Orson Welles, Richard Benjamin, and Buck Henry in starring roles, and directed by Mike Nichols, this screenplay blasted all aspects of military directives and command protocol. Here, in balmy weather, American pilots heard one absurd comment after another about daily mainland bombing runs. "To those of you who won't be coming back, I like to say we're going to do our best to take care of your wives and/or sweethearts," an operations major gibed, "and don't forget, a nice tight bombing pattern on those aerial photographs."

However, one experienced bombardier, Captain John Yossarian (Alan Arkin) reached his limit after thirty-five combat missions and naively asked, "Why are they shooting at me?" A medical deferment went nowhere because regulations clearly stated that any pilot who avoided danger was perfectly sane. As the flight surgeon pronounced, "It's Catch-22." Overall, the base resembled a loony bin. One officer traded parachute silk for cotton, bragging, "We're going to come out of this war rich," while another commissioned man became a squadron commander without earning his wings. A chaplain prepared "a nice snappy prayer that will send the officers out feeling good." A bigwig general flaunted his mistress and barked inconsistent orders while his son-in-law smiled docilely. A medical officer bribed an errant pilot to list his name on the manifest, enabling the doctor to "get my flight pay without doing anything stupid like going up in a plane," while other flyers received decorations for bombing an inlet, killing many fish. A smooth, wheeler-dealer lieutenant arranged a nighttime attack over the base and, finally, the magical go-home number reached eighty missions.

An Air Corps colonel (Martin Balsam) gleefully ups the ante, telling his bomber squadron that the magic go-home number requires eighty combat missions, while his commander (Orson Welles), accompanied by his son-in-law (Austin Pendleton), couldn't care less in Mike Nichols's zany satire, Catch-22. *Courtesy of Paramount Pictures.*

As a runaway 1970 satire, *Catch-22*—with its obvious analogy to the current Vietnam conflict—contained much of the caustic rhythm of Arthur Hiller's 1964 *The Americanization of Emily* with its ongoing put-down of military command. One funny scene depicted a bird colonel (Martin Balsam) bellowing directives while seated on a toilet bowl during a morning self-purification ritual. Later, this commander listened to a smooth-talking lieutenant (Jon Voight) outline a circuitous get-rich scheme involving bartering some base supplies for needed durable goods, while a few yards away, a B-25 crashed and burst into flames. Oblivious to the exploding aircraft, both officers agreed, "There are tremendous profits to be made." As for the one-star general (Orson Welles), his corpulent body oozed opportunism, avarice, gluttony, and sensuality in every frame. Clearly, this motion picture raked every aspect of military life over the coals with its clever depiction of a world gone mad.

Not every storyline was frivolous. In Universal's North African tale *Raid on Rommel*, a captain (Richard Burton), with the unlikely help of a conscientious objector, led a dogged attack team—composed of Jewish refugees fighting for the British—against the strategic fuel depot in Tobruk, halting Field Marshal Rommel's offensive. But in National General Pictures' *Massacre in Rome*, the Welsh-born actor switched sides, portraying a cynical SS colonel who ordered the mass execution of some Italian nationals after a partisan strike in the Nazi-occupied city of Rome. As an antireligious officer, the nasty-talking Burton, a fervent believer in Hitlerism, ridiculed a cleric's plea for mercy, telling the man, "I would prefer a religion that didn't need priests." In Eguiluz Films' *Battle of the Commandos*, a Scottish Colonel (Jack Palance) recruited some British ex-convicts, nudged them with esprit de corps, and then crossed the English Channel, where after hard fighting, they destroyed a huge Axis railroad gun on the Normandy coast hours before the June 6 go-signal. Down in the warm Caribbean, a lone Irish merchant seaman (Peter O'Toole) destroyed a Nazi submarine hiding in an estuary in Paramount's *Murphy's War*. And, in Paramount's *Hitler: The Last Ten Days*, Alec Guinness portrayed an out-of-control führer, hidden deep in his Berlin bunker, screaming one inconsistency after another—including unwarrantable criticism of Wagnerian divas: "Some of our most talented singers have allowed themselves to become absurdly fat"—while aboveground, Soviet troops blasted the German capital. In Fox's D-Day espionage tale, *Fireball Forward*, a general (Ben Gazzara), after some fancy intelligence work, dislodged an Axis spy working in a nearby French town. This discovery provided Allied forces a clear road to Paris. In Universal's *The Young Warriors*, a tough sergeant (James Drury) guided his outnumbered, untried recruits into battle against oncoming Germans. Also, in Brighton Pictures' *Underground*, a maverick U.S. major (Robert Goulet) left his English hospital, parachuted into France, and, after some perilous adventures, thwarted a Nazi general's coastal defense plans, while in Filmstar's *Five for Hell*, a few untoward GIs infiltrated *Wehrmacht* headquarters and walked off with the führer's Italian offensive orders.

What about the home front with its joys and sorrows when American soldiers were fighting their enemies in those faraway places with strange-sounding names? Warner Bros.' beautiful *Summer of '42* told the coming-of-age story of a Nantucket Island teenager (Gary Grimes), infatuated with a lonely woman (Jennifer Jones) whose husband was in an overseas combat zone. When the dreaded telegram arrived—explaining her spouse's death—everything she knew fell apart. In a moment of cathartic weakness she found solace with the boy. A similar photodrama (without the death scene), Columbia's *The Way We Were* spotlighted the wartime courtship of a conservative naval ensign (Robert Redford) and his left-wing girlfriend (Barbra Streisand). In this outspoken screenplay, much of the capitalist system's shortcomings were decried, while, concomitantly, President Roosevelt received ongoing praise as the wartime leader. On the eastern seacoast, Raisen Company's *Remember When* re-created the heartwarming saga of a Connecticut family's four sons in combat zones. In this Norman Rockwell world, every aspect of American life—Mom, apple pie, baseball, and church—confirmed the need for victory.

In sharp contrast, Universal's *Farewell to Manzanar* told the poignant chronicle of West Coast Japanese Americans, rounded up after Pearl Harbor under Executive Order 9066, and their difficult times in relocation camps. Here many good-hearted and patriotic families—victims of wartime hysteria—endured numerous indignities and deprivations during this dark side of national history. A similar title, Aaron Spelling Productions' *If Tomorrow Comes*, told the Romeo and Juliet story of a California girl (Patty Duke) who married a Japanese American (Frank Liu) on Sunday morning, December 7, and the husband's subsequent internment. Another photodrama, Lorimar Productions' *Returning Home* (a remake of the 1946 classic *The Best Years of Our Lives*) depicted the slow integration of three veterans back into their unfamiliar civilian world. With Tom Selleck, Dabney Coleman, and James R. Miller in the starring roles, this lackluster, made-for-television, color version toned down most of the social criticism found in its Academy Award–winner predecessor. Columbia's *Baby Blue Marine* finessed the apple-pie story of an inept recruit (Jan-Michael Vincent) who failed marine boot camp training and was sent home wearing faded baby-blue fatigues, an outfit that symbolized washout. After being knocked unconscious by a battle-fatigued marine deserter, he woke up, discovered his clothes gone, and replaced them with the man's bemedaled uniform. Wearing this spiffy outfit, he soon became involved with local townspeople and was acclaimed a combat veteran. Eventually, the truth came to light and all was forgiven, reaffirming the epistemological maxim that honesty becomes its own virtue. On a supernatural level, Cinema Center's made-for-television clunker, *Sole Survivor*, told the eerie mystery of a B-25 that crashed in the Libyan desert in 1945, killing everyone except the navigator who bailed out to safety. But twenty-five years later, in 1960, this surviving officer (Richard Basehart), now an air force general, learned the plane was unearthed, contradicting his story that the aircraft crashed into the Mediterranean Sea. To complicate matters, the ghosts of the doomed crew, headed by the pilot (Vince Edwards), waited these long years, hoping their bodies would be properly interred. As a supernatural tale capitalizing on the World War II theme, this drama, with its wraithlike twists and turns, resembled any number of episodes from the popular television series *The Twilight Zone*.

In a similar science fiction mood, Viking International's *Flesh Feast* detailed some Nazis in Florida guarding Hitler's corpse and waiting for the right moment to revive him for further conquests, even though a concentration-camp-victim's daughter (Veronica Lake) placed grubs on the restored body, badgering the führer, "What's the matter, don't you like my little maggots?"

Still other motion pictures depicted the human suffering associated with the war. World Wide Pictures' *The Hiding Place* examined the misfortunes of two middle-aged Dutch sisters (Julie Harris and Jeannette Clift), arrested by the Nazis for harboring Jews, and their subsequent ordeal in a concentration camp where their Christian beliefs kept them from total despair. While the older woman died, her sibling lived through the nightmare and, later, in a nod to her religious convictions, learned to forgive her tormentors. In a jurisprudence mode, ABC's 390-minute epic *QB VII* paired an American author (Ben Gazzara) against a German doctor (Anthony Hopkins) in a heated courtroom drama, as British jurors debated the innocence and guilt of wartime crimes. Cinévision's thinly disguised interpretation of the Adolf Eichmann trial, *The Man in the Glass Booth*, retold the story of a New York City Jewish entrepreneur (Maximilian Schell), who was kidnapped by Israeli agents, taken to Jerusalem, and after an emotional courtroom drama, revealed as a concentration-camp commandant. Associated General Films' peripatetic tale of callous indifference, *Voyage of the Damned*, examined the seafaring saga of 937 Jewish refugees, who in 1939 left Hamburg looking forward to a new life in Cuba. However, under Nazi pressure, this island government denied these exiles entrance permits and sent them westward to Florida, where for a second time, national officials refused docking rights. Without hope or recourse, the ship returned to the Fatherland, where a concentration camp awaited them. With Faye Dunaway and Oskar Werner in starring roles, the entire screenplay, from the book by Gordon Thomas, denounced rigid U.S. immigration laws that allowed a democratic country to look the other way.

Another photoplay depicted a nation's shame. Universal's *The Execution of Private Slovik* re-created the heart-wrenching tale of a borderline Michigan draftee and his inability to comprehend military regulations that, eventually, led to his January 1945 execution by firing squad. In his portrayal of the inept Eddie Slovik, Martin Sheen captured every nuance of this unfortunate GI, who, after arriving in France, drifted away from his unit, wandered aimlessly, and, finally, was convicted of desertion, a decision approved by General Eisenhower. Adapted from the scathing book by William Bradford Huie, this made-for-television drama—an indictment of autocratic military power—attacked the high command for its draconian rules.

From a different slant, United Artists' *Beach Red* combined an odd mixture of antiwar sentiments with marine bravado. Here, a captain (Cornel Wilde), leading an attack team on a Japanese-held island, harbored many misgivings about the daily mayhem. Finally, his doubts dissolved in a horrific skirmish, where both American and Japanese forces clawed at each other. A similar screenplay involving a leatherneck's qualms about killing, Warner Bros.' *First to Fight*, re-created a Medal of Honor recipient's gradual metamorphosis from warrior to peacemaker when a rough marine (Chad Everett), after returning stateside and marrying a local girl, reevaluated his outlook about war and its consequences.

Another title that examined a serviceman's change of heart—Cinerama's *Too Late the Hero*—told the repentant tale of a navy officer (Cliff Robertson), whose boyish charms provided a soft life away from hostilities. Eventually ordered to join a reconnaissance patrol, he fell victim to enemy forces in a gory, symbolic ending. In Cinerama's *Hell in the Pacific*, a naval pilot (Lee Marvin), marooned on an uncharted Pacific atoll with a non-English-speaking Japanese officer, forged an uneasy truce for basic survival. Universal's *Flying Misfits* glorified the exploits of the legendary Flying Tiger commander, Pappy Boyington, whose unorthodox methods destroyed the Japanese at every turn over the China skies. After Pearl Harbor, he rejoined the Marine Corps and—following many top-level confrontations—created another fighter squadron, composed of recalcitrants, whose daily sorties harassed the enemy.

The Philippines' jungle fighting contained many perils. In Universal's 100-minute B-yarn *Warkill*, a Marine colonel (George Montgomery) and his Filipino guerrillas fought the Japanese in thick underbrush. Another Universal title, *The Longest Hundred Miles*, explained how a hard-punching American corporal (Doug McClure), an army nurse (Katharine Ross), and a cleric (Ricardo Montalban) saved a busload of children from the advancing Japanese forces, while just a few miles away, in a third Universal screenplay, *Escape to Mindano,* two Bataan Death March survivors (Nehemiah Persoff and

Ronald Remy) fled their jungle compound with a top-secret enemy decoding device. In Manson's B-tale *Mission Batangas*, a mercenary pilot (Dennis Weaver) crash-landed on a small island, and, after a quick transformation, aided the army by caching some gold from the encroaching Japanese forces. In Box Office International's B-yarn *A Taste of Hell*, two American GIs (John Garwood and William Smith) teamed up to rescue a pretty woman (Liza Lorena) from a prison camp. Another reference to the netherworld, Tigielle's *A Place in Hell* positioned a war correspondent (Guy Madison), with the honorary title of major, in the thick of battle destroying an enemy radar station.

By January 1973, after incessant chessboard maneuvering, the United States and North Vietnam reached a cease-fire agreement that ended hostilities, and just two months later, the last ground troops left this faraway battlefield. For most Americans there was a strong feeling of relief—by now the death toll was fifty-eight thousand—even though it meant a strong ally, the South Vietnamese, were on their own. Almost immediately, the fighting resumed, but in April 1975, as expected, Ho Chi Minh's nonstop forces roared into Saigon and took control of the country. Back on U.S. soil, many voices expressed concern about this capitulation. The hawks claimed the nation's honor was impugned, while the doves reiterated the shortcomings that sent GIs to war in the first place. But one thing seemed certain. Hollywood, always ready to capitalize on current themes, lacked material for a rip-roaring Vietnam conflict movie. How could it? If audiences wanted reassurances of the past glories and unbridled triumphs, there was always old faithful—the World War II photodramas, with their uphill pillbox charges and hard-fighting tank breakthroughs—still waving the flag, reminding moviegoers about America's determination, under adverse conditions, to achieve victory.

Chapter Six

The Last Hurrah

1977–1989

"Rock, in the morning, what's it like, a surface battle?"—Commander Egan Powell (Burgess Meredith) feeling apprehensive about an upcoming ship-to-ship battle in Paramount's 1965 tribute to naval prowess, *In Harm's Way*

"Like any other battle, I guess. Maybe a little noisier."—Admiral Rockwell Torrey (John Wayne) trying to downplay the situation

"I'm so scared that my bones are clicking like dice on a Reno crap table. I should be back in Hollywood, sitting in front of a typewriter, making all this up for a movie, not living it."—Commander Powell's wishful thinking

Somewhere in the mid-seventies, many American households could not shake their love/hate relationship with a fledgling technology that promised more enjoyment for a lifestyle already imbrued with instant gratification. In exchange for a monthly fee (that always spiraled upward), local cable television companies provided additional programming that included major sporting events, unbridled pornography, sweet-talking you-must-own-this shop-at-home outlets, and commercial-free, first-run feature films. For many television watchers, this innovative format basically altered leisure time when a small electronic box entered the home. Why bother with the time and expense of driving to a local show when forty, fifty, even sixty channels were available in your living room? And, what about the future? Some companies touted that by the 1980s, every subscriber could access a hundred channels. Clearly, the days of the downtown movie houses—like the small neighborhood theater featured in Columbia's *The Last Picture Show*—were over.

This was not the first time Hollywood found itself on the ropes. During the 1950s, when audience attendance dipped, production companies introduced wide-screen formats—Cinerama, Todd-AO, CinemaScope, VistaVision, plus the three-dimensional photodrama that required cumbersome cardboard glasses—to bolster sales. Now in the 1970s a similar question unfolded. How do you lure audiences away from their cable networks, that once in a while offered a made-for-television movie, and return them to their roots? For the moguls, a simple answer prevailed: build multicomplexes with fifteen, twenty, even twenty-five large-sized screens, install elaborate sound systems, provide unlimited parking, mount coin-operated video games, and offer glamorous concession stands overflowing with food, drink, and cinema paraphernalia. After all, everyone enjoyed a night on the town.

Soon, the megatheater appeared, anchored inside high-powered malls, with acres of parking spots, eclectic fast-food chains, credit-card ticketing, and, of course, numerous motion-picture selections. Clearly, a new era emerged. Moviegoers were no longer restricted to a single title found on the marquee of those old-fashioned neighborhood shows. Now they could pick and choose a photodrama to their liking. Combined with shopping and eating, these user-friendly emporiums quickly found their niche in the American landscape.

As for the World War II action film, these storylines, glamorizing American GIs routing their Axis enemies, still drew excited crowds. In 1977 United Artists released an elaborate 176-minute title that highlighted the planning, implementation, and eventual failure of the September 1944 Market Garden offensive, an unprecedented British, American, and Polish foray into the Dutch countryside where thirty-five thousand paratroopers struggled to secure four strategic Rhine overpasses. Directed by Richard Attenborough and using numerous established actors—Sean Connery, Anthony Hopkins, Lawrence Olivier, Michael Caine, James Caan, and Robert Redford—*A Bridge Too Far* re-created the strengths and weaknesses, the achievements and failures, and the unpredictable serendipity coupled with bad weather conditions affecting both sides during this nine-day invasion.

Even though this photoplay depicted one of the worst Allied defeats of the war, Richard Attenborough fashioned an upbeat, multilayer drama that examined every aspect of this brief campaign, pausing to blame various command personages for their logistical myopia. First, a leading British officer, General Frederick Browning (Dirk Bogarde), eager for a high-profile victory, downplayed reconnaissance reports and, instead, envisioned a quick sweep, reminding various subordinates that this plan "would end the war by Christmas, in less than 100 days." He bragged the airborne invasion—a concept that had "never been attempted before"—would overwhelm the few German defenders, men who "were second-class, not frontline caliber." Adding to this whimsical idea, an operations officer saw nothing wrong with a drop zone approximately ten miles from their target while another colleague, fearful of reporting unpleasant news to General Browning, remained quiet about some malfunctioning field radios, claiming, "If anyone's going to rock the boat, it won't be me." But an intelligence officer, who confronted his general with Panzer tank photographs in the landing area, was quickly scolded: "Are you seriously thinking to ask us to cancel the biggest operation since D-Day? Because of three photographs? Sixteen consecutive drops have been canceled in the last few months—for one reason or another—but this time the party's on! And no one is going to call it off."

Call it off? Who would want to call it off? Certainly not the British high command. Richard Attenborough—in these first thirty minutes—unequivocally placed culpability for this impending disaster on high-ranking English officers, citing their haughty, aristocratic demeanor coupled with a supercilious desire to show up both American and Polish troops. While General "Boy" Browning received the brunt of the blame, Field Marshal Montgomery (Edward Fox) also took it on the chin. Here, the First Viscount, wearing his trademark turtleneck sweater, resembled a cruise-ship recreation director, offering lighthearted pep talks to various staff officers, fast-driving a jeep throughout his convoy, and bantering sophomoric we-will-win shibboleths to the enlisted men, suggesting that when all was said and done, war, like a Caribbean seafaring voyage, was really fun.

Let the party begin. On September 17, 1944, the Market Garden airborne offensive, after weeks of intensive planning, began as hundreds of planes and gliders blackening the skies, lumbering toward the German border. Within minutes, the go-signal flashed, and thousands of paratroopers, many hardened from the Normandy invasion, landed safely over a wide swath of land, quickly assembled, and trekked toward assigned targets. But hopeful success soon turned sour as German troops began an aggressive assault, scattering Allied troops, creating confusion, and blocking roadways. Within hours and then days, the situation seemed marginal as desultory reports reached unit commanders. One logistical officer reported, "We're more or less surrounded. So far we're holding our own but we're desperately short of food, medicine, and above all, ammunition. The Germans have overrun the dropping zones." Another communiqué revealed more bad news: "The Germans have trapped these men in a pocket and they're squeezing it smaller and smaller."

What happened? Why did this carefully plotted assault turn sour? As predicted, the British radios that did not work hampered communications while airborne supply drops, crucial to this offensive, fell into German hands. The Polish troops, held in England by fog, arrived days late, suffered heavy losses, and became inoperative. Soon, a grim reality permeated the Allied camp: the two Panzer divisions, pounding away at their perimeters, were unstoppable. As one British officer lamented, "We just didn't make it this time, did we?" Finally, a disgruntled General James Gavin (Ryan O'Neal) issued the retreat order, "Well that's it, then. We're pulling them out!"

Field Marshal Bernard Montgomery (Edward Fox) slowly digests the news that his highly touted Market Garden offensive has turned into a major Allied debacle in Richard Attenborough's A Bridge Too Far. *Courtesy of United Artists.*

Certainly this fast-moving motion picture, with its rousing military musical score, offered moviegoers many vicarious thrills as American paratroopers, members of the famed 82nd and 101st Airborne, routed their German foes in one skirmish after another as they headed toward their objective until, eventually, the sheer numbers of the *Wehrmacht* proved unbeatable. As for the British, their leadership left much to be desired. One commander ordered his batman to pack both his golf clubs and dinner jacket with his combat gear, while another top-ranking officer pranced around with an umbrella, pointing it in different directions to punctuate an order. Overall, the film implied, the failure of this operation rested with the British. Why not? If this had been an American operation under General Eisenhower's authority, U.S. troops would have seized the bridges in record time. What did the English accomplish? According to an area commander, General Roy Urquhart (Sean Connery), the results demoralized everyone. "I took 10,000 men into Arnhem, and I've come out with less than 2,000." Even General Browning rationalized the failure. Comfortably seated in his leather chair, he proffered a neat throwaway line for the debacle: "Well, as you know I always thought we tried to go a bridge too far."

While the British extended themselves by one bridge, on the eastern front the Russians fared much better with their westward advance. In a typical revisionist storyline, EMI's *Cross of Iron* exonerated most German soldiers from their nation's lebensraum policies and, instead, accused their Prussian-bred officers, those rabid men wearing the coveted Iron Cross, who insisted on death before dishonor as the maddening Russian forces breached their flanks. Here, a resourceful *Wehrmacht* noncom, Sergeant Steiner (James Coburn), fought both Red Army attackers and his superiors' draconian orders, arguing, "God is a sadist, but probably doesn't even know it," as the Third Reich's war machine, once the strongest force in Europe, deteriorated into a mere shell of its former power. Directed by Sam Peckinpah—whose trademark style incorporated slow-motion bullets piercing human organs as an antiwar statement—much of the screenplay insinuated that the Soviet Union, not Nazi Germany, was the Allies' real enemy.

Capitalizing on Sergeant Steiner's heroics, Maverick International's *Breakthrough* transferred this unconventional *Wehrmacht* soldier to the June 1944 Normandy coastline where Third Reich forces, now in a humiliating retreat, suffered many casualties. Once more, Sergeant Steiner disregarded his officer's instructions and, following some close calls, reached Allied headquarters, revealed information about Hitler's planned assassination, persuaded an American colonel (Robert Mitchum) to call a truce, and eventually entered a French town. As with *Cross of Iron*, this 1979 screenplay contained many antiwar, anti-Hitler, and anti-Gestapo remarks and reiterated the prevailing Cold War, backpedaling philosophy that the Nazis, not the German people, were responsible for the horror of World War II.

Another screenplay that humanized the German people, Wardway's *From Hell to Victory*, told the universal story of camaraderie, love, separation, and heartache when six friends gathered at a happy August 1939 Paris party, oblivious that a global conflict loomed weeks away. Soon each person—two Americans, two French, one English, and one German—went off to the war, fighting unseen enemies for unknown reasons. Finally, in a serendipitous nighttime skirmish, the Frenchman killed a *Wehrmacht* officer, unaware that this fallen soldier was the German friend who years earlier sat next to him in that Parisian café. A similar motion picture that used a happy gathering as the jumping-off point, Film Ventures International's *Battle Force* traced the comings and goings of some American, British, and German officers from their affable 1936 Berlin dinner through many battles until they met again in the North African desert, where the Afrika Korps capitulated to Allied forces. With seventy-one-year-old John Huston and seventy-two-year-old Henry Fonda in leading roles, much of the screenplay suggested that wars were fought and won by the geriatric generation. As a low-budget 1977 production, *Battle Force* did not fare well at the box office. Hoping to generate sales, it was released numerous times under different titles: *The Battle of the Mareth Line*, *The Biggest Battle*, *The Great Battle*, and *The Greatest Battle*.

Frequently, a big-scale production, depicting major Allied advances against the German forces, fared much better. United Artists' *The Big Red One* glamorized the army's First Infantry Division beginning with their initial assault-landing in Morocco, through Sicily, Normandy, the Battle of the Bulge, and lastly, a concentration-camp liberation. With Lee Marvin starring as a combat-hardened, World War I veteran, this aged noncom guided his squad through hazardous skirmishes, frequent patrols, ongoing tragedies, castle-in-the-sky dreams, and lost aspirations during their three-year eastward advance, always reminding his charges, "You don't murder animals; you kill 'em." Directed by Sam Fuller, this autobiographical screenplay downplayed heroics and, instead, restated the enlisted man's doctrine that wars were created by politicians and behind-the-lines officers but fought by average soldiers: "You know how you smoke out a sniper? You send a guy out in the open and you see if he gets shot. They thought that one up at West Point."

Sometimes historical events veered off into the galaxy. Associated General Films' *The Eagle Has Landed* told the fictional story of Winston Churchill's planned assassination by some Nazi commandoes led by Michael Caine. United Artists' fast-paced espionage yarn, *Eye of the Needle*, re-created the arduous narrative of a surreptitious Third Reich devotee (Donald Sutherland), working quietly in London, obtaining D-Day information. Eventually, on a remote Scottish island he confronted a determined British woman and realized, "The war has come down to the two of us." In a gruesome finale, she stopped his espionage activities. Fox's *Julia* traced the strained relationship between the noted playwright Lillian Hellman (Jane Fonda) and her mentor and occasional lover Dashiell Hammett (Jason Robards). These two American writers clashed on numerous social, political, and literary issues, including her rapport with a lifelong friend, Julia (Vanessa Redgrave), an outspoken liberal involved in many antifascist causes. After some soul-searching, Miss Hellman threw caution to the wind and smuggled money into Nazi Germany. However, this episode ended badly. Arrested by the Gestapo, Julia died in prison.

In similar chronicles, Paramount's *The Sea Wolves* re-created the unlikely tale of some retired British cavalrymen living in Calcutta who formed an attack team and, after elaborate planning, blew up three Nazi warships moored in a nearby harbor. With Gregory Peck, David Niven, and Roger Moore leading this unorthodox group, success was, of course, guaranteed. Trading International's *Bridge to Hell* allowed three prisoners, including B-actor Andy Forest, to escape from a Nazi camp, team up with Resistance fighters, and locate hidden war booty. In American-International's *Force 10 from Navarone*, good-looking Harrison Ford joined a demolition team that parachuted into Yugoslavia, fought with local guerrillas, infiltrated a Nazi base, and, with the help of a British sergeant (Edward Fox), who claimed, "I'm an expert at blowing them up," destroyed a strategic bridge, bringing the *Wehrmacht* to a grinding halt.

More photodramas depicted breakouts behind enemy lines. MGM's *Victory* told the pie-in-the-sky story of some Allied POWs who agreed to a Paris soccer match with their captors but secretly planned a mass escape, even though an American officer (Sylvester Stallone) complained, "This frigging game is ruining my life." Another meller using Operation Overlord as its backdrop, MGM's *Code Name: Emerald*, elaborated the close calls of a double agent (Ed Harris), who parachuted into France just before D-Day to rescue an American airman familiar with the invasion plans. Satori's *Brady's Escape* detailed the adventures of an American bomber pilot (John Savage) who was shot down over a Hungarian plateau, hidden by some antifascist locals, and—with the aid of Tito's partisans—reached safety in Yugoslavia.

Titles made exclusively for television audiences spotlighted Allied espionage achievements against the Fatherland. Universal's *The Rhineman Exchange*—a five-hour extravaganza—explained the comings and goings of an undercover American plant (Stephen Collins) operating in Argentina, where in a drawn-out storyline, diamonds were exchanged for a needed gyroscope. In Columbia's *Keefer*, beefy William Conrad headed a small group of secret agents working behind enemy lines, while Lorimer's six-hour potboiler, *A Man Called Intrepid*, told the unlikely story of an Allied team privately funded by a wealthy Canadian (David Niven). Over in North Africa, Nazi spies vied against British interests in Lawrence Productions' four-hour tale of intrigue, *The Key to Rebecca*. With Cliff Robertson in the leading role, this cat-and-mouse tale featured David Soul as an elusive German spy, while, in bizarre casting, Robert Culp played General Erwin Rommel, the famed Desert Fox.

Another farfetched idea, HBO's *To Catch a King* low-keyed the convoluted propaganda scheme employed by some Axis agents hiding in Lisbon, hoping to kidnap the Duke of Windsor. However, a well-known man-about-town and nightclub owner (Robert Wagner) sidetracked their plan. With a slight nod toward *Casablanca*, this made-for-television dud proved, once again, that no German undercover agent could outwit a fast-moving American. A similar oddball story, Warner Bros.' *Lassiter*, placed a handsome, smooth-talking London jewel thief (Tom Selleck) in an awkward situation. After an embarrassing arrest, the second-story man must choose between imprisonment or a government-approved burglary of the heavily guarded German embassy, a feat that would help his country. "Why not?" the experienced burglar groused, "I'm standing in a frame and you're gonna wrap me in the flag, too."

In Phoenix Entertainment's made-for-television dark thriller, *Monte Carlo*, sexy Joan Collins, working as chanteuse, spied for the Allies on the eve of World War II. In a flippant mood, Universal's burlesque *The Gypsy Warriors* paired Tom Selleck and James Whitmore Jr. as two American intelligence officers who, after some silly cloak-and-dagger escapades, destroyed a German chemical-weapons factory. In MTM Enterprises' espionage suspense film, *Behind Enemy Lines*, a professor-turned-spy (Hal Holbrook) planned a rescue mission to Nazi-occupied Norway, where a prominent scientist with doubtful loyalties was holed up. Another action screenplay depicting capture and escape, TNT's *Breaking Point* (a remake of MGM's 1964 intrigue, *36 Hours*), retold the roundabout tale of an American intelligence officer (Corbin Bernsen), who, after being drugged and tortured by Nazi operatives, escaped with important information.

Two other made-for-television programs examined familiar stories. Columbia's *The Caine Mutiny Court Martial* detailed the vitriolic courtroom battle between an aggressive navy defense attorney (Eric Bogosian) and a neurotic senior officer, the vulnerable Captain Queeg (Brad Davis), resulting in an acquittal for his clients. Directed by Robert Altman, this updated version, laden with the director's trademark—background scenes juxtaposed against the main frontal action—complemented the earlier Humphrey Bogart and José Ferrer version, even though much of the action took place in a gymnasium (with anachronistic basketball floor markings) instead of a staid military chamber. NBC's *Mister Roberts* used Charles Durning and Robert Hays in the James Cagney and Henry Fonda roles about seafaring shenanigans aboard a supply vessel hovering in the noncombatant South Pacific, where an irrational captain sparred with his ensign about decorum. Basically a comedy with a few somber overtones, this 100-minute version reminded audiences that laughter was still the best way to handle an out-of-control officer.

Sometimes World War II made-for-television photodramas emphasized distaff members and their role in the global conflict. Penthouse Productions' *The Secret War of Jackie's Girls* re-created the spirited adventures of five female pilots—stationed in England and using experimental helicopters—flying covert missions behind enemy lines. With Mariette Hartley in the title role, this exaggerated storyline stretched aviation history with its anachronistic scenes depicting helicopters in aerial combat. Another potboiler, Harlech's *Jenny's War*, told the unusual saga of an American mother (Dyan Cannon) who learned that her RAF son (Hugh Grant) was shot down over Germany. Soon she traveled to Berlin where her ex-husband—now a Nazi major—rejected her pleas for help in finding the airman. After a series of arduous exploits—including working as a maid in a fancy brothel, killing an SS officer, struggling in a Russian POW camp, and escaping in an onion sack—she went into hiding after a Gestapo agent (Robert Hardy) ordered, "If you find her, shoot her on sight."

Hitler's world-domination plans were a popular theme. Circle Films' *Inside the Third Reich* heralded the career of the führer's architect, Albert Speer, the man who once rebuked a field marshal by asking, "Do you realize who you are talking to?" With Rutger Hauer in the title role, every aspect of Germany's grandiose project for a New Order was examined in this five-hour epic. Time-Life Productions' 180-minute re-creation of Hitler's final days, *The Bunker*, starred Anthony Hopkins as an obsessive megalomaniac führer, switching between hot and cold moods, speaking incoherently—"I've never acquired anything of value in my life"—as fast-moving Soviet troops entered the capital city. Metromedia's *Hitler's SS: Portrait in Evil* dissected the Gestapo's fourteen-year history, so enveloped in brutality that it prompted an imprisoned professor (José Ferrer) to contemplate, "I wonder what Goethe would have to say now."

Other motion pictures presented similar problems. Cannon Group's *The Assisi Underground* showcased the cat-and-mouse efforts of some Italian priests hiding Jewish nationals in their village church, while outside the cloister walls Third Reich officers nonchalantly strolled by, harassing the townspeople and examining resident permits. With James Mason as a levelheaded bishop orchestrating many ruses necessary to avoid detection, and Ben Cross as his youthful cleric, these hapless victims remained hidden until war's end. A similar storyline, ITC's *The Scarlet and the Black*, honored a Vatican official (Gregory Peck) who hid many downed pilots, escaped prisoners, and Resistance members inside the Holy City. Anthea's *Forbidden* examined the clandestine love affair between a German countess (Jacqueline Bisset) and her Jewish lover (Jürgen Prochnow) as the Berlin Gestapo hovered nearby, unaware that their fugitive was ensconced in a windowless apartment. In Castle Hill Productions' *Reunion*, two secondary-school friends, one Jewish, the other Christian, enjoyed many carefree days, oblivious to emerging ideologies in 1933 Stuttgart. After Hitler seized power, the Jewish boy, Hans, left for America while his Christian pal, Conradin, remained behind. Years later, an older Hans (Jason Robards) returned to his birthplace and searched for his lost chum, only to learn about his execution in the failed 1944 Hitler assassination plot.

Over in France, HBO's *The Blood of Others* depicted the ordeals associated with the New Order's occupation of this Gallic country, while another melodrama, Newland-Raynor's *Arch of Triumph* (a remake of the 1948 Charles Boyer and Ingrid Bergman classic) paired Anthony Hopkins and Lesley-Ann Down as star-crossed lovers being harassed by their Nazi nemesis, Donald Pleasence. Another Sunday-night photodrama, NBC's *The Great Escape II: The Untold Story*, served as a sequel to United Artists' popular 1963 screenplay about Allied soldiers who tunneled out of their stalag, fled into the countryside, and were captured and hastily executed by German soldiers. In this awkward, nonsequential account, two American officers (Judd Hirsch and Christopher Reeve) pestered their captors for straight answers about missing men.

Other titles continued the fight against heel-clicking Nazis in more flamboyant terms. Capitalizing on the success of its 1967 blockbuster *The Dirty Dozen*, MGM produced three made-for-television sequels heralding the misadventures of these ill-disciplined soldiers, who for survival, formed a tough fighting unit. *The Dirty Dozen: The Next Mission* brought members of the original cast on another high-risk Fatherland operation. Once more, Lee Marvin—now eighteen years older—led a motley team of murderers, degenerates, and rapists behind German lines to disrupt a Hitler assassination plot, because an army general (Ernest Borgnine) claimed, "Hitler is our best ally, we need him alive." Two years later, with Telly Savalas in charge of this unsavory group, they destroyed a nerve-gas plant in *The Dirty Dozen: The Deadly Mission*. The following year, in the third installment, *The Dirty Dozen: The Fatal Mission*, Major Savalas took these mavericks into the hot Middle East to obliterate an elite Nazi team, twelve handpicked Hitler devotees planning an insurgent Fourth Reich movement, capable of continuing the war.

Copycat versions of *The Dirty Dozen* saga soon followed. Film Concorde's *Deadly Mission* involved the misadventures of five imprisoned GIs, who, after a strafing attack, escaped from their guards and headed toward Switzerland. Following an array of comic-strip events—where they strangled, speared, shot, and stabbed many Germans—they inadvertently joined a

French Resistance team, entered a V-2 plant, and, following a wild railroad ride, grabbed a gyroscope. An American colonel, holding this crucial part, bragged, "That's what we came for." As a ninety-nine-minute B-travesty, this film, like the phoenix, had numerous rebirths. Reissued four times, the producers deftly created spiffy titles with different twists: *Counterfeit Commandos*, *GI Bro*, *Hell's Heroes*, *The Dirty Bastard*, and *Inglorious Bastards*.

American cast-offs were not the only group in hot water with their superiors. Another spin-off of the renegade-soldier motif, Panorama's *The Misfit Brigade* bellowed the same shenanigans except this time, the heroes were slovenly *Wehrmacht* prison battalion recalcitrants. Sent on a suicide mission, they fought not the Americans but, instead, the encroaching Red Army. After some Looney Tune adventures, this dysfunctional unit killed many Russians, lost some of their own men, and finally reached a village, where—to their surprise—they found both German and Soviet soldiers romping harmoniously in a nude swim fest with pretty girls. Basically an antiwar tract, this B-spoof contained one caricature after another, including the pompous SS colonel fingering his monocle and the pudgy general threatening to execute everyone within hearing range. One scene in particular, the screening of some Soviet propaganda call-to-surrender motion pictures in a no-man's-zone, pushed the misfits over the edge. This Red Army ploy promised a beautiful woman, wearing a gossamer nightgown, in exchange for capitulation. Besides their sexual frustration, these men realized the futility of Hitler's expansionism and, coupled with the SS's fight-to-the-death dictum, understood everything was lost, prompting one man's facetious observation, "If we lose the war, we win."

Frequently, a screenplay emphasized the difficulties of the heart when American soldiers found new love interests. In a mushy tale, Columbia's *Hanover Street* re-created familiar problems when a carefree B-25 pilot (Harrison Ford) fell for a lonely, married British woman in war-torn London. To complicate matters, the husband and lover were paired on an intricate French intelligence mission. After some close calls dodging Nazi troops, both men returned to England, where the conscience-bound aviator, sadder but wiser, walked away from this ill-fated romance. Another American who also walked away from his British girlfriend, General Dwight Eisenhower, was detailed in ABC Circle Films' *Ike: The War Years*. The Kansas-born commander's private relationship with Kay Summersby, his driver, offered some insight into wartime separation, especially for the man responsible for the Operation Overlord implementation. Here, Robert Duvall captured the mannerisms of the levelheaded general who frequently argued with Field Marshal Montgomery and, in a jocular mood, kidded his English chauffer for "seeing too many Hollywood movies."

Still other American GIs kept chasing British women. In Universal's *Yanks* the problems associated with sexual frustration exploded when thousands of American soldiers stationed in Northern England came to town looking for fun, happiness, and romance with the local women whose husbands and boyfriends were off fighting on foreign battlefields. As expected, a congenial mess sergeant (Richard Gere) quickly fell for a local beauty whose beau was in the combat zone, while his commanding officer (William Devane) courted a married woman whose husband likewise was in the service. Eventually, the sergeant and the English lass became lovers and, days before his Normandy departure, pledged everything, while the Captain, standing quietly off to the side, stared lugubriously as his British sweetheart, now reunited with her spouse, waved goodbye. He was remembering her prophetic words uttered weeks earlier, "Perhaps, I'm not a woman of the world."

In an offbeat mode, the popular horror film genre, always a staple for youthful audiences, offered many sadomasochistic productions using the war as a peripheral backdrop. General Film's *The Passage* told the macabre story of a simple Basque shepherd (Anthony Quinn) and his misadventures while guiding a fleeing family through the Pyrenees to neutral Spain while a demented Nazi psychopath (Malcolm McDowell), determined to catch these escaping refugees, followed closely. In true Caligula fashion, this repulsive German, wearing swastika-embroidered underwear, raped the daughter, chopped off and cooked a peasant's finger while strumming "chop, chop, chop, chop," and burned a gypsy alive, bragging, "I'm sending him exactly where he told me to go—Hell," before he fell victim to his own brand of cruelty. As an R-rated motion picture, the entire screenplay, imbued with one violent, nasty, deplorable scene after another, echoed Stanley Kubrick's *A Clockwork Orange*, where a deranged Malcolm McDowell portrayed another antisocial misfit, spouting blood and mayhem in futuristic London. On a lesser scale, Associated Capital's paranormal photoplay, *The Keep*, recounted the uncanny happenings in a Romanian citadel located high on a mountain pass, where *Wehrmacht* soldiers died mysteriously. Suspecting some isolated partisan activity, the Gestapo command, after an inept investigation, confronted an evil force trapped within this fortress, determined to kill anyone that prevented its escape, which prompted a professor's daughter (Alberta Watson) to exclaim, "We're dealing with a gnome! A devil!"

But *The Keep* was not the only picture to depart from a conventional mode and stray cautiously into the science fiction realm. United Artists' *The Final Countdown* gathered momentum from *The Twilight Zone* in creating the eerie story of a modern aircraft carrier—laden with sophisticated tracking equipment—on an early December 1979 patrol north of Hawaii. Inexplicably, the carrier sailed into a preternatural mist. Emerging a little shaken but unscathed from this eerie experience, the ship's leader (Kirk Douglas) realized that his modern-day flattop, the pride of the navy's fighting armada, had entered a time warp and returned to Sunday morning, December 7, 1941. After the captain explained to the crew, "I believe what we stumbled across is not man-made but a phenomenon of nature," everyone seemed confused. Now what? Should the navy launch its F-15s and destroy the approaching Japanese attack planes or simply allow history's ineluctable forces to run their course?

A copycat version of this oddball storyline, Cinema Group Ventures' *The Philadelphia Experiment*, highlighted the frolicking jaunts of two navy men who, in October 1943, somehow wound up in 1984 because of an electronic testing mishap—involving some radar and camouflage techniques—aboard their destroyer, dry-docked in Philadelphia. A wide-eyed tar (Michael Paré) seemed confused by his new surroundings and pondered, "How is this sort of thing possible?" Even so, he took the future in stride, including a childlike addiction to video games. In a similar strained photodrama, Thorn's *Holcroft Covenant* told the convoluted tale of a German boy, who was adopted by an American family during the closing weeks of World War II, lived in New York, and—as a middle-aged man (Michael Caine)—learned his father, a confidant of Adolf Hitler, left him $4 million for victims of Nazism. Now in Europe and running for his life, he discovered that a latent Fourth Reich organization planned to steal this money for their cause.

As President Roosevelt often proclaimed, any overseas combat victory first began in Pittsburgh's round-the-clock steel mills. While many factories publicized their daily outputs as morale boosters, other industrial units were strictly hush-hush institutions. Paramount's *Fat Man and Little Boy* detailed the unparalleled secrecy and intricate logistics required for the Manhattan Project, where thousands of scientists, physicists, and mathematicians gathered to plan, construct, and, subsequently, implode the first nuclear bomb. Under the leadership of J. Robert Oppenheimer (Dwight Schultz), these handpicked technicians worked assiduously, while in the background, ever mindful of security leaks, General Lester Groves (Paul Newman) glared suspiciously at the many leftists assigned to his base. The participants were often at odds with each other about politics, morality, and expediency. The hard-nosed officer hammered away at the importance of victory. "We could give this country the biggest stick in the playground, and I intend to do that." His civilian nemesis listened politely and puffed his pipe as the harangue continued, "We gotta come down out of the clouds, and get into the business of winning the war." BBC's *Oppenheimer*, another photodrama but with stronger liberal leanings, allowed Sam Waterston more philosophical latitude, permitting the scientist to ruminate, "I have become Death, the destroyer of worlds." Spelling Productions' *Day One* retold the volatile Manhattan Project story from a third perspective.

This time Brian Dennehy portrayed General Leslie Groves as a pudgy, in-your-face officer, who worked, argued, and then compromised with J. Robert Oppenheimer (David Strathairn) to construct America's first nuclear weapon. After this atomic bomb imploded on the New Mexican desert, the Army Air Corps reconfigured a B-29—one of the new high-altitude superfortresses attacking Japan—as the delivery system for this advanced weaponry. Viacom's 156-minute drama *Enola Gay: The Men, the Mission, the Atomic Bomb* praised the intricate organization that culminated when this state-of-the-art bomber became airborne on August 6, 1945, flew westward, and eventually dropped this explosive on Hiroshima. The bomber was named after the mother of the pilot, Colonel Paul Tibbets (Patrick Duffy).

Other famous war personages appeared in made-for-television productions. HBO's *Mussolini: The Decline and Fall of Il Duce* starred Bob Hoskins as the Italian leader who bellowed many orders, winked at women, and kowtowed to Adolf Hitler. Trian Productions offered a more positive interpretation with George C. Scott's performance in *Mussolini: The Untold Story*, in which the fascist leader pooh-poohed Hitler. "I don't like him; Genghis Khan in a raincoat." Stonehenge Production's *Wallenberg: A Hero* narrated the mysterious saga of the Swedish diplomat who rescued 120,000 Hungarian Jews right under Eichmann's nose and later entered the Soviet Union, never to be seen again. Richard Chamberlain portrayed the international champion. Back on U.S. soil, in Titus Productions' *F.D.R.—The Last Years*, Jason Robards depicted the American leader implementing his Doctor-win-the-war strategy. In a similar vein, BBC's *Churchill and the Generals* placed Roosevelt (Arthur Hill), Eisenhower (Richard Dysart), and Churchill (Timothy West) in a 180-minute re-creation of their ongoing discussions, arguments, and decisions.

Entertainment Partner's *Last Days of Patton* positioned George C. Scott back in his Academy Award role as the braggadocio-spouting general who died in a freak German automobile accident, while Circle Films' *Young Joe, the Forgotten Kennedy* re-created the story of this prominent family's oldest scion (Peter Strauss) and his airborne death. Globe Film's *Casablanca Express* told a convoluted story about an attempted assassination of Churchill during his North African visit. In this revisionist screenplay, the prime minister confessed to an American general that England "had a spy in Japan who was able to let us know at the end of November that three Japanese aircraft carriers were heading toward Hawaii. The most logical target was Pearl Harbor." Aquarius's *Nazi Hunter: The Beate Klarsfeld Story* recounted the turbulent experiences of a German housewife (Farrah Fawcett) who, along with her husband, organized a grassroots movement to bring Nazi war criminals before the bar. In a slightly different mode, Fawcett took another starring role as the unorthodox photographer—whose many black-and-white stills recorded the war's shaded nuances—in TNT's biographical sketch, *Margaret Bourke-White.*

Another title highlighting a wartime personage, Universal's *MacArthur*, magnified the five-star general many regarded as the war's messianic savior, the commander who pushed the Japanese back to their homeland even though numerous critics, fearful of his popularity, denounced him as a modern-day Caesar. With Gregory Peck in the leading role, the storyline began during the darkest hour of the Pacific fighting, when outnumbered and ill-supplied U.S. and Philippine troops struggled hopelessly against Japanese forces on the Bataan Peninsula. With defeat a certainty, MacArthur, now ensconced in Australia, issued his famous "I shall return" dictum and eventually organized his armed forces for the northward offensive. Always reminding his subordinates, "We are attacking," MacArthur's troops captured strategic islands while leapfrogging others. Finally, on October 20, 1944, he waded ashore at Leyte Beach and traveled inland, where in an emotionally charged scene, he reunited with the Bataan survivors. Months later, standing on the USS *Missouri*, he presided over the Japanese surrender.

Always imperious, MacArthur demanded complete authority. When ordered from Corregidor, he initially balked, threatening "to resign my commission and fight on here as a private." Later he disagreed with Roosevelt's Luzon's bypass proposal, countermanding his commander in chief, asserting, "I'm going back there next fall, even if I had to paddle a canoe." Other times, he chided indecisive officers demanding, "I want action, not complaints." Finally on Philippine soil, he pleaded with the guerrillas, "Rise and strike, in the name of your sacred dead, strike!" But with the Bataan survivors he appeared humble, apologizing to the emaciated soldiers, "Sorry I'm so late, we're long overdue."

Later, his liberal policies transformed Japan from a feudal society to a fledgling democracy by invoking land reforms and trade unions, which underscored what he told his officers: "The Japanese must be treated with courtesy and respect." But in 1950, with this conquered nation stabilized, another problem surfaced: the Korean invasion. Initially on the defensive, MacArthur's forces slowly retreated until he launched the September 15, 1950, Inchon landing, cutting his enemy's supply line. Now on the offensive, American troops moved forward. With Harry S. Truman in the White House, he promised the president a quick victory. But a few months later, Chinese forces crossed the Yalu River and attacked U.S. outposts, prompting MacArthur to exclaim, "We are now facing a new, fresh, highly trained army." Frequently at odds with Truman—who nicknamed him "His Majesty"—MacArthur issued an ultimatum to the Chinese. Tempers flared until finally the president exclaimed, "I'm going to fire that brass hat prima donna, right now." Relieved of his command, MacArthur returned to Washington, declaring, "War's very object is victory,

Puffing on his trademark corncob pipe, five-star general Douglas MacArthur (Gregory Peck) contemplates his next strategic move against Japanese fortifications in Joseph Sargent's photodrama MacArthur. *Courtesy of Universal Pictures.*

not prolonged indecision." Feted by Congress, MacArthur's famous Old Soldiers Never Die speech brought everyone to their feet in stupendous applause.

But not every screenplay ended triumphantly. Always depressing, the concentration-camp titles—the darkest side of World War II history—mirrored the horror of Hitler's Final Solution in seven made-for-television motion pictures. Time-Life's *The Wall* reenacted the April 1943 Warsaw Ghetto uprising where approximately six hundred Polish fighters held off thousands of Nazis in a fight to the finish that culminated with a German takeover. As a tough-talking resistance fighter, Tom Conti exemplified the strength of this beleaguered group that preferred death to imprisonment. Katz-Gallin's *The Diary of Anne Frank*, another version of the famous novel and play, retold the heart-wrenching story of the Amsterdam family hiding in a cramped attic, their arrest, and concentration-camp deaths. Here, Melissa Gilbert played the budding adolescent whose posthumous diary became an acclaimed international best seller. Another version of this poignant story, Telecom's *The Attic: The Hiding of Anne Frank* placed Lisa Jacobs in the leading part.

Syzygy Productions' *Playing for Time* told the surreal saga of some Auschwitz inmates, all accomplished musicians, who formed a bizarre welcoming committee for confused prisoners arriving at the death camp. With Vanessa Redgrave in the starring role, this 180-minute drama reiterated the depths of Nazi cruelty. Titus Productions' *Holocaust* traced the joys, sorrows, and life-and-death experiences of two German families caught in the lebensraum vortex. This elaborate nine-hour drama was summarized by a sadistic SS officer's (Michael Moriarty) remark, "We must keep killing them, don't you see? If we stop it's an admission of guilt!" Zenith Entertainment's *Escape from Sobibor* re-created an actual 1944 breakout from a notorious Polish death camp by six hundred Jewish prisoners who overpowered their guards and ran from the compound. Eventually, almost three hundred survived this ordeal. With Alan Arkin leading this revolt, the photodrama described the stark brutality of Hitler's Final Solution and called into question how a production company that made such a detailed Holocaust motion picture, graphically depicting torture and cruelty, could lackadaisically place the word "entertainment" in its logo. Likewise, Citadel Entertainment heralded the same misnomer in their logo when producing *Max and Helen*, another retelling of concentration-camp misery for a simple Polish couple. Yet another photodrama picture denouncing the terror of German captivity, Golan-Globus's *Hanna's War*, told the horrific story of an Israeli immigrant (Maruschka Detmer) who joined a British commando unit and returned to her native Hungary, where she was quickly captured, imprisoned, and tortured. The entire 150-minute screenplay described her Axis tormentors as savage, inhuman beasts.

In an equally horrific title depicting the Nazi war machine, International Films' *Triumph of the Spirit* narrated the true story of Greek middleweight boxing champion Salamo Arouch, who along with his entire family was shipped to Auschwitz, where he alone survived because the guards forced Jewish boxers to fight, gladiator-style, for their perverse entertainment. Starring Willem Dafoe, this poignant drama reiterated the unspeakable conditions in Hitler's extermination program. Similarly, Universal's *Sophie's Choice* told the excruciating story of an Auschwitz survivor (Meryl Streep), ordered to choose which of her two children must die in the camp. Told in erratic flashback from a postwar Brooklyn apartment, this cathartic screenplay offered graphic testimony about Nazi bestiality.

On the other side of the globe, a few motion pictures examined the sadistic nature of Japanese imprisonment. Jeni Productions' *Women of Valor* restated the misery imposed upon a group of American army nurses taken at Bataan. With Susan Sarandon in the leading role, this made-for-television screenplay—modeled after MGM's *Cry Havoc!* (1943) and Paramount's *So Proudly We Hail* (1943)—re-created the three-year struggle as beatings, rape, torture, and execution became common Japanese practices. Similarly, Yorkshire's *Silent Cries* detailed the three-year nightmare of many Australian, British, and American women captured at Singapore and sent to Sumatra. With Gena Rowlands and Annabeth Gish in principal roles, this graphic motion picture detailed the brutal treatment that caused hundreds to die from starvation and disease. Victorian Film's *A Town Like Alice* followed two lovers (Bryan Brown and Helen Morse) across three continents over a twenty-year period, including a barbaric crucifixion scene in a Malaysian camp, in this 301-minute made-for-television remake of the 1956 production. A similar drama depicting the agony of Allied soldiers in a Javanese camp, Asahi's *Merry Christmas Mr. Lawrence* explained the depravity imposed by a draconian commander (Ryuichi Sakamoto)—whose Bushido philosophy maintained that prisoners were cowards for accepting capture instead of suicide—and his interaction and possible latent homosexual desire for a British officer (David Bowie).

Another B-title elaborating the fanatical Japanese soldier obsessed by his Bushido credo, Pathfinder's *The Last Warrior* recounted the unusual circumstances of an American marine (Gary Graham) and a Japanese officer (Cary-Hiroyuki Tagawa) finding themselves stranded on a remote Pacific island in April 1945. With little chance for rescue, the Oriental soldier, hoping to die as a warrior, staged a ritualistic samurai sword-fighting contest, but the sinewy leatherneck, determined to stay alive, taunted his foe with a facetious remark, "Don't get too excited, Tojo." Then, in a gory finale, the American killed this last warrior, reaffirming that even with superior martial-arts training, the Japanese could not overpower Yankee intransigence.

Nathaniel Productions' *Pacific Inferno* offered a different perspective, depicting life in a Japanese POW camp for the Bataan survivors as a Sunday walk in the park, where navy divers received good food, pleasant housing, clean clothing, and, once in a while, a little physical romance. Here, a seaman (Jim Brown) feigned working for his captors, while in his nocturnal hours, he tiptoed out of the compound, met with some guerrillas, and then removed vast quantities of silver from Manila Bay. Eventually, the Japanese discovered his ploy, and now with his back to the wall, he chose death before capture. With numerous flashbacks to stateside cultural disparities, the photodrama took some nasty digs at contemporary racism, including a contrived scene where a navy lieutenant rationalized his behavior, "We don't bunk down with Negroes; on the ship they have their quarters, we have our quarters."

Occasionally, Hollywood toned down the horror of the Greater East Asian Co-Prosperity Sphere's occupation policies. Yanco Films' Academy Award winner, *The Last Emperor*, re-created the layered life of China's last ruler, Pu Yi. Born in 1906, he witnessed many upheavals, including the Japanese invasion, and finally in 1934 became Manchukuo's puppet head. With John Lone in the leading role, this elaborate storyline skirted historical events. In a similar vein, Warner Bros.' *Empire of the Sun* detailed the confusion experienced by a precocious eleven-year-old British boy growing up in an affluent Shanghai neighborhood when enemy forces invaded the city. Separated from his parents and interned in a civilian detention center until war's end, this free-spirited adolescent (Christian Bale) adapted to camp life, taking lessons from a Fagin-type American (John Malkovich), even though on one frivolous occasion he sang a nationalist battle hymn with some Japanese pilots.

Sometimes fictitious ideas stretched the limits of credibility. Orion Pictures' *Farewell to the King* traced the unusual odyssey of an American GI (Nick Nolte) stationed at Bataan, who spotted the Japanese approaching his perimeter, left the peninsula and, after some elaborate escapades, reached Borneo's northern coast, befriended the aborigine tribesmen, and eventually became their barefoot ruler. After three years of carefree living that included good food, pretty women, long hair, and warm breezes, a British reconnaissance patrol arrived, headed by a major (Nigel Havers) who ordered this AWOL soldier to fight some retreating Japanese forces, reminding him, "You cannot turn your back on this war." Finally, in a bloody confrontation, the GI-turned-monarch now understood the futility of battle and promised, "From this day forward, I will raise my hand against no man." With numerous nods to the Noble Savage theory, this screenplay took a few swipes at English imperialism and attitude toward people of color.

Other titles presented the global conflict in slightly different formats. Comworld's made-for-television melodrama, *The Execution*, told the unusual predicament of five San Diego women, all survivors of a Nazi concentration camp, and their involvement in the death of a local restaurant owner, a former Nazi camp doctor (Rip Torn) who, years earlier, performed gruesome experiments on young girls. Paramount's *Islands in the Stream* traced the gradual transformation of a Bimini recluse (George C. Scott) from apathetic beachcomber to hardened antifascist and his deadly confrontation with a German

U-boat while smuggling Jewish refugees to Cuba. Columbia's *A Time of Destiny* reminded audiences that the U.S. Army contained its fair share of psychotic soldiers. Here, William Hurt stalked a fellow GI, waiting for the opportune moment to kill him. Another made-for-television nine-hour saga, Universal's *Once an Eagle*, paralleled the lives of two Army officers—one (Sam Elliott) a World War I Medal of Honor winner, dedicated soldier, and straight arrow, and another (Cliff Potts) a West Point graduate, bag-of-wind conniver, and self-serving womanizer—and their many wartime experiences. A similar storyline, but twice the length, Paramount's *The Winds of War*, pushed the made-for-television concept to new dimensions with its multilayered plots, big-name stars, and varied locales. Created from Herman Wouk's best-selling novel, this eighteen-hour extravaganza traced the comings and goings of the Henry family, where the father (Robert Mitchum) became an eyewitness to military strategy, partisan politics, ill-fated romance, family conflicts, war crimes, and bumbling bureaucracy. The sequel, *War and Remembrance*, continued the saga to V-J Day even though Hitler, hiding in his bunker on April 29, 1945, declared, "I should have won this war. I did not make a single mistake."

Back on Hawaiian shores, Columbia's elaborate six-hour made-for-television remake of the 1953 classic, *From Here to Eternity*, brought back Sergeant Warden (William Devane), Karen Holmes (Natalie Wood), and Robert E. Lee Prewitt (Steve Railsback) in the multitiered storyline about sadistic NCOs, an ambitious commanding officer, a brutal stockade sergeant, a kindhearted prostitute, and, finally, the Pearl Harbor attack. In this fancy Technicolor version all the GIs wore anachronistic black neckties instead of the authorized khaki shade. Not to be outdone, Warner Bros. used the same Hawaiian locale for its spin-off version of James Jones's famous novel in their six-hour television drama *Pearl*. In this production, Angie Dickinson, Dennis Weaver, and Robert Wagner kept the soap-opera pot boiling with their many social, political, and romantic maneuverings until the early-morning Japanese aircraft rewrote history, even though most of the bombing scenes were lifted from *Tora! Tora! Tora!*

Stateside life, while far away from the hostilities, still contained its own share of problems, frustrations, and anxieties. Paramount's *Racing with the Moon* championed the high-jinks story of two California lads, anxiously waiting their eighteenth birthday to report for Marine Corps basic training. With Sean Penn and Nicolas Cage in the leading roles, the two happy-go-lucky teenagers spent their last weeks flirting with girls, imbibing some underage drinks, and fooling around with old friends. Another screenplay centering on military enlistment, Kraco Productions' *Coward of the Country* was less frivolous. Here a young southern townsman (Frederic Lehne) refused to enlist after Pearl Harbor because of a pacifist promise made to his dying father. After some unpleasant events involving his girlfriend's rape, he changed his mind, rebutted these men, and, with the help of his preacher uncle (Kenny Rogers), signed up for military duty.

On a different note, Warner Bros.' *Swing Shift* took an ambiguous look at some marital infidelity when a lonely wife (Goldie Hawn), working in an aircraft factory while her navy husband was overseas, fell for a 4-F coworker (Kurt Russell), even though the inexperienced assembler could not find a left-handed screwdriver. In an offbeat made-for-television tale, Highgate Pictures' *Summer of My German Soldier* recounted the bittersweet experiences of a Jewish teenage girl who fell for an escaped Nazi POW in a small town in Georgia. In nearby Mississippi, where a young draftee (Matthew Broderick) experienced the many vagaries of World War II military training in Universal's *Biloxi Blues*, the Brooklynite quickly realized, "It's hot. It's like Africa hot. Tarzan couldn't take this kind of hot." In a more somber mood, Columbia's *A Soldier's Story* told the unusual tale of violence, strife, and murder at a segregated training base. In CBS's *Too Young the Hero*, teenage idol Rick Schroder portrayed the real-life story of Calvin Graham, a twelve-year-old boy, who, because of his mature looks, hoodwinked navy recruiters, joined this service, and, at Guadalcanal, earned the Purple Heart. Later, after some military mix-up, he was imprisoned until everything straightened out in this made-for-television photodrama.

MGM's *Maria's Lovers* showcased the problems a returning POW (John Savage) encountered when his marriage unraveled in this sudsy, domestic melodrama. In war-torn London, Columbia's *Hope and Glory* looked at the blitz through the eyes of a nine-year-old boy (Sebastian Rice-Edwards) who imagined only fantasy and games as Luftwaffe bombs dropped near his parents' home. Village Roadshow's *Rebel* revealed more problems of the heart when a wounded American marine (Matt Dillon), recuperating in an Australian hospital, fell for a local singer, tiptoed away from a military infirmary, and moved in with the comely chanteuse. Eventually, the young leatherneck saw the light and, in a moment of reconciliation, returned to his outfit. Sometimes human emotions superseded the combat experience. TriStar Pictures' *Every Time We Say Goodbye* told the unusual situation of an idealist American flyer (Tom Hanks) who joined the RAF months before Pearl Harbor and, after some complicated adventures, wound up in a Jerusalem hospital, convalescing from a leg injury. Soon, he was romantically involved with a devout Jewish girl, but as the son of a pacifist Protestant minister, the religious differences presented numerous obstacles for a permanent relationship. In another lost-love episode, United Artists' *Captive Hearts* belabored the unlikely story of an army flyer (Chris Makepeace) who parachuted from an exploding B-25 into an isolated northern Japan region. Quickly apprehended by nearby villagers, the next few days included making friends with locals, repairing a dilapidated roof, demonstrating basic baseball rules to children, staying clear of an overage militarist, learning some falcon commands, and, finally, falling for a pretty widow, who quickly turned him into mush. Eventually, the village patriarch (Pat Morita), spotting Japanese forces nearby, trekked him to the Sea of Japan, found a small boat, and pointed to the China coast. Now, in the sudsiest of farewells, the crestfallen lovers, realizing they were "two countries, one heart," stared lugubriously at the water, fully aware, as the torch song prophesized, they may never meet again.

A few titles examined the antipodean aspect of the war. In Fauna Productions' *Attack Force Z*, some fast-moving Australian commandos, spearheaded by Captain Mel Gibson, landed on a well-guarded Japanese island, moved inland, and rescued survivors of a recent plane crash before top-secret information fell into enemy hands. With Sam Neill as the radio operator, this low-budget production reminded audiences that Anzac forces played an integral part in the victory effort. Belinon Productions' *Emma's War* examined an Australian family's difficulties revolving around a father fighting in New Guinea, a fourteen-year-old daughter's coming-of-age in a boarding school, a mother coping with separation, and a conchie (conscientious objector) trying to maintain his beliefs, especially after the Japanese bombed Sydney. Lee Remick starred in this domestic potboiler. Suatu Film's *Death of a Soldier* portrayed the negative side of the U.S. military justice system, when a mentally deranged GI was expeditiously executed for local murders. Loosely based on the Brownout Strangler incidents, this storyline portrayed MacArthur as an imperious officer, lacking remorse or forgiveness. Another screenplay depicting the five-star commander's influence, *The Last Bastion*, wove in and out of historical events and famous personages gathered in Sydney and their various roles, both defensive and offensive, against the Japanese.

Frequently, Hollywood producers opted for laughs, pratfalls, and contretemps, using the war as a convenient backdrop. In an offbeat take suggesting that the Pacific war resembled nothing more than a balmy day at the beach, Universal's remake of *Operation Petticoat* offered one gag after another when some smiling nurses came aboard a submarine operating in the Pacific theater, repeating most of the shenanigans found in the 1959 original. In this version John Austin and Richard Gilliland copycatted the Cary Grant and Tony Curtis roles in a harmless romp that included a buxom nurse blocking a narrow walkway, a smooth-as-glass ensign bird-dogging needed supplies, and, of course, an inadvertent pink paint job on the underwater vessel's hull. Another remake of an established war comedy, Fox's *To Be or Not to Be*, spoofed the Third Reich's expansion policies, mimicking Hitler when a group of Polish actors, plotting an escape from Warsaw, created a theatrical diversion and, after some fancy legerdemain, sang a few bawdy songs (including an anachronistic Pakistan reference), impersonated the führer, and finally, after a bouncy Mack Sennett car chase, flew off to freedom. With Mel Brooks and Anne Bancroft re-creating the Jack Benny and Carole Lombard 1942 roles, this 1983 screenplay rehashed much of the earlier dialogue, including Hitler's phony tantrum, "All I want is peace. Peace! Peace! A little piece of Poland, a little piece of France."

Likewise, Universal's frolic spoofing patriotism, *1941*, ran amok with its burlesque of stateside fears and widespread paranoia hours after the Pearl Harbor attack, when many West Coast residents, certain that Japanese warships were in their harbors, resorted to numerous schemes to repel these invaders. Highlighting Dan Aykroyd, Ned Betty, and Treat Williams in featured roles, this entire lark resembled the monkey business found at fraternity parties, including the madcap antics of John Belushi, who as Air Corps pilot Wild Bill Kelso flew aimlessly over the California skies proclaiming, "I've been chasing a Jap squadron for a day and a half. I lost 'em somewhere over Fresno." Another made-for-laughs title, Pimlico's *Escape to Athene*, depicted the playful adventures of some Allied POWs (Elliott Gould, David Niven, Richard Roundtree, and Sonny Bono) stashed away in a Greek island prison and their frequent fooling around with the commandant (Roger Moore). With one gag after another, including references to the greed associated with British imperialism, a quick spoof of B-Westerns, and a take on future Volkswagen sales, this film purported that the Nazi control of Greece, another dark episode of the war, resembled nothing more than a Sunday afternoon picnic.

In a similar vein, but back on home soil, Universal's made-for-television mistaken-identity gag, *Don't Push, I'll Charge When I'm Ready*, recapped the oddball adventures of an Italian POW (Enzo Cerusico) who—following one misunderstanding after another—was drafted into Uncle Sam's army. Another popcorn production, Empire's *Zone Troopers*, pushed World War II verisimilitude to its limit when a group of GIs, squirreled away in the Italian foothills from encroaching *Wehrmacht* troops, located an extraterrestrial ship and quickly struck up a friendly relationship with the funny-looking inhabitants. Soon these two groups teamed up, and within minutes, using their ray guns, routed their adversaries. With Tim Thomerson and Biff Manard in the main roles, the eighty-eight-minute put-on resembled those Saturday-afternoon cliffhangers popular during the 1930s and 1940s.

Another 1940s parody, Universal's *Dead Men Don't Wear Plaid*, rounded up numerous clips from well-known film noir classics—including *The Big*

An unnamed, friendly alien, whose flying saucer recently landed in the Italian countryside, offers his "hands" in camaraderie to American GIs in Danny Bilson's science-fictional romp Zone Troopers. *Courtesy of Empire Pictures.*

Sleep, *Sorry, Wrong Number*, *Johnny Eager*, and *Suspicion*—and incorporated these short segments into a storyline that placed a Los Angeles gumshoe (Steve Martin) one step behind a Nazi spy ring operating in his hometown, even though a field marshal's plan "to wipe out hunger, by aging cheese faster" seemed innocuous. Another spoof, Paramount's *Top Secret*, took numerous swipes at the many World War II B-quickies in an updated screenplay. Instead of swastika-wearing Nazis and banzai-spouting Japanese lurking in every frame, the 1984 villain, the East German Communists, were outfoxed by an American rock-and-roll singer (Val Kilmer). In a continuation of these parodies, an outlandish Harrison Ford played the flamboyant adventurer, erudite professor, and international roamer, Indiana Jones, in three running-wild romps, *Raiders of the Lost Ark*, *Indiana Jones and the Temple of Doom*, and *Indiana Jones and the Last Crusade*. In all these moving pictures, the famous archeologist butted heads with numerous Third Reich officers and their minion sheikhs, quipping, "Nazis. I hate these guys."

Once in a while, Hollywood drifted into la-la land. Vista's low-budget *The Lucifer Complex* told the aftermath of a 1986 nuclear war where deep in the South American jungle, escaped Nazi leaders, under Adolf Hitler's command, cloned numerous American officials hoping to disrupt the recovery period. With Kenneth Wynn, Robert Vaughn, Leo Gordon, and Aldo Ray in leading roles, the entire mishmash, replete with one loose end after another, drifted aimlessly, even though the führer bragged, "The Fourth Reich continues to move forward." Fox's *The Boys from Brazil* entered the same science fiction realm when an escaped Nazi doctor, Josef Mengele (Gregory Peck), now hiding in Paraguay, bred ninety-four identical Hitler clones—hoping to resurrect a new Reich—and reminded a charge, "You are the duplicate of the greatest man in history." His plans, likewise, were wrecked by Lawrence Olivier, an aged Simon Wiesenthal–type Nazi hunter.

When the 1980s came to a close, the Hollywood World War II motion picture still attracted many admirers who applauded America's fighting men leaping out of Higgins boats, running inland, and blasting their foes from their pillboxes, even though most of these viewers cheered from their living-room sofas. With their red-white-and-blue credo, frontal attacks, and hand-to-hand fighting, these screenplays highlighted major victories and recalled glorious moments from recent history. Why wouldn't they? For many young men, these cinematic adventures provided vicarious thrills about a global war that produced straightforward heroes, indisputable issues, and discernible foes.

With its ups and downs, vacillating ideologies, and skewed revisionism, these war films, in one form or another, offered tangible proof of the nation's prowess. For Hollywood this was reassuring news. But one thing seemed certain. In a few years, elaborate semicentennial celebrations would venerate this victory. Why not? Almost fifty years ago the nation's youth fought overseas, and now it was time to revere these aging veterans. And, how should the film industry join the commemoration? The answer seemed simple enough. Keep producing more spectacular motion pictures portraying U.S. forces defeating the Axis scourge. After all, as the popular song proclaimed, "Everybody loves a winner." Conversely, the lyrics continued, "But when you lose, you lose alone."

Chapter Seven

Going, Going, Gone!
Cable Television Explains the War

1990–2007

"Most people gaze neither into the past nor the future, they explore neither truth nor lies, they gaze at the television."—Czech pastor Daniel Vedra, observing his countrymen's reaction to the Communist breakdown, in Ivan Klima's 1997 novel, *The Ultimate Intimacy*

Sometime in the 1980s—an exact date is impossible to pin down—the video-cassette recorder emerged as a dominant force in most American living rooms. With two competing formats (Beta and VHS), sales of this popular electronic device soared, and by decade's end over 70 percent of all households could watch their favorite motion pictures at home, either by renting titles at local stores or taping a movie from the airwaves. For many viewers this was the ideal way to enjoy a popular photodrama, even though the setup process, for the all-thumbs crowd, seemed cumbersome. Seizing on this national "problem," president George H. W. Bush—in a moment of executive levity—prophesized that by 1990 all Americans would know how to program their VCRs.

Even with its meteoric rise—by the mid 1990s many children watched VCRs in their bedrooms—this exciting technology suffered the same fate as its electronic cousins, the 78s, LPs, and 45s—when a better mousetrap appeared, the digital video disc, a compact recording that offered a sharper picture. Dubbed the DVD (since most adults associated the initials VD to mean venereal disease, the manufacturers added the superfluous letter D to steer clear of any ambiguity), sales of this equipment took off, and by 2006 the VCR, like scratch cakes, all-cotton socks, letterpress, and local bookstores, faded from the national landscape.

Hollywood, of course, moved quickly to adapt to this expanding technology. Realizing the financial impact at the box office, the moguls recognized they could sell current releases or, for greater profit, delve into their elaborate

libraries and copy motion pictures onto this format. Naturally, factory-pro-
duced movies, first on tape and later on disc, proved popular, and consumers
bought them by the handfuls. For the first time in cinema history, viewers—
instead of heading to a theater—could own (or rent) their favorite titles and
leisurely watch them. As expected, World War II dramas remained high on the
sales chart. Why wouldn't they? Ever since Pearl Harbor, these photodramas
with their red-white-and-blue endings offered tangible reminders of victory.

And what better place to show victory than France's western coastline,
where on June 6, 1944, American troops landed on Omaha Beach, ran many
yards inland, reached a tenuous seawall, and—following deadly setbacks—
destroyed the Axis bunkers, securing a wide area? Soon additional men and
matériel poured ashore and within hours, General Eisenhower announced
that, after months of logistical planning, Allied forces were on French soil.

With this historic invasion as its backdrop, DreamWorks Pictures produced
an elaborate photodrama recreating the D-Day invasion as seen through the
eyes of a small infantry squad. Directed by Steven Spielberg, *Saving Private
Ryan* expanded the boundaries of combat films with its graphic portrayal of
death, destruction, and mayhem. Probably no other Hollywood screenplay
has ever equaled the first twenty-eight minutes of this motion picture for its
realism, pathos, and horror as U.S. troops struggled forward, desperately trying to grab a foothold on Fortress Europe.

In the early hours of June 6, as hundreds of Higgins boats lumbered
through the turbulent Normandy waters toward the French coastline, one
Ranger squad stared apprehensively from their small landing craft, pondering
the next few minutes. Under the command of Captain John Miller (Tom
Hanks), these men were frightened, nauseous, and bewildered by the looming
beachfront. Suddenly, the navy driver yelled, "Thirty seconds, God be with
ya." Moments later the ramp dropped, but immediately scores of bullets entered the hull, killing and wounding the startled GIs. From their hilltop advantage, German soldiers, firing incessantly at this vulnerable landing craft,
seem indestructible. American bodies quickly filled the small boat.

"Over the side," the captain yelped, and terrified infantrymen plunged into
deep water. Some died instantly, killed by stray bullets. A few, unable to un-
tangle themselves from heavy gear, drowned, but a handful reached the surface and crawled onto the beach. Dead bodies strewed the water's edge as
American soldiers dropped rapidly from German machine-gun fire. Arms,
legs, heads, torsos, and intestines bobbled in the surf. Expiring GIs cried out
for their mothers or called upon patron saints. Some soldiers exploded from
artillery shells, others were immolated. Everywhere death and destruction assaulted the moviegoers' senses, echoing Henry V's observation, "Those who
die in battle do not die well."

Sidestepping this carnage, the squad finally regrouped, reached a small sea-wall, and following Captain Miller's orders, "Let's get back into the war," charged uphill, routing Axis defenders from their fortified lairs. Slowly, the tide changed as additional GIs joined the fray. Now, dead Germans lined the hillside as American forces plunged upward. Moving quickly, angry infantrymen killed anyone in their path, while their captain watched reflectively. For this small squad, this moment of triumph, a bittersweet victory, seemed tempered by the hundreds of American bodies scattered on Omaha Beach. Slowly panning across this deadly landscape, director Spielberg's camera lugubriously zoomed downward, pausing at water's edge on one isolated soldier. A name was sten-ciled on the fallen man's musette bag. This dead soldier was Sean Ryan.

Two days later, standing in his Washington, D.C., office, General George C. Marshall listened attentively to a report about an unusual casualty situa-tion. Two brothers, Sean and Peter Ryan, were killed on Omaha and Utah Beaches, while a third, Daniel Ryan, died the previous week in New Guinea. For the army's chief of staff this news was exasperating because a fourth son, James Ryan, parachuted behind enemy lines on June 6, his status unknown. Recalling Abraham Lincoln's letter to a mother who lost five sons during the Civil War, the four-star general spoke bluntly, "If this boy's alive, we are go-ing to send somebody to find him."

Back in France, Captain Miller heard his orders: select seven men, travel quickly into the Normandy countryside, locate Private James Ryan, and re-turn him to headquarters for immediate deployment to the zone of interior. A few hours later, one GI in this small squad, miles from the safety of their front lines, grumbled openly, badmouthing the mission's logic. "You wanna ex-plain the math of this to me? Where's the sense of risking the lives of eight of us to save one guy?" In a facetious tone, Captain Miller retorted, "Our duty as soldiers! We all have orders—we have to follow them." With this com-mand, the Rangers trekked inland. After a few diversions—that included fighting in a village, locating the wrong James Ryan, attacking an Axis radar station, incurring two combat deaths, and destroying an SS armored truck—the Rangers finally found Private James Francis Ryan, from Iowa, holed up in an abandoned town, ready, with his platoon, to blow a strategic bridge. Quietly, Captain Miller explained his assignment. "Our orders are to bring you back." Somewhat shaken, but firm, the young paratrooper balked. "I have my orders too, Sir, they don't include me abandoning my post."

Now what? Should the straight-arrow field officer pull his rank, assert his au-thority, and order Ryan back, or did the GI have a point? Should they hold their position or return to the beachfront? After some soul-searching, Captain Miller issued new directives, "Disperse, you know what to do." This order needed no explanation. His troops were not leaving. For Miller, this change of heart reiterated his credo that their "objective was to win the War." German soldiers soon attacked, and, after a fierce battle, the GIs held the town. But one casualty stood out. Captain Miller—the man who once taught Ralph Waldo Emerson to high school students—had fallen on the bridge, another dead soldier miles from his Pennsylvania home. As for Private Ryan, he remained unscathed and now was heading back to his Iowa farm. For him, the war was over.

An elaborate motion picture, *Saving Private Ryan* touched every human emotion. No viewer could remain oblivious to the horrific opening scene in which untold American bodies permeated the Normandy beachfront, or a follow-up sequence back in the nation's capital, where speedy typists prepared thousand of condolence letters informing families about their sons' combat deaths, or a few scenes later when a clergyman quietly appeared in Mrs. Ryan's doorway. Clearly, the cost for the Normandy victory was immeasurable. As for the mission, the search for Private Ryan brought out the best about America. Following General Marshall's directive, no mother should bear an unreasonable burden. With soft-spoken references to the Sullivan brothers' tragedy (these five sailors, who perished on the USS *Juneau*, came from Iowa; likewise, Private Ryan was from Iowa), the senior officer's words resounded, "We are going to get him the hell out of there."

Certainly director Spielberg stretched a point here—logistically, accurate Normandy casualty information could not reach Washington the next day—but this embellishment created the storyline. With subtle elements of Fox's *The Fighting Sullivans* and *A Walk in the Sun*, this motion picture—a classic retelling of the World War II squad story—reiterated why combat men bonded, protected, and, occasionally, died in each other's arms. As for finding Private Ryan, perhaps Captain Miller had the right idea: "Ah, Ryan. I don't know anything about Ryan. I don't care. The man means nothing to me. It's just a name. You know if finding him so that he can go home—if that earns me the right to get back to my wife, then that's my mission."

Other soldiers fighting the Axis also wanted to see their friends and family. Beacon's *A Midnight Clear* recalled the adventures of six GIs from an intelligence squad, tiptoeing around the Ardennes Forest during the December 1944 Battle of the Bulge. Soon, these Americans ran into some young Germans, but instead of firing their weapons, the two sides pitched snowballs back and forth in a playful, schoolboy manner, suggesting that war—a concept created by elderly statesmen but fought by much younger people—was really a game. Basically an antiwar allegory, the photodrama downplayed all heroics but instead disparaged various officers for their callous behavior, allowing a sergeant (Ethan Hawke) to complain, "Nobody in the army ever admits that someone on our side is killed. They're either lost, like Christopher Robin, hit, as in a batter hit by a pitched ball, or they get 'it' like in hide-and-go-seek."

In sharp contrast, another portrayal of a cold December 1944 offensive, HBO's *When Trumpets Fade*, steered wide of allegory but, instead, graphically re-created the horrendous Battle of Hurtgen Forest, a confrontation in which American casualties rose every hour. With Ron Eldard in the starring role as a skeptical GI, quickly promoted to sergeant and then lieutenant, this made-for-television drama reiterated that most soldiers considered survival, not patriotism, their primary goal, echoing their leader's words, "If I can help in any way without endangering my life, I won't hesitate." A parallel storyline, with close ties to *Kelly's Heroes*, Carnaby International's *The Last Drop* recounted the misadventures of Allied soldiers, dropped behind Dutch lines during the Market Garden offensive to retrieve stolen art treasures before the Germans shipped this booty to Berlin. With Captain Billy Zane piloting the glider, "Everything," he quipped, "was on a need-to-know basis," even though two rogue Nazis were after the same plunder.

In a similar vein, Anthem Pictures' *The Fallen* focused on the October 1944 northern Italian campaign, where Axis and American troops cautiously eyed each other's movements. Loosely modeled on *The Young Lions*, this four-tier storyline reflected both sides' hopes and fears. Certainly, these ambivalent days created unprecedented problems: the ragtag German soldiers, with a handful of Italian soldiers, facing certain defeat, struggled to maintain discipline while the local partisans bickered about the merits of communism versus fascism, promising, "One day, all wars would be fought on chessboards." On the other side, the GIs—determined to stay out of harm's way—waited apprehensively, not wanting to be the last casualty.

But some Americans were less fortunate. Go Films' *Saints and Soldiers* re-created the December 1944 Malmedy Massacre where dozens of GIs—captured during the Battle of the Bulge—were machine-gunned by German soldiers near a small Belgian town. During the confusion, four infantrymen darted into the woods and for a few days dodged enemy patrols, always fearful, as one airborne sergeant warned, "They're shooting prisoners." With no weapons and little food, the foot soldiers eked out a precarious existence until a rescued British pilot, clutching a map folder, revealed he was "in possession of some crucial intelligence" and needed help. Many close calls followed this haggard group, but their luck ran out near their front lines after *Wehrmacht* forces killed three members. Following another skirmish, the two lone survivors, evading Nazi bullets, stumbled into the Allied camp, delivering the needed information. With numerous biblical, mystical, and ontological references, this ninety-minute screenplay also downplayed heroics, suggesting in an unobtrusive way that survival, a basic human instinct, was the GI's only credo.

Certain screenplays, of course, depicted the global conflict in elaborate, almost mythical proportions. DreamWorks' ten-part, made-for-television homage

to a single company from the elite 101st Airborne, *Band of Brothers*, placed
these men under a microscope by retelling their three-year odyssey, beginning
with the unit's formation, through numerous major campaigns, until the joyous
V-E Day celebration. In a 705-minute tribute, this all-volunteer group experienced every human emotion—apprehension, angst, vigilance, vengeance, eu-
phoria, exultation, triumph, and, of course, death—testifying to the cohesive
spirit that centuries earlier bonded Shakespeare's Henry V, "We few, we happy
few, we happy band of brothers."

Beginning in the hot 1942 Georgia sun, a disparate group of inexperienced
army men, eager for adventure and the extra allotment, worked assiduously,
hoping to earn the coveted paratrooper insignia, an emblem awarded after
five jumps. While this schedule pushed most GIs to their physical limits, their
psychological health suffered from the frequently irrational and occasionally
sadistic badgering by their commanding officer (David Schwimmer), a
blowhard first lieutenant seemingly bent on proving himself. After weeks of
hard training—and with some encouragement from a second lieutenant
(Damian Lewis)—these newly appointed troopers bonded into the Easy Company of the 506th Regiment, realizing, as one GI exclaimed, "It don't matter
where we go—once we get into combat, the only person you can trust is yourself and the fellow next to you."

Now for the war. After a cramped Atlantic crossing, Easy Company
reached their English countryside base where the training intensified. Then,
on the evening of June 4, the troopers geared up, ready to mount their C-47s
for their invasion drop, while the company sergeant waggishly reminded his
pals, "If you did not sign your GI life insurance policy, go over to Headquarters Company. Boys, don't let your families miss out on $10,000." Then the
stand-down order arrived: no takeoff tonight. But the next night, all was
ready. Easy Company boarded their aircraft, slid into their bucket seats, and
as the carrier plane gained altitude heading for France, each man sat taut,
backpedaling unknown fears.

Suddenly explosives filled the skies as German ack-ack bursts forced the
troopers to hook up, stand by the door, and, as flames engulfed their aircraft,
make an early jump. Now on French soil, the men of Easy Company—scattered over many miles—fought Germans, bumped into French nationals, and
finally regrouped as a cohesive unit. With an operational command post del-
egating orders, the fast-moving squad, sensing that *Wehrmacht* forces were
everywhere, stood ready to fight. Soon, they attacked an Axis weapons post
and, after a fierce battle, destroyed their artillery, allowing safe access for the
GIs who were storming the beaches eight miles away. With this initial victory,
a stark reality emerged. Easy Company—created two years earlier with a
group of green, rough-and-ready volunteers, high-spirited lads who boasted

the world was their oyster—suffered its first casualties. Two men were dead and others wounded.

As an elaborate motion picture, based on Stephen Ambrose's best-selling book and utilizing fourteen directors, *Band of Brothers* downplayed flag-waving histrionics and, instead, focused on each trooper's hopes and dreams, fears and aspirations, strengths and weaknesses, in a subdued manner that allowed the group's heroism to speak for itself. For the next eleven months this unit fought at Carentan, Market Garden, and Bastogne, suffering unbearable casualties. During these encounters myriad problems and personalities emerged: one officer turned into an alcoholic while another lieutenant fell apart during enemy shelling, became mute, and was quickly relieved. A third officer became a one-man show, firing his machine gun from the hip, charging German fortifications. Enlisted men died regularly from explosives or sniper shots while ammunition, clean uniforms, and hot meals never materialized. Even the winter weather, the coldest in recent years, offered more headaches because of inadequate protective clothing. Untried replacements created added concerns because these men were either cocky or naive, unaccustomed to warfare's nuances. And sometimes, in moments of expediency, Americans shot German prisoners. Once, a U.S. captain, realizing the dangers of a nighttime patrol, fudged a morning report, claiming the nonexistent reconnaissance produced negative results.

Finally, Allied forces crossed the Rhine, and within weeks the German military collapsed, revealing unbelievable horror for Easy Company when they liberated a concentration camp, staring at the hollow-eyed, near-dead inmates. Many of these hardened paratroopers simply stared in disbelief, unable to comprehend Hitler's Final Solution, pondering the evil forces that created such despair. Even their captain looked confused: "The locals claimed that they never knew the camps existed—they say we [the Americans] are exaggerating." Days later, the men raced toward their victory prize, the führer's exclusive Bavarian hideaway, Eagle's Nest.

Why shouldn't this battle-worn group receive the lion's share? After all, one officer observed, Easy Company's goal was "to move the ball forward, one yard at a time," and ignore vulnerabilities. "We're paratroopers, we're supposed to be surrounded." But not everything worked out well. A junior officer, who landed in Normandy and suffered many close calls, waved his Dear John letter, moaning, "My wife is divorcing me. She's taking everything, taking the house, taking the kid, taking the dog." As for the notifications of combat deaths, that, too, was never pleasant, requiring proper comportment: "You tell them [the families] what you always tell them. Their sons died as heroes." And, unfortunately, that rate was high. Easy Company's attrition stood as a grim but tangible reminder of this group's achievements. As reiterated by

A paratroop officer (Neal McDonough) examines his options before ordering his squad onto a French roadway in HBO's testimony to the men of Easy Company, 506th Regiment, 101st Airborne, Band of Brothers. *Courtesy of HBO.*

a surviving member, interviewed in the late nineties for this motion picture, "I treasure my remark to a grandson who asked, Grandpa, were you a hero in the war? No, I answered, but I served in a company of heroes."

Every branch of service contained its own peril. Warner Bros. airborne saga *Memphis Belle* focused closely on the exploits of the first B-17 crew to fly the enviable twenty-fifth mission in the European theater. With Matthew Modine in the pilot's seat, this arduous flight from the bucolic English countryside to the

German port city of Bremen contained one hazard after another as Axis ack-ack blanketed the skies, and Luftwaffe fighters attacked furiously. Finally, the aircraft reached its target, and the crew—inspired by their captain's words, "If we don't drop these bombs right in the pickle barrel there are going to be a lot of innocent people killed,"—released the explosives. Following hours of white-knuckle situations, the aircraft landed safely at its home base.

The high seas presented similar risks. Castle Hill's *Proud* recounted the adventures of the first all-black destroyer crew that manned the USS *Mason* during the ship's many perilous Atlantic crossings at the height of Nazi wolf-pack attacks. Told in flashback by a surviving member (Ozzie Davis), this Eleanor Roosevelt experiment proved that black enlistees were capable and loyal mariners, men who would not flinch from duty. Reminiscing about this experience—over fifty years later—the words of a crewman said it all: "This is my land, I defended it, and the 160 Black men on the USS *Mason* defended it too!"

Over in North Africa, Allied soldiers fought tenaciously. Showtime's *Sahara* starred James Belushi as the tough-talking tank commander (Humphrey Bogart's role in the 1943 production), who with a handful of Allied soldiers prevented hundreds of haggard Nazis from obtaining needed water at an isolated desert well. Completely outnumbered, Belushi regularly taunted the Germans by suggesting his small group could drink and bathe all day long, boasting to a Nazi major that he was not "the guy with a bunch of casualties lying around for the buzzards to pick." In a different vein, Paramount's *Enemy at the Gates* examined the Stalingrad siege where Red Army and *Wehrmacht* forces collided while—off in their private war—two sharpshooters, one Russian (Jude Law), the other German (Ed Harris), trained their scopes across no-man's-land, hoping to locate their adversary. With an opening scene similar to *Saving Private Ryan*, the photodrama clearly explained how this battle became a turning point, even though an explanatory map depicted Switzerland as a recent Nazi conquest.

Wartime, of course, produced convoluted intelligence missions. Ecosse Films' *Charlotte Grey* lauded a heroic Scottish woman (Cate Blanchett), who in 1943 parachuted into France as a Resistance operative but spent much time searching for her boyfriend, a young airman (Rupert Penry-Jones). Along the way, she encountered local collaborationists, numerous infightings, and Communist sympathizers. Canal+'s *A Woman at War* recounted the harrowing adventures of a Belgian loyalist (Martha Plimpton), who became a translator for the Gestapo and sent privileged information to the underground, even though her lover (Eric Stoltz) was a traitor. Fox's *Shining Through* watched an OSS director (Michael Douglas) move unobtrusively through numerous European capitals gleaning needed war information before the Day of Infamy. After America's entry, his German-speaking secretary (Melanie Griffith)—who

passed an arbitrary, ad hoc test, "to stand up, turn around, and close your eyes
and tell me everything you see in the room," even though a fifty-star U.S. flag
adorned the office—entered the Fatherland, and, following some comic-strip
adventures, slithered into Nazi headquarters, photographed classified documents, and, with her supervisor's help, finally reached Switzerland.

Intermedia Films' *Enigma* glossed over the complex work of the Bletchley
Park British code breakers, who, after much trial and error, unraveled the secrets of the German ENIGMA box, an intricate device used to relay messages
between commands. Working day and night, a top-notch mathematician
(Dougray Scott) finally cracked the Nazi permutations, even though "The
machine has a hundred and fifty million, million, million ways of doing it, according to how you set these three rotors, and how you connect these plugs."
With a new girlfriend at his side (Kate Winslet), the twosome, in a surreal
subplot, stumbled upon top-secret Soviet information about the infamous
Katyn Forest massacre, where Russian soldiers slaughtered most of the Polish officers corps. Loosely based on the life of famed cryptologist Alan Tur-
ing, the storyline adeptly sidestepped any mention of his homosexuality, persecution, and eventual suicide. Two other screenplays used this German
machine as their fulcrum. Universal's *U-571* detailed the adventures of some
U.S. sailors on a search-and-seize mission, who boarded a U-boat, overpowered the crew, and seized a code box. With Matthew McConaughey leading
this American assault team, the bluejackets moved quickly to secure their
prize and, for good measure, torpedoed a Nazi destroyer.

Another screenplay, Artisan Entertainment's *In Enemy Hands*, pushed cred-
ibly to the edge of space when a group of U.S. seamen—drifting helplessly in
the Atlantic—were rescued by a benevolent U-boat commandant who, contrary
to Hitler's take-no-prisoners policy, offered sanctuary. Then, in a surprising
volte-face, the commandant requested help operating the submarine, because a
runaway meningitis epidemic had crippled his crew. With basic survival at
stake, this symbiotic relationship reached the straining point when, above the
waves, Allied and German vessels battled. With an American victory in sight,
the U.S. chief (William Macy), as a benevolent gesture, looked the other way
as the Nazi officer destroyed the ENIGMA machine, rationalizing, "A promise
is a promise." As a 2004 revisionist fairy tale, the entire motion picture sugarcoated every aspect of the Third Reich's brutal open-seas policy, pathetically
suggesting that Nazi officers acted chivalrously in the Atlantic Theater.

The fight against Germany continued in other formats. Fine Line Features'
black comedy, *Mother Night*, based on Kurt Vonnegut's novel, told the strange
story of an American playwright, Howard Campbell (Nick Nolte), who married a German actress, moved to Berlin, and—dismayed by National Socialism—returned to New York. Quietly recruited by U.S. intelligence officers for

espionage work, a handler politely warned him, "Your role will remain classified and Uncle Sam's official position is you're the scum of the earth." During
the War, his daily anti-Semitic, anti-American radio broadcasts—employing
an intricate system of pauses and coughs—contained valuable information for
the Allies. After V-E Day, he slipped back into New York City, where he lived
uneventfully for fifteen years until Mossad agents arrived in 1961 and, after
some fancy maneuvering, spirited their prized war criminal to Israel. Now, sitting alone in a spartan cell, abandoned by everyone, he chatted amicably with
Adolf Eichmann, another prisoner awaiting trial.

In a different vein, Butcher's Run Films' *The Man Who Captured Eichmann* praised the Israeli intelligence service that finally uncovered the high-
ranking Nazi responsible for much of the Holocaust, Adolf Eichmann, who
fled to Argentina in April 1945 and lived furtively for fifteen years under an
assumed name. With Robert Duvall in the starring role, this made-for-television production glamorized the diligence of these agents—hardened men who
patiently eyed their target, seized him off the street at an opportune moment,
and, finally, returned him to Israel. Another spy screenplay, Miramax's multilayer tale of romance and intrigue, *The English Patient*, recounted the comings and goings of a Hungarian count (Ralph Fiennes), who in prewar Egypt
flew over the desert, ostensibly taking photographs for a geographical society
but, in reality, preparing maps for the English military. Now ensconced in a
Tuscan hospital, a horribly burned combat victim unable to move, he slowly
assembled segments from the past, including an adulterous relationship with
a fellow-pilot's wife. Similarly, Remstar Films' *Head in the Clouds* involved
the playful experiences of three friends—a Spanish Civil War nurse, a French
Resistance operative, and a Nazi colonel's mistress—who frivolously experiment in some 1944 Paris ménage à trois escapades, hoping to escape from
the political realities unfolding around them.

Sometimes the Italian and German forces flaunted their political differences. Universal's *Captain Corelli's Mandolin* re-created the tense mood
when both armies occupied a small Greek island. Initially formal to each
other, the German commandant soon locked horns with an Italian officer
(Nicolas Cage) about his lackadaisical approach to military discipline and obvious interest in food, wine, music, and women. But the happy-go-lucky captain shrugged off the Nazi's complaint. "I have always found something in
life worth singing about and for that I cannot apologize." However, Mussolini's departure changed everything, and now both sides battled each other.
With Penélope Cruz appearing as the village beauty and, eventually, the
sweetheart of the strutting, mandolin-playing captain, the storyline sugarcoated Italy's Axis Pact role, suggesting this nation was, basically, an unwilling participant. One anachronistic scene—a June 1944 radio announcement

that Rome had fallen and Italy surrendered—missed its mark by almost nine months, since the Italian government capitulated in September 1943 and one month later declared war against Germany. Consequently, a good part of this screenplay was historically inaccurate.

In a lighthearted mood, Hallmark's *In Love and War* recounted the youthful adventures of the popular travel writer Eric Newby (Callum Blue) who—in 1943, as a British lieutenant—was captured by the Italians, placed in an orphanage-turned-prison, flirted with local women, and finally escaped, hiding in a nearby village with an antifascist's daughter. As a Sunday-night feature produced by a popular greeting card company, the entire screenplay depicted most Italians as totally inept fighters, solely interested in finding some vestiges of *la dolce vita.*

Life in occupied countries contained its fair share of uncertainties. In a slightly upbeat tone, Blue Wolf Productions' *Jakob the Liar* told the story of a mild-mannered shopkeeper (Robin Williams), living in an unnamed Polish ghetto amid suicide and depression, and his uncanny ability to spread phony news reports from a "secret" radio, creating a sliver of optimism for his doomed neighbors. Hollywood Pictures' *Swing Kids* recalled the problems some German students—all fans of American swing music, British fashions, and Harlem slang—endured, including their ongoing conflicts with the Hitler Youth brigades, when the Third Reich banned these decadent foreign influences. With Frank Whaley as a long-haired teenager enamored of the exuberant sounds of Benny Goodman and Count Basie, his disdain toward political issues was obvious: "No one who likes swing can become a Nazi."

The New Order disrupted everything. Stillking Film's *The Ring* rekindled the arduous struggle of a young German woman (Nastassja Kinski), who was separated from her family, imprisoned by the Nazis, released, and finally married a *Wehrmacht* officer. Then, in 1945, after the Russians entered Berlin and killed her husband, she fled to America hoping to find her family. Based on a best-selling Danielle Steele novel, this made-for-television soap opera, filmed in various locations, restated the emotional problems that nations experienced during this global upheaval. In a similar heartthrob vein, Paramount's *The Garden of Redemption* recalled the inner conflicts of an Italian priest (Anthony LaPaglia), who could mislead SS officers but could not shake off his sexual feelings for a woman in the Resistance.

Castle Hill Productions' *A Day in October* praised the quiet heroism of a Danish family's involvement with the underground movement, smuggling Jewish refugees into neutral Sweden and doing some sabotage work in a munitions plant. Amy International Artists' *That Summer of White Roses* remembered the simple lifestyle of ordinary people in a Yugoslavian riverside resort town and their ordeal when German invaders entered their lives. Hallmark's fairy tale, *Silent Night*, told a dubious 1944 Christmas Eve parable about a German mother and her son who took refuge in a family cabin near the snowy Ardennes' war front. Soon three American GIs jumped into this shelter, and moments later, three lost German soldiers arrived. Initially, the two sides behaved belligerently. One U.S. private (Romano Orzari) badmouthed the Axis, "I had a whole life planned until you guys invaded Poland," but eventually the *Mutter*—after some warmhearted yuletide season dialogue—convinced the combatants to halt their differences and share a Christmas dinner. Supposedly based on a true story, much of the storyline overlooked Hitler's expansionism and, instead, suggested that the war could easily be won through kindness and brotherhood.

Motion pictures about the Holocaust overwhelmed every viewer. Another depressing Auschwitz story, Lions Gate Films' *The Grey Zone*, rationalized why a few Jewish prisoners guided inmates into the gas chamber and later disposed of the ashes. With David Arquette in a leading role, this brutal screenplay pushed cinematography to its limits with unremitting scenes of torture and suffering. In somewhat better circumstances, Focus Features' *The Pianist* told the remarkable story of a Polish Jew who, with the help of some underground members and kindhearted friends, survived the war by hiding in various Warsaw locations. Based on the autobiography of Wladyslaw Szpilman, this accomplished musician (Adrien Brody) did everything to save himself, vowing, "If I'm going to die, I prefer to die in my own home." Completely surrounded with deprivation but determined to stay alive at any cost, he managed, with some unexpected good luck, to avoid capture.

Other elaborate made-for-television productions appeared on Sunday-night programming. Avnet/Kerner Productions' *Uprising* recalled the pitiful existence that thousands of Polish Jews—jammed inside Warsaw's old slum district—experienced as hunger and disease routinely claimed many lives. But in April 1943, these hapless victims, realizing that survival was impossible, armed themselves and, for the next thirty days, battled the Axis forces from street barricades, hidden tunnels, and dark cellars. Unable to continue this uprising, they were quickly overrun and subsequently annihilated. With Donald Sutherland as the Jewish Council chairman struggling with Third Reich leaders for leniency ("I try to minimize the damage"), the entire 177-minute docudrama mirrored German brutality. Foxboro Company Productions' *In the Presence of Mine Enemies* offered additional evidence regarding the Warsaw Ghetto. Here, a pacifist rabbi (Armin Mueller-Stahl) watched helplessly as ongoing deprivation and death took its toll in this imprisoned enclave. As a test of faith, he urged tolerance, while his nineteen-year-old son—full of unrealistic expectations—demanded reprisal. With many examples of Nazi cruelty, the screenplay, remaining steadfast to historical reality, retold this sad episode with dignity and clarity.

Other Sunday-night titles reminded viewers about Germany's infamous Final Solution. HBO's *Conspiracy* highlighted the 1942 Wannsee Conference, where fifteen Nazi and SS leaders gathered in a Berlin suburb to resolve what they euphemistically called the Jewish Question. Supervised by Reinhard Heydrich (Kenneth Branagh), these high-ranking officials, comfortably ensconced in a luxurious mansion, lackadaisically decreed that the Jews of Europe, regardless of their age, would be exterminated. In typical bureaucratic manner, Heydrich ordered, "From Lapland to Libya, from Vladivostok to Belfast, no Jews, not one," facetiously reminding his small audience, "Dead women don't get pregnant." Dorothy Pictures' *Anne Frank: The Whole Story* took a slightly different approach than earlier motion pictures about the Amsterdam teenager (Hannah Taylor Gordon) and her world-famous diary portraying the numerous adolescent vagaries associated with growing up—"I like watching people. I make up stories for them"—while her mother, suffering from a midlife crisis of sorts, appeared unhappy with her marriage. After months of confinement in their cramped attic and eventual deaths in the concentration camp, this gloomy drama detailed the poignancy, expectations, and fears of an ordinary family caught up in the throes of Hitler's maddening expansionist policies.

Another agonizing Holocaust story, Leucadia Film Corporation's *Alan and Naomi*, told of the simple maturation of an awkward American Jewish adolescent, Alan (Lukas Haas), living in 1944 Brooklyn, where he routinely played stickball in the crowded Williamsburg neighborhood, while his father, obsessed by the war news, listened to radio programs, studied newspaper reports, and placed colored pins on an international map. When a young, almost catatonic, French refugee, Naomi (Vanessa Zaoui), moved into an upstairs apartment, Alan's mother instructed her son to befriend this new neighbor, explaining the girl's problems stemmed from witnessing her father's brutal death at the hands of storm troopers. Unable to comprehend the girl's reticence, the fourteen-year-old Alan, eager to join his pals on the stickball field, challenged his parents' decision asking, "Why me?" But his father set him straight: "Because you're one of the lucky ones." Soon, Alan befriended the troubled Naomi and, using some ventriloquistic skills, slowly elicited from her those terrible memories of Nazi occupation until a tenuous closeness developed, culminating with an upbeat, this-too-shall-pass message.

Following the German surrender, the Allies denounced former Nazis for their role in perpetrating these atrocities. Alliance's *Nuremberg* detailed the November 1945 courtroom procedures of this international tribunal that levied one charge after another against high-ranking supporters for implementing Hitler's genocidal policies. With numerous concentration-camp newsreel inserts, this made-for-television indictment clearly documented the guilt of the Axis defendants as Chief Justice Robert Jackson (Alec Baldwin) explained point by point each man's participation in these crimes against humanity. His nemesis Reichsmarshal Hermann Göring (Brian Cox), taken aback by these accusations, proffered his own rationalization: "Everything Hitler did before the war was right. One day the German people will remember that." Finally condemned to death, Göring's suicide—he swallowed cyanide hours before his execution—remained mysterious, even though the screenplay suggested that perhaps a U.S. Army guard, out of misplaced loyalty, slipped the prisoner a poisonous ampoule.

Famous personages, always an appealing topic, received their share of made-for-television cinematic history. Gideon Productions' *World War II: When Lions Roar* re-created the November 1943 Tehran Conference when the Big Three—Franklin Delano Roosevelt (John Lithgow), Winston Churchill (Bob Hoskins), and Joseph Stalin (Michael Caine)—discussed, argued, and negotiated many issues vital to the victory effort. With much of the dialogue improvised, this 194-minute docudrama detailed an array of topics, including the upcoming Normandy invasion, Poland's demarcation, and Russia's declaration against Japan. Likewise, A&E's *Ike: Countdown to D-Day* reconstructed the months of intricate planning for Operation Overlord. Here, General Dwight Eisenhower (Tom Selleck) wrestled with thorny logistical and personnel problems, explaining to Winston Churchill, "I'm expendable, you are not," until a misty June evening when he issued the go-order, sending thousands of armed forces onto the French beaches. This biopic captured most of the general's mannerisms, idiosyncrasies, and strategies in a clear and forceful way in spite of many anachronisms: The concept of the jet stream, which began with the B-29 Japan bombings, was not understood or even named by June 1944. The acclaimed British propaganda film *Henry V* (which Ike and his staff viewed in March) was not completed until fall 1944. The Canadian maple-leaf flag insignia (prominently displayed on a Juno beach map) was not operational until 1965. And the famous walk among the airborne troops, where the supreme commander bantered and offered cigarettes, occurred on the evening of June 5, not June 6. Similarly, HBO's *The Gathering Storm* lauded Winston Churchill for his untiring leadership. This time, Albert Finney portrayed the prime minister as a pugnacious optimist, a man who asserted, "Mr. Hitler and his Nazi thugs had better look out. We're going to teach them a lesson that they'll never forget."

Other noteworthy achievements were unearthed years later. Universal's *Schindler's List* praised the real-life story of a German national—whose wartime privileges included drinking, gambling, and womanizing—and his gradual transformation from a greedy materialist to an acknowledged humanitarian, a man who risked everything to save thousands of Polish Jews scheduled for deportation and death. In his characterization of a roué turned altruist, Liam Neeson depicted Oskar Schindler as a complicated individual whose prewar ambitions included becoming a millionaire. Four years later he spent his fortune rescuing Jewish workers while defrauding the Nazis by manufacturing defective munitions, saying, "If this factory ever produces a shell that can actually be fired, I'll be very unhappy." With Ralph Fiennes and Ben Kingsley in supporting roles, the 184-minute, black-and-white, Academy Award Holocaust film paid tribute to one man's triumphs during a nightmare period. As an added acknowledgment, Ardent Productions' *Varian's War* told the quiet story of a New England idealist, Varian Fry (William Hurt)—often called the American Schindler—who unobtrusively smuggled hundreds of Jewish refugees, during the volatile pre–Pearl Harbor days, out of France, via Spain, into the United States.

On the other side of the world, Hollywood explained the Pacific fighting. Touchstone's elaborate 183-minute special-effects version of the December 7 sneak attack, *Pearl Harbor*, detailed the Japanese planning and implementation of that morning's assault, and, as a bonus, provided a goofy American love triangle. Directed by Michael Bay, this storyline traced the friendship of two Tennessee boys, Rafe McCawley (Ben Affleck) and Danny Walker (Josh Hartnett), who enlisted in the Air Corps, graduated from flight school, and were assigned to Colonel Jimmy Doolittle's (Alec Baldwin) squadron. Quickly enamored of nurse Evelyn Johnson (Kate Beckinsale), Lieutenant McCawley left for London, joined the Eagle Squadron, and fought the *Luftwaffe* during the Battle of Britain. Back in Honolulu, American admirals—studying their defensive posture against an air assault—concluded, "Pearl Harbor is too shallow for an aerial torpedo attack, we're surrounded by sub nets. All we have to worry about here is sabotage, so we bunched our planes together to make them easier to protect." Meanwhile, Japanese officers in Tokyo, examining military photographs, concluded that these clustered ships and planes made "perfect targets."

As always, the course of true love never ran smooth. From England came word that Lieutenant McCawley died in an aerial fight. Devastated, the pretty nurse fell into a depression but, a few months later, began a shaky romance with her deceased lover's best friend. After all, one onlooker quipped, "She's gotta be with someone, it might as well be you." As expected—after some moonlight coitus—this couple developed a meaningful relationship, only to learn that Lieutenant McCawley was, in fact, alive and back in Honolulu, arriving on December 6, 1941. What a predicament for the two best friends and their girlfriend.

Personifying the worst of Nazi Germany's Final Solution, a concentration-camp commandant (Ralph Fiennes) stares menacingly at the main yard, pondering the fate of hapless inmates in Steven Spielberg's epic Holocaust production, Schindler's List. *Courtesy of Universal Pictures.*

But a few hours later this problem dissipated as Japanese bombs destroyed most of the Pearl Harbor fleet. Determined to avenge this Day of Infamy, President Roosevelt ordered a Tokyo retaliatory raid. Four months later, Colonel Doolittle led this attack, and (according to Touchstone Pictures) damaged many enemy factories before veering west toward China. At the controls of two B-25s, a couple of Tennessee boyhood friends dropped their bombs, crash-landed on the mainland, fought a Japanese patrol, and later returned to Washington, D.C. Only Captain Danny Walker came home in a casket, a wartime casualty. Soon Captain Rafe McCawley and nurse Evelyn Johnson reconciled, married, and, in a typical Hollywood send-off, lived happily ever after.

Overall, *Pearl Harbor* took many liberties and employed spectacular special effects in retelling America's entry into the Second World War. Japanese aircraft zoomed through the skies, explosives shook the ground, and bombs blew apart naval vessels in such a fashion that, at times, the December 7 attack resembled a cacophonic, computerized pinball-machine game. As for the American airmen, how did they learn to fly different aircraft? Could a fighter pilot simply take over the controls of a bomber? A British Spitfire? Also, what happened to cigarettes? In the smoking-was-glamorous 1940s decade, puffers were everywhere. But in this screenplay no one smoked. Was this for real? Soldiers, sailors, and marines without their nicotine pleasure? Even President Roosevelt—whose famous cigarette holder often graced stateside newspapers—refrained. And what about that I-can-stand scene, where the chief executive rose like Lazarus from his chair without any help from his aides? Was that physically possible?

The war against Japan claimed many Americans. Fries Entertainment's *Mission of the Shark* re-created the worst World War II naval casualty. It was about the USS *Indianapolis*—a seafaring cruiser torpedoed in the Pacific Ocean—and the four-day ordeal of its crew, struggling helplessly in the water as prowling sharks killed dozens of sailors, while back in port, no record of this downing reached headquarters. Eventually rescued by dumb luck, navy commanders, in a heartless manner, moved quickly to assert blame, pointed their fingers at the captain (Stacey Keach) for various policy breaches, and convened a court-martial. Years later, however, at a 1960 shipmates' reunion, this officer received a standing ovation from the survivors, a testimony to his wartime leadership. With many close-ups depicting the savagery of the shark attacks (this entire historical episode—with all its gory details—became a prominent scene in Universal's 1975 summer blockbuster *Jaws*), it seems Kafkaesque that the film company producing this Sunday-night made-for-television drama, like many of its competitors, placed the noun "entertainment" in its trademark.

Two wartime lovers (Kate Beckinsale and Ben Affleck) struggle to maintain a modicum of normalcy against the backdrop of the December 7 sneak attack in Michael Bay's Pearl Harbor. Courtesy of Touchstone Pictures.

South Pacific island victories did not come easy. In MGM's *Windtalkers*, a marine sergeant (Nicolas Cage) received a difficult assignment for his unit's impending Saipan invasion. Designated a personal bodyguard for one Navaho code talker, his orders required killing a fellow jarhead—whose esoteric language formed the basis of an intricate message system—rather than allow capture by the Japanese. Fox's *The Thin Red Line* (a remake of Allied Artists' 1964 B-clunker) retold the famous James Jones novel about the army's difficult task of securing Guadalcanal. With Nick Nolte as a gung-ho infantry colonel, the elaborate screenplay provided many frontal assaults as the GIs labored to destroy the Japanese.

Other invasions offered similar risks. Many miles to the north, U.S. Marines landed on a strategic island, Iwo Jima, charged forward, and after weeks of deadly fighting, secured this sulfuric landmass. Originally the subject of the 1949 John Wayne classic, *Sands of Iwo Jima*, this victory uplifted most Americans after a photograph, depicting six Americans raising Old Glory on Mount Suribachi, appeared in daily newspapers. Taken by Joe Rosenthal, this picture made instant heroes of these five marines and one navy corpsman. In 2006, DreamWorks released its interpretation of this famous battle and its aftermath. Directed by Clint Eastwood, *Flags of Our Fathers* detailed the intricate planning, implementation, and success of the invasion, followed by the stateside problems when the three surviving flag raisers embarked on a bond-selling drive.

With Ryan Phillippe, Jesse Bradford, and Adam Beach in leading roles, *Flags of Our Fathers* traced these spirited marines' shipboard preinvasion jitters, the beachfront assault, and the many close calls from Japanese artillery until February 23, 1945, when six men raised a second, much larger American flag on the island's summit, while an Associated Press photographer snapped their picture. By evening's end, three of these Marines were dead. The survivors—after some fancy brass-hat maneuvering—were removed from combat and ordered stateside. Arriving in Washington, D.C., and acclaimed as heroes, the two leathernecks and the bluejacket balked at their accolades but eventually—after a public relations officer moaned, "The last four bond drives came up so short we just printed money"—agreed to appear at rallies. After V-J Day, the threesome took their discharges and returned home. A few years later, Ira Hayes, the Pima Indian who helped raise the Stars and Stripes on a distant island battlefield, died ignominiously in the Arizona sun, a victim of alcohol abuse and wartime guilt.

In retelling this story, director Clint Eastwood pulled out every plug with his stark depictions of beach carnage where marines died violently from explosives, fires, shrapnel, and, later, banzai charges. For the Japanese, the invasion meant American forces were defiling holy ground, since this island, geographically, was part of the mainland. Later, when the three flag raisers toured the States, different problems arose. As a Pima Indian, Ira Hayes endured numerous racial taunts and soon turned to alcohol, while his two pals had other issues. For these three men, their welcome-home-hero reception—with flashbulbs popping, firecrackers crackling, and brass-band music blaring—offered little comfort; instead, all the noise and commotion brought back deadly memories of the Iwo Jima invasion.

Clearly, this motion picture delineated the Iwo Jima fighting in unequivocal terms. On one side, eager American marines, the best of the nation's youth, moved forward to secure this strategic island. Always rough and ready, these leathernecks fought tenaciously, protected each other, and upheld the tenets of semper fidelis. As for their Japanese enemy, that was a different matter. These Japanese soldiers, imbrued with emperor-worship and a medieval death-before-dishonor mentality, mutilated American prisoners, staged numerous banzai assaults, and committed hara-kiri. The advancing marines understood their peril. Be careful at all times. The Japanese attackers wanted to kill Americans.

But a few months later, in December 2006, another motion picture, also directed by Clint Eastwood, took a different look at the Iwo Jima invasion, depicting the Japanese defenders as kind and decent people, helpless pawns in uniform, caught up in the vortex of a war created by militarists so long ago that the reasons seemed obscure, while their nemesis, thousands of offensive American marines, were determined to eradicate every Japanese they saw. Using a predominately Japanese cast, DreamWorks' *Letters from Iwo Jima* portrayed these ill-fated soldiers—waiting for the inevitable arrival of the Western barbarians—as protectors of their emperor and families. Led by a Harvard-educated general (Ken Watanabe), this officer's credo, "I am determined to serve and give my life for my country," provided inspiration for his worn-out battalion, while another shibboleth, "If our children can live safely for one more day it would be worth the one more day that we defend this island," revealed the grim truth.

For these troops, digging trenches, erecting fortifications, enlarging tunnels, and reinforcing cave entrances took their minds off the looming American invasion even though their commander's words, "Our duty is to stop the enemy right here. Do not expect to return home alive," provided little comfort. Farewell letters were written. A few reached the mainland but most never left the island. Decades later, they were unearthed in a bombed-out cave and provided worthy reading. According to the tattered letters, one soldier recalled happy hours working as a baker, another pined for his children, a third remembered his wife's softness, and an officer reminisced about cheerful horseback-riding trips. Overall, these letters limned a Norman Rockwell nation, where thoughtfulness and tenderness, not militarism and aggression, filled the air. Golly!

Swearing to uphold the Bushido creed of death before dishonor, a bemedaled Japanese officer (Ken Watanabe) salutes his beleaguered troops in Clint Eastwood's revisionist retelling of a costly U.S. Marine battle, Letters from Iwo Jima. *Courtesy of Touchstone Pictures.*

Eventually, the Marines landed, ran forward, and after weeks of fighting, captured Iwo Jima. Virtually every Japanese soldier died, most from fire-power or hillside accidents. A handful were self-inflicted. A few surrendered. As for the Americans, their casualties climbed into the thousands, but one un-fortunate marine, wounded near a cave, experienced kindness. Looking at the bleeding leatherneck, an English-speaking general reassured the frightened man and ordered rudimentary medical care. Hours later, however, the marine died. Staring at a dead enemy and listening to their officer read a letter from his mother, the Imperial soldiers realized this young man—over three thou-sand miles from his hometown—imaged themselves: peaceful, happy, and friendly. Peaceful, happy, and friendly? What kind of revisionism was Clint Eastwood peddling? Were these the same Japanese who bayoneted emaciated GIs on the Bataan Death March? Was this the military machine that routinely decapitated civilian prisoners? How about the Rape of Nanjing? Were some of these peaceful, happy, and friendly Imperial soldiers involved in that six-week orgy? How about Shanghai? How many bed-ridden patients did the Japanese slaughter? Should the moviegoer believe, as Clint Eastwood expa-tiated, that these troops quietly arrived, like a deus ex machina, on Iwo Jima without any prior military experience, fresh from their mainland families, to become fodder for some I-want-to-kill-you, sadistic U.S. marines?

Clearly, many World War II combat pictures contained subtle pacifist messages that echoed General MacArthur's dictum, "Only the dead have seen the end of war," and *Letters from Iwo Jima* dramatically mirrored this viewpoint. Certainly, every story has two sides, and history is always written by the winners, but it's difficult to view the Imperial Japanese army as victims. As Jerry Della Femina quipped, weren't the Japanese those wonderful folks who gave us Pearl Harbor?

As for the Japanese prisoner-of-war camps, most photodramas left nothing to the imagination in depicting the barbaric treatment imposed upon all captives. Planet Pictures' *Paradise Road* told the uplifting saga of some women from different countries and social levels who organized a vocal ensemble—in spite of their guards' resistance—to maintain a peripheral level of sanity in these untried circumstances. With scene after scene of Japanese depravity—including setting a prisoner on fire and forcing another to kneel in the afternoon sun inches away from a fatal sword—the women struggled against innumerable hardships, always mindful that, as one victim uttered, "The will to survive is strong, stronger than anything," while their Japanese tormentors grimaced menacingly. Loosely based on the aftermath of the infamous Bangka Island massacre, where Japanese soldiers, on February 16, 1942, forced twenty-one women into waist-high ocean water and then machine-gunned everyone, this Hollywood production offered quiet praise for these survivors and their three-year ordeal. A similar screenplay involving another Indonesian POW camp, NBC's *Silent Cries*, told the harrowing, three-year story of Japanese torture, starvation, rape, and beatings of helpless women, a situation so deplorable that nearly half died from their captors' treatment. Together, these two titles portrayed the Japanese soldier—some fifty years after V-J Day—in terms that few moviegoers could comprehend: uncaring, bestial, and vindictive behavior, supported by historical records.

If such blatant atrocities were routine in the female compounds, how did male prisoners of war survive Japanese captivity? Blood Oath Production's *Prisoners of the Sun* articulated the grisly story of three hundred liberated Australian soldiers from the Ambon Island compound—where Japanese guards, during a three-year period, beheaded over eight hundred prisoners and tossed the bodies into an unmarked gravesite—and the subsequent war tribunal, revealing more gruesome torture, that prosecuted the Japanese officers responsible for these atrocities. Argyll Film Partners' *To End All Wars* recounted the harsh treatment inflicted on many Scottish soldiers forced to build a railroad in the difficult Burmese underbrush. Frequently beaten and given only meager rations, the Highlanders, despised by their captors because they accepted surrender before death, gradually learned survival techniques: "Always bow before a guard, Korean or Jap. And never look 'em in the eyes when they pass you—that's pure defiance. Always look away. Rules of Bushido." Likewise, Roadshow Productions' *Return from the River Kwai* explained the depravities experienced by the Allied prisoners—who built a bridge in the Thailand jungle for their Japanese captors—and their subsequent sea voyage to their enemy's homeland. With Edward Fox and Denholm Elliott in starring roles, this screenplay depicted the sadistic, uncaring, and inhumane behavior of the Japanese soldiers.

A similar storyline, but with a strong flag-waving ending, Miramax's *The Great Raid* re-created the daring January 1945 rescue of hundreds of U.S. captives taken at Bataan three years earlier and held in the Cabanatuan camp in the Philippine jungle. U.S. Rangers trekked inland, attacked the compound, and returned the emaciated GIs to safety, validating their commander's promise: "We're going to push through our front lines right into the Japs' backyard and rescue 500 hundred American prisoners of war." With scene after scene of Japanese atrocities, including the burning alive of hapless Americans, the final moments of this red-white-and-blue extravaganza—with strong echoes of the rousing 1945 John Wayne breakthrough title *Back to Bataan*—reminded audiences, once more, about America's great World War II victories.

Sometimes the war took a back seat to lost love. Miramax's *Map of the Human Heart* traced the mushy regrets of a young Inuit from his playful Eskimo days, months in a Montreal hospital, youthful infatuation, unrequited affection, and finally, combat service in the RAF when in February 1945, on a strategic bombing run over Dresden, his aircraft exploded. Forced to bail out, his slow parachute descent into the burning city brought his life into focus, proving that true love, unlike gravity, plots its own course. With Jason Scott Lee in the leading role, the screenplay's unhappy ending reiterated the popular song's lamentation, "For all we know, we may never meet again." Another Romeo and Juliet romance, New Line's *The Notebook*, utilized the war as a backdrop, attesting that love and separation go hand in glove. Here, a young Carolinian from the wrong side of the tracks (Ryan Gosling) unsuccessfully wooed the girl of his dreams. Pearl Harbor changed everything; first enlistment, then North Africa, the Battle of the Bulge, and, finally, an army hospital. His stateside return to a lonely house retold the saddest of tales experienced by thousands of GIs.

Occasionally, a love story made a disastrous, left-hand turn, destroying everyone in its path. HBO's made-for-television *The Affair* indicted the U.S. Army for perpetuating the same old-boy, racist policies—found in southern states—on its British bases, where thousands of Americans amassed for their D-Day embarkation. Here in a small village, a soft-spoken black soldier

(Courtney B. Vance), haphazardly became involved with an introverted, married woman (Kerry Fox). When the affair became public, the confused wife, unable to handle peer pressure, cried "rape," charging the GI with this violent act. He was quickly arrested, tried, and executed. This story line blamed numerous officers for their uncaring, unconscionable attitude toward African Americans. Columbia's multitiered morality tale of adultery, Catholic guilt, jealousy, and self-doubt, *The End of the Affair*, depicted a delicate ménage à trois—a novelist, a government official, and his future wife—during the height of the London blitz. With Ralph Fiennes, Stephen Rea, and Julianne Moore in leading roles, this fleeting triangle proved once again that all was fair in love and war. A similar storyline, Fox's *For the Moment*, recounted the summer 1942 romantic entanglements among various Commonwealth airmen training in rural Manitoba and their newfound girlfriends. This time a spirited Aussie flyer (Russell Crowe) fell for a lonely married woman (Christianne Hir), even though, he mused, "The average life expectancy of a bomber pilot [in combat] is six bloody weeks." After earning his wings and embarking for England, these star-crossed lovers politely waved goodbye, realizing—for better or worse—their wartime affair combined both joy and sorrow.

The American home front, with its roller-coaster lifestyle, contained another set of problems. IRS Media's *December* examined the youthful side of unbridled patriotism, when on December 7, news of the Japanese attack resounded in the hallways at an elite, all-male, Vermont preparatory school, inciting the students into a vengeful mood. After days of debate—a mixture of solipsistic and chauvinistic arguments—a busload of seniors, with the administration's blessing, left the campus and were transported to a nearby induction center. Paramount's *A Separate Peace*—also set in a boarding school at the war's height—examined those ambiguous days where fourth-year classmates realized that graduation meant military service, bringing an end to the simplicity associated with carefree, learning days. Orion Pictures' *Radio Days* centered around a Jewish family living in Queens, spending many hours listening to war news in their modest apartment. Written and directed by Woody Allen, this droll screenplay re-created many well-known personages whose daily broadcasts molded opinions and disseminated international stories. These prompted a geography-deficient spinster aunt (Mia Farrow) to ask, "Who is Pearl Harbor?"

Fox's *For the Boys*—a peripatetic tale about two USO entertainers (James Caan and Bette Midler) who sang and danced at makeshift military sites—offered such double entendres as "Well, alone in the dark with thousands of men. There is a God after all!" to many GIs, even though one song, "Come Rain or Come Shine," was not composed until 1946. Sometimes a returning soldier learned that loneliness did not make the heart grow fonder. In another Fox production, *A Walk in the Clouds*, a decorated hero (Keanu Reeves) returned to San

Francisco, discovered his marriage in shambles, and—after some Cinderella adventures—agreed to pose as the husband of a pregnant, unmarried college student (Aitana Sánchez-Gijón), hoping this ruse would placate her domineering,
oenologist father. With numerous flashbacks to his South Pacific combat days,
this bittersweet storyline, with fairy-tale deftness, blended good wine, young romance, and wartime memories into the obligatory happy ending.

Another home-front title, Fox's *Come See the Paradise*, tackled the embarrassing question of President Roosevelt's Executive Law 9066, the thorny
legislation that authorized immediate internment of all West Coast Japanese
Americans to remote, bleak camps. Based on the fearful, racist assumption
that fifth columnists would aid their motherland through sabotage and dissension, these U.S. citizens—the majority were women and children—endured
many months of hardships and deprivation in spartan compounds. In this barren landscape, a leftist labor organizer (Dennis Quaid), married to a Japanese
American, struggled unsuccessfully to convince military officials that their actions represented innumerable violations of law, fair play, and morality. A similar storyline, Kennedy/Marshall Company's *Snow Falling on Cedars*, reiterated this dark side of national history by recreating the many indignities this
hapless minority underwent during their illegal internment. Warner Bros.'
American Pastime also examined this unsavory period, only this time the GI
guards played the Japanese Americans a highly charged baseball game that
came down to the ninth inning with two outs. With a fifty-star flag flying overhead, the home team batting first, and a bigoted coach warning his daughter,
"You're not going to see that Jap!" the entire 2007 photodrama—using a popular sport as metaphor—offered many parallels to the current Iraqi War.
HBO's *The Tuskegee Airmen* posited the inspiring story of the real-life African
American pilots, from their early Alabama flight training to becoming a legendary fighting unit noted for protective air support of Allied bombers in the
European theater. As tenacious aerial attackers, most of the flyers echoed a
senior officer's words, "As pilots we live in the air, but we die by fire."

Overall, many made-for-television productions that used the Second World
War as backdrop contained the usual Norman Rockwell pabulum needed for
Sunday-evening audiences. Disney's crowd-pleaser *Chips, the War Dog* told
the happy story of a hard-to-discipline family canine that was placed into the
army and, with the help of a new master, became a valuable war-effort asset.
With Brandon Douglas in the leading role, this photodrama offered strong appeal for most pet owners. A similar Pollyanna interpretation of Trillium's remake of the Rodgers and Hammerstein classic, *South Pacific*, updated the
musical wartime tale. This time Glenn Close crooned she would "wash that
man right out of my hair," while a young army lieutenant, good-looking
Harry Connick Jr., claimed that true love could make anyone feel "younger

than springtime." Castle Rock Entertainment's *The Majestic* provided quiet praise to Bedford, Virginia, a small town that sent 134 men—the Bedford Boys—into combat, but only a handful returned. Jim Carrey sparkled as an amnesia-stricken patient who in 1951 stumbled into a tiny, Capraesque Californian hamlet, where some locals, mistaking him for a long-lost hero, explained, "All told, this town gave sixty-two of its young men to the War—more than our share; seventeen of them in Normandy alone." After some goofy Jimmy Stewart–type up-and-down adventures, everything came to light in an all-was-forgiven, brass-band ending.

Hallmark's *Decoration Day* honored a southern black tenant farmer and the problems associated with a belated Medal of Honor presentation. Here, a recluse neighbor (James Garner) stepped out of his private world to help this former GI. Quinex Entertainment's *The Incident* examined a small town's anger when a German POW at a nearby internment camp—accused of killing a popular doctor—denied this charge. Soon, a slow-talking lawyer and World War I veteran (Walter Matthau) unraveled evidence proving his client's innocence, even though the physician's widow, unable to accept her husband's medical peccadilloes, screamed, "I don't think you have the right to call yourself an American anymore!" Another title dealing with intricate legal maneuverings, Turner Pictures' *Never Forget*, told the unusual story of a concentration-camp survivor (Leonard Nimoy) and his courtroom battle with a neo-Nazi organization's claim, using discursive logic, that the Auschwitz gas chambers never existed. With Dabney Coleman portraying his attorney, the two men slowly unmasked the screwball world of Holocaust deniers, a fringe movement with a small but vociferous band of supporters. Another Hallmark Sunday-night picture, *The Little Riders*, told the quiet story of a young American girl stranded with her Dutch grandparents right after the Nazi takeover of Holland and the problems associated with the occupation, seen from a child's perspective. Sometimes a motion picture raised moral issues. A more balanced look at the Japanese home front that examined the lives of diehard Imperial officers, small children, stoic family members, and many foreigners, Greenwald Production's *Hiroshima: Out of the Ashes* detailed the traumatic seventy-two hours before and after the August 6, 1945, atomic bombing of this major seaport. Intertwining the lives of a few desperate inhabitants—an American prisoner of war, Japanese civilians, and European diplomats—and their subsequent struggle for survival amid conflagration, ruination, and radioactive fallout, the photodrama—created for Sunday postprandial entertainment—weighted the efficacy of this first nuclear explosion against various humanistic principles.

As expected, the science fiction market—with its strong box-office appeal—offered its own interpretation of the global conflict. Trimark's *The Philadelphia Experiment II* kept the preternatural kettle boiling with the same shenanigans of the original, nine years earlier. In this sequel, a modern (1993) U.S. Air Force stealth bomber vanished into a time void, reappeared in Hitler's Germany, and subsequently dropped a nuclear bomb on Washington, D.C., enabling the Nazis to win the war. However, an American hero (Brad Johnson), whose unique DNA permitted unlimited linear travel, returned to 1943, and after some Captain Marvel adventures, changed the time sequence and thwarted the German victory, allowing "real" history to continue. With one subplot contradicting another, the whole mishmash resembled wartime *Popeye* cartoons, in which America's favorite spinach-eating sailor continuously ran the Axis forces into the ground.

Dangers lurked everywhere. Dimension Films' *Below* suggested that a U.S. submarine operating in the North Atlantic—making creepy, metal-against-metal sounds—was haunted by its former skipper's ghost, while above the waves a German ship, concerned with more practical matters, dropped explosives. With Bruce Greenwood holding a steady course, everyone's nerves snapped when an unexplained recording of Benny Goodman's "Sing, Sing, Sing" resounded throughout the hull, even though a chief petty officer concluded, "We got mechanical problems, that's all." Replete with typical *Twilight Zone* metaphysics, the entire underwater drama, with its eerie noises, occasional apparitions, and wraithlike mirrors, rattled everyone.

Science fiction travesties frequently were off the wall. King Picture's *Treasure Island* spoofed the comings and goings of two American code specialists (Lance Baker and Nick Offerman) working on a classified naval base in San Francisco Bay, deciphering Japanese messages. Basically a parody of Fox's 1956 thriller, *The Man Who Never Was*, these two men planned to drop a dead body with false documents into the Pacific near Japanese forces. Laden with soft pornography, this screenplay's many skits—Charles Atlas and his ninety-seven-pound weakling, race relations, wartime epithets, and victory celebration photographs—were overshadowed by the prurient scenes involving latent homosexuality, voyeurism, polygamy, and nymphomania.

Another screwball idea, Lions Gate's *The Empty Mirror*, rationalized Adolf Hitler's dysfunctional behavior, suggesting that the führer's problems originated in his youth. With Norman Rodway as the German leader, Camilla Soeberg as his mistress Eva Braun, and Joel Grey as Josef Goebbels, much of the screen time contained one diatribe after another as top officials blamed each other for the Third Reich's shortcomings, even though the führer denounced Joseph Stalin as "a footnote, a footnote if he is fortunate." A third photodrama, Silver Bullet's *Straight into Darkness*, depicted a group of abandoned French children—programmed by a loose-cannon caretaker (David Warner) to kill Nazis quickly and efficiently—who eventually reached safety thanks to the efforts of two U.S. Army deserters

(Scott MacDonald and Ryan Francis). Another plotline involving children, Columbia's *Hellboy*, re-created the comic-strip adventures of some Nazi weirdoes, who in spring 1945 planned to summon forth the Seven Gods of Chaos. Thwarted by U.S. soldiers and President Roosevelt's personal psychic adviser (John Hurt), this squad rescued a little red baby—equipped with horns and a tail—and subsequently raised this child to become Hellboy (Ron Perlman), mankind's greatest warrior, the sworn enemy of all evil forces.

Other supernatural storylines provided many face-covering screams for science fiction fans. Arbor Avenue Films' *Horrors of War* pushed the envelope when American troops, patrolling German forces, ran into werewolves, mutants, and zombies, unaware that Hitler's mad scientists had hatched these secret "weapons." Soon, OSS operatives, headed by Lieutenant John Schmidt, prowled the forests, discovered the sources, and finally destroyed these unusual creatures. Not to be outdone, Combat Productions' *SS Doom Troopers* fashioned additional fodder for *Frankenstein* aficionados after a U.S. intelligence squad, headed by Corin Nemic, uncovered a zany Nazi experimenter (Ben Cross) amalgamating some unexplained atomic-energy particles. He was creating a twenty-foot, hulking, megamuscled supersoldier that resembled a huge plastic action figure and was impervious to heavy gunfire, grenades, flamethrowers, tank blasts, and multiple explosions. He bragged, "An entire army of such creatures could crush the Allied advance and guarantee absolute victory for the Fatherland." Using a variety of offensive maneuvers, the GIs, after numerous setbacks, finally cornered this laboratory contraption and, with a little help from the French Resistance, destroyed the Third Reich's behemoth.

Sometimes, a Nazi monster became airborne. Concrete Productions' *Reign of the Gargoyles* provided many thrills when German soldiers uncovered some medieval pagan ruins embellished with stone gargoyles. Using the latest Third Reich incantations, these inanimate creatures were brought to life and, after some preternatural events, downed many Allied aircraft, causing a flight commander to ask, "What the hell are those things?" One bomber crew, headed by Joe Penny and Wes Ramsey, parachuted to safety, teamed up with Resistance fighters, eluded Nazi pursuers, and—using the Spear of Destiny (a weapon that once pierced Christ's side)—slew the gargoyle king, rendering all its minions helpless. With numerous scenes depicting explosions, shootouts, disintegration, and decapitations, the entire screenplay, with all its bells, whistles, and bows, resembled nothing more than a contemporary video game.

Occasionally, a screenplay floated into outer space putting an eccentric spin on world history. HBO's *Fatherland* expostulated that in 1944 the Normandy invasion failed, forcing a truce between Germany and the Allied

Powers. Twenty years later, Hitler still ruled Germany, Albert Speer created an elaborate monument to the Thousand Year Reich, Joseph Kennedy Sr. was America's president, General Eisenhower and Prime Minister Churchill died in exile, and King Edward and Queen Wallis sat on England's throne, while eighty-five-year-old Joseph Stalin, still at war with Germania (its new name) pondered his nation's next move. With numerous inconsistencies and illogical premises, this made-for-television travesty—with Rutger Hauer in a leading role—jumped from one implausible scene to another, ignoring logic, continuity, or substance, even though one Nazi general bragged, "This is the age of detente."

Certainly moviegoers witnessed many changes since the early, two-dimensional 1942 propaganda titles appeared, in which good and evil stood clearly apart. Later, colorized, wide-angled, then digital photodramas chronicled the war with expanded technology. Hollywood, of course, abandoned its antiquated back lots and filmed on locations all over the world, working in countries that offered the best tax loopholes, while at the same time distributing many foreign-made titles. At the beginning of the twenty-first century, World War II movies still appeared, albeit intermittently. But what about the audience? Was there still a market for a rousing, flag-waving go-get-'em screenplay? Would this genre survive or would the war become a spin-off, reduced to commercialized science fiction stories or comic book adventures designed for young audiences?

Chapter Eight

Sixty Years of Fighting

Why Should It End?

"What, are my deeds forgot?"—Achilles, a Greek warrior, at the gates of Troy, asking his compatriot Ulysses for clarification about his recent battlefield achievements in William Shakespeare's tragic story of unfulfilled love, *Troilus and Cressida*

"Those scraps are good deeds past, which are devoured; As fast as they are made, forgot as soon as done."—Ulysses' pragmatic reply explaining victory's ephemeral nature

"What do wars ever prove? Men, women, and children are slaughtered and a generation later, friends are enemies and enemies are friends and the whole stupid cycle starts over again."—Marlon Brando, as an anti-Nazi, German national, expatiating about wartime's chiasmatic nature in Fox's 1965 sea-voyaging saga, *Morituri*

"I loved it. I loved the war. I didn't want it to end. The idea of the war continuing on and on was really great for me."—Cult-film director Russ Meyers—whose 1965 black-and-white romp *Faster, Pussycat! Kill! Kill!* started him on the road to stardom—recalling his World War II combat experiences

When the Second World War ended in September 1945, most Americans literally jumped for joy in madcap celebrations. Why wouldn't they? The Japanese unconditional surrender meant only one thing: our boys were coming home. A few months later, when the servicemen began returning, the good times moved up a big notch. Festive parties heralded wonderful celebrations and now, the GIs—finally reunited with friends and family after years of separation—sat down and recounted wartime experiences. And what stories were told! Throughout 1945 and into 1946, one question greeted every veteran, "What did you do in the war?" Sometimes the answer was terse, in other situations, complex. Occasionally a veteran became reticent, other times, everything spilled out in a torrent of words.

But wartime jubilation eventually wore down, and by 1947, just one year later, new problems gripped the country. Unemployment fueled economic anxieties, while a former ally, the Soviet Union, repudiated its friendship with an Eastern Europe expansionist policy. On a positive note, the Marshall Plan aided Germany's recovery, while over in Japan, democratic reforms, under General MacArthur's benevolent eye, moved forward. By 1949 both Germany and Japan—two nations that once launched an unprecedented and brutal war against the United States—were now good friends with their former adversary. And not a moment too soon. On June 25, 1950, just five short years since V-J Day, the North Korean army, an acknowledged Russian puppet, attacked their southern neighbor. Within hours, U.S. troops, rifles in hand, were in a hot zone. Almost overnight, the Second World War became ancient history as a worried nation turned their eyes toward a small Southeast Asian peninsula.

Three years later the Korean conflict ended, but peace seemed as distant as the moon because two superpowers—the United States and the Soviet Union—aimed nuclear missiles at each other. Dubbed the Cold War, this unprecedented conflict shaped American life throughout the fifties and sixties as each side wondered who would launch the first explosive. In an age of jet aircrafts, low earth-orbit satellites, and computer-guided missiles, World War II armament—now squirreled away in museums—seemed, like the conflict itself, a quaint relic from the outlying past. In 1958 a realistic motion picture reflected these mainstream ideas. Directed by Edward Dmytryk, *The Young Lions* synchronized the adventures of two American draftees and a *Wehrmacht* officer. In one scene, a smooth-talking, New York City ladies' man (Dean Martin), annoyed about his upcoming induction, offered a dire prediction: "Look, I've read all the books. I know that in ten years we'll be bosom friends with the Germans and the Japanese. Then I'll be pretty annoyed that I was killed." How prescient was that?

By the early sixties, most Americans watched an impending problem festering on the other side of the world. In Southeast Asia, a jungle conflict brought U.S. troops to Vietnam, causing stateside tempers to flare about this distant entanglement. Still waving Old Glory, the World War II generation argued for a decisive victory, only to watch in dismay as college students burned flags and draft cards while taunting President Johnson with a derisive litany, "Hey, hey, LBJ! How many babies did you kill today?" Clearly, the "we're-all-in-this-together" days of twenty-five years earlier—like loose-lips-sink-ships, blackout shades, and aluminum pennies—vanished from the landscape. For all its glory and sacrifice, the Second World War, with its poignant monuments, gold-star mothers, and foreign burials became, as the popular Carole King song lamented, "so far away."

Far away? By the 1970s this global conflict seemed as remote as the Peloponnesian Wars. In 1973 a Hollywood motion picture poked fun at the nation's historical awareness. Directed by John G. Avildsen, Paramount's scathing black comedy *Save the Tiger* traced the downward spiral of a World War II veteran, Harry Stoner (Jack Lemmon), who fifteen years earlier landed in Anzio but now operated a California dress-manufacturing company teetering on bankruptcy. Frequently remembering the Italian beach invasion, he could not comprehend how "In 1944 that sand was made in blood and last year it was covered with bikinis." Soon, he ran into an offbeat, college-age hitchhiker, Myra (Laurie Heineman), and after some double-entendre generational banter (she wanted to save the tigers from extinction) the two wound up in a cozy room. Eventually undressed, she eyed his scars and innocently inquired what happened. "I got those in Italy," he mumbled. Impressed, she continued, "In a fight?" Shaking his head, he explained, "In the war." Puzzled, she asked, "In Italy?" Nodding, he confirmed, "In Italy." Looking nonplussed, the free-spirited student blurted out, "We never fought a war with Italy."

Italy? Why would the United States fight a war with such a fun-loving nation, a country with a reputation for pretty women, succulent pastas, aromatic wines, spiffy sports cars, and high-fashion clothing? By the mid-1970s—over thirty years since V-J Day—how many university-aged Americans understood the war's intricacies, its combatants, its issues, and, finally, its conclusion? How many knew that fascist-controlled Italy, under the heel of Benito Mussolini, invaded neighboring countries, deported hapless civilians to concentration camps, and as a major component of the Axis tripartite, fought against Allied forces?

If by the 1970s World War II resembled, as the love ballad suggested, "faded photographs," what about the new century? Would old deeds, as Achilles pondered, be soon forgot? At Tokyo's venerable Yasukuni Shrine, a Shinto religious site that commemorates Japan's World War II dead—including General Hideki Tojo and other convicted Class-A criminals—a new extension, the Museum of Military History, contains hundreds of mementos glorifying the nation's past. Opened in 2002, most of exhibits claim that Japan fought a war not to subjugate other countries but, instead, to gain independence from outside influences. Citing the two thousand years of freedom from invading foreigners, one display after another tones down the 1941–1945 aggression. Poignant farewell letters from kamikaze pilots highlight the virtues of sacrifice, while the 1937 Rape of Nanjing—where estimates of Chinese deaths reach three hundred thousand—is simply called the

Totally worn out from an evening with a silly coed, a former infantryman (Jack Lemmon), who was wounded during the 1944 Anzio invasion, cannot fathom the university student's marginal understanding of World War II in John G. Avildsen's black comedy, Save the Tiger. *Courtesy of Paramount Pictures.*

Nanjing Incident, an event euphemistically described as Japanese forces bringing stability to a troubled region. As for Pearl Harbor, a text from Emperor Hirohito rationalized the attack, expounding the military had no choice but to go forward because the United States, a belligerent Western nation, planned to force Japan into a confrontation simply as a means to end its Great Depression. Perhaps that explains a commemorative statue of India's Judge Radhabinod Pal, the only jurist who handed down a not-guilty verdict for Japan's leaders during the postwar tribunals.

Even most textbooks downplayed the war. References to the Korean occupation, including the Comfort Women, do not appear, echoing Tokyo's governor Shudo Ishihara's directive that the Nanjing Massacre never took place. At the same time, in March 2002, the Japanese appeals court ruled their government did not have to pay $7,260.00 damages to three Korean women because these sexual violations—committed by the occupying Japanese army—did not breach their nation's constitution. Earlier, in January 2000, organizers at the Osaka International Peace center called the Nanjing Massacre the biggest myth of the twentieth century. Unwilling to confront its past with anything remotely unpleasant—a Class-A war criminal was elected prime minister in 1957—the director of the Nagasaki Atomic Bomb Museum, in 1996, removed some 1937 photographs of women being jostled in Nanjing, claiming these images upset children. A chairman of a nationalist group and war veteran, Sunao Nishi, claimed categorically that Japanese troops did not kill Chinese in Manchuria, sentiments that appear in the nation's textbooks. Written by nationalist scholars, these books consistently deny historically documented atrocities committed during the war and often refer to Japanese invasions into Asian nations as "advances." Even the 2001 prime minister, Junichiro Koizumi, approved these changes. To maintain national honor, another government-endorsed textbook revision deleted all references to Japanese troops ordering the 1945 mass suicides of Okinawan villagers.

How quickly events fade. Not wanting to upset an upcoming summit applecart, on July 6, 2000, a U.S. Marine general, Earl B. Hailston, dutifully apologized to the Okinawan governor for the behavior of a nineteen-year-old serviceman in his command. The young leatherneck, who was not charged with anything, was accused of trespassing and an indecent act against a minor. In a scene echoing any number of Hollywood POW atrocity pictures—*Prisoner of the Sun* or *The Great Raid*, for example—the high-ranking officer bowed contritely and expressed his regret, while grimfaced Japanese officials stood quietly. In a similar situation in March 2001, Admiral William Fallon and the U.S. ambassador—hoping to allay some anti-American anger—bowed submissively to the homeland prime minister and apologized for a U.S. submarine accident that killed nine Japanese students in the Hawaiian waters. A few days later, the vessel's commander, Scott Waddle, also leaned forward in a gesture of submission to the parents, offering handwritten letters as a tangible token of remorse.

Music and veneration, two needed components of militarism, offered Japanese students a chance to evaluate their past. In 2004 the Tokyo Board of Education—hoping to foster ethnic pride and national identity—mandated that every school day, all students must stand, face the rising-sun flag, and sing the national anthem. During World War II, this patriotic song, "Kimigayo" (translated as "His Majesty's Reign"), was heralded by Japanese troops during their Asian invasion forays, while the prominent red-and-white flag, always displayed in public arenas, was a grim reminder to captive people everywhere of their unwanted colonial rule.

And what about Hideki Tojo, Japan's wartime prime minister who in 1948 was hanged as a Class-A criminal? Over fifty years later, his granddaughter Yuko Tojo works assiduously to transform the image of the general, who ordered the Pearl Harbor attack, from villain to national hero, a soldier who died defending his country. Her best-selling 1997 revisionist book, *My Grandfather Hideki Tojo*, extolled his patriotism, portraying him as a victim of Allied politics. The following year, a film production company used this text as the screenplay for *Puraido: Unmei no toki* (translated as *Pride: The Moment of Truth*), another slanted motion picture depicting Tojo as the nation's savior. With Masahiko Tsugawa in the starring role, this skewed photodrama became the highest-grossing Japanese movie of 1998, even though in one Tokyo suburban theater, protesters, angry at the positive portrayal of the wartime leader, slashed the screen.

Japanese revisionism lurks everywhere. In the southern town of Chiran, an elaborate kamikaze museum, opened in 1975, glorifies young pilots' sacrifices against the encroaching blue-eyed devils. The museum, which draws over half a million visitors a year, displays farewell letters and photographs that nationalists argue preserve their noble sacrifice against a barbaric enemy. This type of adulation for the approximately four thousand Special Attack Corps pilots assigned to crash their bomb-laden aircraft into Allied ships, blends nicely with current official policies to expunge Japanese atrocities from history books and reinstate patriotism into public education. At the same time, a popular 2007 motion picture, *I Go to Die for You*, written by Tokyo's governor, magnified the defensive effort as honorable and the kamikazes' role as righteous heroes who died for the common good in an idealistic crusade to free Asia from Western domination. By fall 2007, this somber motion picture, depicting the worship and enshrinement of these rightists' ideals, grossed over two billion yen in Japan. Prime Minister Yoshiro Mori's appraisal, made on May 19, 2000, was that, "Japan is a divine nation with the emperor at its core and we want the people to recognize this." Why doesn't he just yell, "Banzai?"

Across the ocean in the Mississippi Delta, a similar drama played out in the New Orleans World War II Museum. As in Chiran, each year thousands of visitors examine the many artifacts associated with America's victory effort. One of the volunteer guides, Tom Blakey—a former paratrooper who fought on D-Day and, later, across Europe—spent six years answering questions and relating his combat days to interested groups, many of which, he realized, did not know much about the war. Sometimes, the octogenarian mused, people asked, "What side were we on?" or worse, "Did we win the war?" These inquiries resounded in the lobby of an elaborate building dedicated to explaining the Second World War. A similar story, recounted by Bobbie Hamilton, detailed her childhood experiences living in Corregidor before the Japanese takeover, where playful children swam in the South China Sea right near the Malinta Tunnel. Today, the Florida resident reflected, "Very few people have heard of Corregidor and that includes many young Filipinos." Why is this? What happened? How did World War II awareness fall to the wayside? Maybe someone should ask Joe Foss.

Born in 1915 on a South Dakota farm and raised in a hunting and marksmanship environment, Joe Foss became enamored of flying—according to local folklore—when Charles Lindbergh landed at the nearby Sioux City Airport. In 1940 he earned a bachelor's degree, a civilian pilot's license, joined the Marine Corps, graduated from flight school, was commissioned a second lieutenant, and, the following year, on December 7, was the Pensacola officer of the day. On October 13, 1942, over Guadalcanal, he destroyed his first Japanese Zero. A few more kills followed until October 25, when he shot down five enemy aircraft, becoming the Marine Corps' first ace-in-a-day.

On November 7, his luck soured when his plane crashed into the Pacific waters. Initially discombobulated, he climbed aboard a raft, floated for a few hours, and was rescued by nearby locals off Malaita Island. Back in the air, his tally reached nineteen kills. On November 9, Admiral Halsey awarded him the Distinguished Flying Cross. Four more enemy aircraft dropped from the skies, but—a few days later—malaria caught up with him. Hospitalized in Australia, he returned to his unit on January 1, 1943, and on January 15 he shot down three more aircraft, bringing his total to twenty-six, equaling Eddie Rickenbacker's World War I record. All of this took place in a mere eighty days, including six weeks of convalescing. Apparently, President Roosevelt thought that was enough. Ordered stateside, on May 18 Captain Joe Foss cautiously leaned forward while the chief executive pinned the Congressional Medal on his blouse and, according to personal recollection, called the airman "young feller." A few days later, his picture appeared on the cover of *Life*. Acclaimed a national hero, he served as a training adviser for the rest of the war.

After V-J Day, more recognition followed. Initially one of the organizers of the South Dakota National Guard, he joined the House of Representatives, returned to active duty during the Korean conflict, served four years as governor of South Dakota, and from 1959 to 1966 reigned as commissioner of the American Football League. Always in the public eye and a popular speaker, retired Marine Corps general Joseph J. Foss openly greeted friends and admirers at functions, meetings, sporting events, even on the street. But years later, on January 11, 2002, at the Phoenix International Airport, everything changed abruptly. Foss became—like a character from Yevgeny Zamyatin's dystopian novel *We*—a nonperson.

After placing his jacket into the X-ray machine, the eighty-six-year-old Marine Corps ace was questioned by security personnel about a small pentagonal object inside a fancy case, whose rounded metal edges represented a potential threat to airline safety. For over forty-five minutes, Foss recalled, about eight or nine people passed around the Congressional Medal of Honor without any real understanding of what they were holding. Certainly, none of these security workers had the vaguest notion what this decoration represented, even with the inscription on the reverse side. None, of course, knew anything about Guadalcanal. For all practical purposes, that South Sea island was a planet in outer space. And World War II? What was that? Something you see in the movies? Finally, after some unpleasant back-and-forth discussion, an America West Airline representative intervened. The World War II fighter pilot—who fifty-nine years earlier went airborne for different reasons—was finally allowed on the commercial aircraft. Quietly he sat down, fastened his seat belt, and stared pensively out the window.

At least he sat quietly. Back on January 17, 1994, in Oakland, California, approximately seventy Castlemont High School students—on a special Martin Luther King Day field trip—were taken to a local theater to see Steven Spielberg's Holocaust film, *Schindler's List*. According to news accounts, most of the adolescents seemed disinterested, even bored watching this slow-moving, black-and-white picture about a subject that lacked teenage appeal. About an hour into the drama, a small but loud group laughed, joked, and cheered when a Nazi officer shot an old Jewish woman point-blank in the head. When other viewers complained, the manager halted the projection and summarily ejected every student. Someone called the local newspaper, and within hours this incident became a national front-page story.

Immediately, the board of education worked on damage control. Students apologized, and local Jewish organizations offered help in explaining the Holocaust. Even Steven Spielberg and Governor Pete Wilson showed up at an elaborate meeting in the school's auditorium. For the next few months, the controversy rebounded in school hallways. Finally, the summer vacation arrived and, like most unpleasant episodes, the events of that January afternoon faded away. Why wouldn't they? As one fourteen-year-old sophomore explained, she meant no disrespect in the theater. "World War II," she continued, "was long ago and far away and about people we never met."

At least these California teenagers did not wear a swastika to the movie house. In January 2005, twenty-year-old Prince Harry—third in line to the British crown—donned a Nazi uniform to a costume bash, hoping, one can only speculate, to impress his friends with this sartorial grand entrance. When photographs appeared in *The Sun* depicting the young prince soul-kissing a pretty partygoer, also dressed in Nazi regalia, the royal family, no stranger to scandal, issued a formal apology, claiming that young people's knowledge of World War II was limited.

British tabloids—always eager for the jugular—suggested that if this merry-making had taken place a few weeks later in the Austrian Obersalzberg Mountains, the young prince might have been spared the embarrassment. In February a luxury hotel opened on the site of Adolf Hitler's alpine German retreat. Berchtesgaden, the Third Reich's second seat of power, where the führer romped with his selected inner circle, boasts 138 rooms and twelve suites. While condemned by Jewish leaders as a place inappropriate for holiday recreation, the Bavarian State minister claimed this new five-star resort, with daily rates from 270 to 1300 euros, would give the local tourist industry a needed shot in the arm. What's next? An elaborate luxury hotel—situated majestically on Berlin's brightly lit Kurfürstendamm—named the Hotel Hitler?

Why not? As one of France's great heroes, Napoleon Bonaparte's reputation remains unblemished. Squares, streets, hotels, alcoholic beverages, clothing, logos, even a multilayered, creamy pastry use his name or image lavishly as a testimony to his many deeds. None of his admirers, of course, mentioned Napoleon's 1802 Haitian decree ordering the death of every black male over the age of twelve. How about Hitler? In the early 1960s—fifteen years after V-J Day—the hang-ten surfing crowd proclaimed the führer's coveted Iron Cross their pelagic symbol. Why shouldn't they? Doesn't this metal image enhance the appearance of any young surfer? How about the future? In two hundred years, will Hitler's cropped mustachioed image appear on commercial products? Maybe on the label of a robust Bavarian beer? By 2200 will revisionist capitalists argue Hitler only wanted to improve his country but went about it the wrong way? Maybe someone should talk to Punit Sabhlok, an aspiring entrepreneur who, in 2006, opened an eatery in Mumbai, India, called Hitler's Cross. Taking his cue from the führer, this owner boasted that he, too, wanted to conquer the world, not militarily, but by "his food and service." What a wonderful name for a restaurant!

As for the zone of the interior, how well do most Americans remember the war some sixty years later? On May 26, 2001, Michael Bay's *Pearl Harbor* opened nationwide. To commemorate this event, a New Brunswick, New Jersey, megatheater invited members of the Pearl Harbor Survivors Association as their guests. Idling in the lobby, one of the veterans, Ernest Renda, stared incredulously as an usher, speaking with his wife Bebe, stumbled over his words. The twenty-year-old seemed confused. Wasn't *Pearl Harbor* just a movie, like *Jurassic Park* or *Field of Dreams*, he asked? Sheepishly, the young man listened to an impromptu history lesson explaining this film was not a story that some Hollywood screenwriter made up.

Maybe a few German nationals need an extemporized history lesson. In early November 2004, England's Queen Elizabeth II arrived in Berlin for a climate change conference, held informal talks with Chancellor Gerhard Schroeder, and—two nights later—attended a festive concert to raise funds for the rebuilding of Dresden's *Frauenkirche*, an elaborate, eighteenth-century cathedral destroyed by Allied bombers in February 1945. Throughout her stay, German newspaper editorials berated Her Majesty's government, the Royal and American Air Forces, and various leaders, including the late General Arthur "Bomber" Harris for the three-day aerial attack of almost sixty years ago and demanded the queen apologize for this wartime act. Undaunted (and probably confused), Queen Elizabeth, who lived through the 1940 London blitz, demurred and, after a few ceremonial functions, politely returned to London.

Apologize? Were German headlines demanding an apology from the royal family for bombing a World War II enemy target—the former Third Reich nation whose unrelenting Luftwaffe attacks destroyed city after city, including Rotterdam, during the peak of their westward offensives? What is next? Maybe the U.S. Army should apologize for liberating the concentration camps and forcing nearby adult townspeople to view their führer's final solution. Or how about the Nuremberg Trials? Maybe the Allies should apologize for prosecuting known war criminals.

As always, a fine line divides capital interests and historical realities. On Waikiki's main shopping street, Kalakaua Avenue, an elaborate twin-story hotel dominates this prime beach area. With its startling lobby, indoor waterfall, and prized oceanfront rooms, the hotel attracts many well-heeled visitors, especially Japanese nationals, who arrive in busloads, ready to enjoy the balmy Honolulu weather. For many of these tourists, this ivory-colored hotel is a honeymoon retreat where smiling couples arrive, *en famille*, for elaborate Hawaiian-style weddings and receptions.

With friendly, pleasant service as its watchword, the hotel staff offers one useful suggestion after another to comfort its guests. Fascinated by Polynesian artifacts, its island activities sheet inquires, Why not visit the famous Bishop Museum? How about an excursion to the only royal mansion on American soil? Head over to the Iolani Palace, the staff advises, to see this grand structure completed in 1882. Interested in twentieth-century history? Why not visit Pearl Harbor? Here, on December 7, 1941, the hotel's directory informs, enemy dive-bombers nearly destroyed the U.S. Pacific fleet that fateful morning.

The U.S. fleet was attacked by *enemy* dive-bombers? Where did these aircraft come from? Enemyland? On a bright, happy August 2002 afternoon, an energetic, smiling assistant manager offered a facile explanation for the hotel's language. The Pearl Harbor attack occurred nearly forty years before anyone on the staff was born, she began, and since her formative years were spent in California, the historical events were a little fuzzy. But if the Japanese actually dropped those bombs, they probably were sorry. After all, look around, she gestured. Look at all these happy people from Japan. Besides, why bring up the past? Really, she concluded, what's done is done and prudent hotel management requires simplicity. Don't you understand, her smiling faced beamed, that was long ago. Yes, it was long ago, but it certainly wasn't far away. The attack happened a few miles from the hotel. Maybe this polite representative spent the previous evening watching Columbia's 1957 desert saga *Bitter Victory*. Here a British major (Richard Burton), preparing to attack an Axis stronghold, speculated about the raid's long-term effects: "I wonder why people have short memories. Do they forget what they want to forget or don't they care?"

Maybe Hollywood can refresh past events. In the fall 2000 issue of *Voices*— a quarterly magazine published by the Pfizer Pharmaceutical Company to promulgate their blue, erectile dysfunction pill, Viagra—an unsigned article explained some seductive traits to "warm up those cool fall nights." Some suggestions included long walks, fresh flowers, stargazing, and romantic movies. Motion pictures, of course, can inspire some intimacy, and the writer singled out *From Here to Eternity* as a mood-setting title. Romance? Intimacy? Did anyone on the Pfizer staff watch this picture? Where is the romance when a sadistic stockade guard bludgeons a helpless prisoner? Will anyone feel like some intimacy after watching Japanese planes strafe Hickman Field, killing many GIs? How about the vicious treatment of an idealist bugler by some nasty sergeants? Will that instigate some lovemaking? Need more inspiration? Why not swoon over that back-alley stabbing scene where one soldier knifed another? Or, for the pièce de résistance, maybe the couple should watch *Schindler's List*. That should clinch the evening.

Certainly there were difficult experiences on the road to victory, and Hollywood—never shying away from the horror, mayhem, or destruction— would gleefully summarize the four-year conflict with a colorful noun. Photodramas such as *A Place in Hell*, *A Taste of Hell*, *Back Door to Hell*, *Between Heaven and Hell*, and *Bridge to Hell* retold many problems associated with combat. Other screenplays, *Five for Hell*, *From Hell to Victory*, *Hell Commandos*, *Hell in Normandy*, and *Hell in the Pacific* offered ongoing praise for America's champions. Likewise, *Hell Is for Heroes*, *Hell River*, *Hell Squad*, *Hell to Eternity*, *Hellboy*, and *Heroes in Hell* described numerous victories, while *Seven Women from Hell*, *Surrender—Hell*, *Ten Seconds to Hell*, *and The Walls of Hell* fought more battles. Lastly, *The Walls of Hell*, *To Hell and Back*, and *When Hell Broke Loose* demonstrated, when all was said and done, American prowess remained undaunted.

For better or worse, Hollywood remains the leading teacher of World War II, offering one version after another about America's four-year ordeal. With its ubiquitous visual appeal (even though GIs wear lipstick), high-powered amplifications, and elaborate special-effects system, their many interpretations still hold court. Can anyone doubt the influence of John Wayne, the tough American who never lost a battle? How about Clark Gable? Didn't he send those B-17s into Germany's heartland, wrecking their matériel industries? Look at Henry Fonda. Wasn't that a smart idea, attacking the Japanese at Midway? Do not forget Gregory Peck. After many setbacks he finally waded ashore, godlike, at Luzon, keeping his "I Shall Return" promise to the Philippines people. Remember to clap for Robert Taylor. He and his *Enola Gay* crew brought the war to a dramatic end. Wave the flag for James Garner and his fine-tuned Rangers. Didn't they blast those Nazis out of their mountain stronghold? Give credit to Jeff Chandler. His Red Ball Express kept the French eastward advance moving unobtrusively. Do not leave out young Audie Murphy and his daring exploits routing the Germans. What about James Cagney? His quick thinking wrecked the Japanese navy.

As for the future, where will Hollywood venture next? Can World War II screenplays remain a viable commercial interest, or is this subject, like its predecessor the Great War, dated? Will the motion-picture industry keep Old Glory, frontal beachhead assaults, commando raids, and precision daytime-bombing attacks in its production schedule, or has this subject, like the 1940s propaganda pictures, also run its course? One point is certain. Future generations will learn about this conflict from the movies they watch. No one can deny—as Marshall McLuhan told the Vietnam generation—the medium is the message. And certainly, no one can overlook Paul Fussell's prescient words, "The real war will never get into the books." Maybe a coda is needed: the real war will never reach the silver screen.

Selective Filmography of
World War II Motion Pictures

1946–2007

Above and Beyond

MGM, Directed by Melvin Frank and Norman Panama,
Released 1952

A sudsy, hearts-and-flowers soap opera that details the marital problems
caused by the elaborate security necessary for the crew training to drop the
first atomic bomb. Good-looking Robert Taylor excels as Colonel Paul W.
Tibbets Jr.—the fly-by-the-book Air Corps pilot—who demands rigid discipline for his top-secret assignment, while his wife (Eleanor Parker) cannot
fathom warfare's realities. (Robert Taylor, explaining to his spouse the nature
of Japanese aggression: "To lose this war to that gang we're fighting would
be the most immoral thing we could do to those kids in there—and don't you
ever forget it.") Eventually, the *Enola Gay* completes her mission—bringing
the war to a dramatic climax—and after months of separation, the happy couple, in a corny tearjerker ending, reunite at the Washington, D.C., airport.

Act of Love

United Artists, Directed by Anatole Litvak, Released 1954

A wonderful boy-meets-girl romance in which true love takes the proverbial
wrong turn and ends disastrously. Kirk Douglas radiates as a combat-experienced PFC, who in winter 1945 is assigned to Paris command headquarters.
Soon, the dimpled-chin GI falls for a sweet French girl (Dany Robin), and after a whirlwind courtship the twosome agree to marry. (Douglas, explaining
why he cannot stay the night: "The Army doesn't know anything about "just
once"—when they say eleven o'clock, they mean eleven o'clock.") Hampered

by a loudmouthed captain, Douglas is reassigned, and after a failed last-ditch effort both lovers are permanently separated. Then, in a Javert-type finale, the distraught female drowns in the Seine. As a social protest, the photodrama blasts away at those American opportunists fueling the black market and the nasty, undemocratic behavior of the officer caste system.

The Affair

Home Box Office, Directed by Paul Seed, Released 1995

A critical, no-holds-barred indictment of the U.S. Army's officer cadre system that blatantly enforces Jim Crow laws when hundreds of black GIs arrive in a British village, months before the Normandy landing. Well-mannered Courtney B. Vance sparkles as an ordinary foot soldier unaccustomed to the civility proffered by his host nation. Following a series of romanticized coincidences, he becomes the lover of a lonely married woman (Kerry Fox). Eventually discovered, the comely wife—completely discombobulated—cannot stop those events that allow a kangaroo court-martial to execute Private Vance on a trumped-up rape charge. Supposedly inspired by a "true" story, this made-for-television drama reiterates that racism and fascism permeate the commissioned ranks. (Colonel Ned Beatty, explaining why he wants an immediate execution: "We are shipping out any day. In France, the nigger boy's gun will be loaded; we estimate to lose 50,000 good men there! So, I'm not about to worry about one bad one.")

Ambush Bay

United Artists, Directed by Ron Winston, Released 1966

A slow-moving, disjointed, don't-ask-any-questions trek through the Japanese-held Philippine jungle by a wily group of U.S. Marines hoping to infiltrate an enemy camp days before General MacArthur's historic 1944 "I shall return" invasion. Here, a close-to-the-chest sergeant (Hugh O'Brien) watches helplessly as one by one his elite squad falls victim to the hostile terrain. Eventually, the resourceful noncom, along with a nineteen-year-old radio operator (James Mitchum), creates a loud diversion, sneaks into a guarded compound, and—after some fancy hand-grenade throwing—detonates a Japanese underwater mining complex, a feat that ensures the U.S. Navy safe passage for their attack vessels. Worst typecasting: former Andy Hardy all-American boy and song-and-dance man, Mickey Rooney, as a rough-and-tumble, sangfroid marine gunnery sergeant. (Sergeant Rooney, ruminating about his precarious situation: "I can't figure it out—feel like I'm in a stadium with a bunch of Jap spectators.")

An American Guerrilla in the Philippines

Twentieth Century–Fox, Directed by Fritz Lang, Released 1950

Another strong testimony to American individualism, proving once again that prowess, integrity, and determinism always lead to victory regardless of the odds. Tyrone Power moves quickly as a navy officer stranded on a Philippine island in 1942, when his command retreats to Australia. After a shaky start, this resourceful ensign—along with other isolated GIs—mobilizes villagers and, for the next three years, destroys enemy installations, harasses Japanese forces, and maintains morale, while radioing important logistical information to Allied headquarters. (Ensign Power, summarizing his work: "In short, we built an army, restored a government, sought to imbrue the people with an unconquerable faith and an inevitable victory.") Best scene: the guerrillas beam with pride as their hero, five-star General MacArthur, keeping his "I-shall-return" promise, enters their village hideout much to the acclaim of the flag-waving, native population.

The Americanization of Emily

MGM, Directed by Arthur Hiller, Released 1964

A wacky, off-the-wall, farcical, black comedy—probably the funniest World War II movie ever made—that grinds the U.S. military into the ground with its irreverent spoof of authority, leadership, and interservice rivalry. Always resourceful and quick on his feet, James Garner coruscates as a goldbricking naval aide who supplies women, booze, elaborate London hotel accommodations, and favors to numerous admirals planning the massive D-Day assault. Off to the side, his English girlfriend, Emily (Julie Andrews), slowly learns that the American method of waging war requires an oleaginous public relations staff. (Admiral Melvyn Douglas, explaining the importance of usurping any army glory: "The first dead man on Omaha Beach must be a sailor.") After a series of madcap, turnabout events—that include blatant opportunism, poor planning, unbridled alcoholism, and a canceled invasion date—the first "dead" naval man returns alive, much to the confusion of the senior officers who must scramble to reverse this unexpected contretemps.

Anzio

Columbia, Directed by Edward Dmytryk, Released 1968

An outspoken commentary pointing the finger at the U.S. Army's high command for the severe casualty rate during the January 1944 Italian campaign. Here, an accredited war correspondent living with a combat squad

(Robert Mitchum) witnesses many examples of ineptitude responsible for the decimation of an inland patrol. (Newsman Mitchum, lambasting General Arthur Kennedy: "Of 767 men there are seven survivors left to see the results of one more royal foul-up.") As a fervent Nazi officer in charge of an ill-supplied garrison, Wolfgang Preiss keeps the Allied forces bogged down on the Anzio beachhead until German reinforcements arrive. Eventually, the U.S. Army—after some leadership shuffling—initiates a dramatic breakthrough, allowing the ground pounders their first victory on the slow road to Rome.

Attack

United Artists, Directed by Robert Aldrich, Released 1956

A blatant, no-holds-barred, both-barrels salvo exposing the U.S. Army officer old-boy network where cronyism, nepotism, favoritism, and occasional incompetency flourish with impunity in a frontline outfit. Eddie Albert is outstanding as an unstable, indecisive, southern National Guard captain whose numerous blunders create many casualties during the November 1944 French hostilities. Eventually confronted by a squad lieutenant (Jack Palance), the two men square off. (Lieutenant Palance threatening his commanding officer: "Listen to me, Cooney! If you put me and my men in a wringer—if you send us out there and let us hang—I swear, I swear by all that's holy, I'll come back. I'll come back and take this grenade and shove it down your throat and pull the pin!") Basically an outspoken, leftist film, the photoplay emphasizes the futility of combat, but—in a faltering shift—its weak, Pollyannaish, red-white-and-blue ending softens the blow, reducing the screenplay's antiwar message to mere pabulum.

Attack on the Iron Coast

United Artists, Directed by Paul Wendkos, Released 1968

Another explosive damn-the-torpedoes-full-speed-ahead aquatic yarn, this one heaping dollops of praise on a fast-moving Canadian commando unit. These commandos' daring 1943 attack on a German-occupied Normandy seaport destroyed an important component of Hitler's so-called impregnable Iron Coast. Led by tough-talking Lloyd Bridges, the knife-wielding night fighters must live up to his exacting standards. (Major Bridges to staff: "Postponement is out of the question. We gotta move within six days or not at all.") With the help of a diehard naval officer (Andrew Keir), this raid, after some initial setbacks, restates the indomitable spirit of the British Empire. Best scene: Major Bridges, learning that an apprehensive sailor is only sixteen years old, gives the lad his prized cigarette lighter.

Away All Boats

Universal, Directed by Joseph Pevney, Released 1956

A quintessential 1950s Cold War–era naval adventure that highlights America's seafaring forces as indomitable sailors who methodically blast their Oriental foes out of the water. Promoted to captain of an amphibious launch vessel, hard-talking Jeff Chandler slowly hones his inexperienced tars into a first-class assault team. (Captain Chandler, laying down the law: "The singular duty of this ship is to carry a combat-loaded battalion right into the laps of the enemy.") After months of vicious fighting, the ship's luck runs out when a kamikaze, dodging hundreds of rounds over Okinawa, rams its starboard side. Unwilling to accept defeat, the fast-moving bluejackets, inspired by their officers, clear the deck, patch the hull, and literally tow their damaged vessel to safety. Using many pelagic stereotypes—including the loneliness of command, the disgruntled officer, and the innocent bumpkin—this wonderful ending reaffirms the U.S. Navy's credo that the unassailable bond between crew and ship never falters.

Band of Brothers

DreamWorks, Directed by David Frankel et al, Released 2001

An elaborate, made-for-television, straightforward account about the men of Easy Company, 506th Regiment, 101st Airborne. Beginning with their arduous Georgia basic training, they are followed through their jam-packed Atlantic crossing, nighttime D-Day drop behind German lines, difficult fight for Carentan, Market Garden, and Bastogne, poignant concentration-camp liberation, and, finally, the glorious capture of Hitler's prized Bavarian hideaway, Eagle's Nest. With a large supporting cast and utilizing eight directors, this 705-minute tribute offers strong testimony to an outfit that by war's end suffered a 150 percent casualty rate. (Lieutenant Damian Lewis, explaining his company's philosophy: "You know why they volunteered? So when things got really bad, the man in the foxhole next to them would be the best, not some draftee who's going to get them killed.") With numerous interviews of surviving members, this cinematic epic details those wartime emotions—fear, anxiety, disappointment, caution, elation, retribution, elitism, and victory—as these paratroopers move forward, mindful of the company clerk's directive, "Anyone who has not made a will, go to the supply office."

Battle Cry

Warner Bros., Directed by Raoul Walsh, Released 1955

A chest-pounding 155-minute Marine Corps hagiography—based on Leon Uris's best-selling novel—which traces the joys, camaraderie, and sorrows of some young men from their shaky San Diego boot-camp days to their eventual rendezvous with Japanese forces in the South Pacific campaign. Van Heflin stands tall as the hard-nosed father-figure commander, ordering extensive physical training for his youthful charges. (Colonel Heflin, explaining the rationale for his unremitting all-day, all-night marches: "When we go into battle again, not one of my boys will die because he's a straggler—no one's going to die because he's weak."). With James Whitmore, Tab Hunter, and Aldo Ray in supporting roles, the screenplay blends family values, the contribution of the Navaho Indian code specialists, and semper fidelis with the larger backdrop of the nation at war in a style reminiscent of the 1940s propaganda films.

Battle Force

Film Ventures International, Directed by Umberto Lenzi, Released 1977

Another low-budget, Italian-made hoopla that chronicles the glory and defeat of a small group of American, British, and German officers from a 1936 Berlin dinner through numerous battles. Finally, the combatants converge in the North African desert, where, in an elaborate tank offensive, they witness the capitulation of Rommel's Afrika Korps. Here, a seventy-one-year-old war correspondent (John Huston) watches the Nazi surrender, while back at West Point his pal, a seventy-two-year-old general (Henry Fonda), receives personal messages from the front lines. Loosely modeled on *The Young Lions*, this copycat version contains one disjointed vignette after another that caricatures both Axis and Allied soldiers. Worst German accent: *Wehrmacht* soldier (Stacy Keach) explaining lebensraum. (Lieutenant Keach to party guests: "I can guarantee, the führer has no intentions of starting a war.")

Battle of Blood Island

Bickman/Rapp Productions, Directed by Joel Rapp, Released 1960

Another grainy, B-for-bad, hackneyed sixty-four-minute earsplitter—based on a short story by Philip Roth—describing the ordeal of two GIs, who in January 1945 survive a botched Pacific island raid. Then, they spend the next few months hiding in makeshift areas, dodging Japanese patrols, and arguing ad infinitum about extraneous issues not pertinent to the war. Both Richard Devon and Ron Kennedy talk incessantly but never make a point or reach a conclusion. (Private Devon, expatiating on survival instincts: "What kind of guts does it take to stay alive?" while his pal, Private Kennedy retorts: "Do you always have to be kidding around?") Unknown to the Americans, V-J Day arrives, and in a ritualistic mood, the Japanese commit hara-kiri, allowing the soldiers two more months of prosy and tedious loquacity until a rescue party, searching for a suitable atomic bomb testing site, locates them.

Battle of Bloody Beach

Twentieth Century–Fox, Directed by Herbert Coleman, Released 1961

A bottom-of-the-barrel, 100 percent hokum, B–soap opera that follows the misgivings of an American construction worker, who roams around various Philippine islands delivering matériel to resistance groups while searching for his wife during the precarious 1942 Japanese-occupation days. Acting more like a lovesick student than a guerrilla fighter, Audie Murphy frequently stares out into space hoping to locate his missing bride, while his sidekick (Gary Crosby) suggests more vigilance. (Lieutenant Crosby, summarizing various dangers: "Last time I listened in on Tokyo Rose, they upped the reward on you to 50,000 pesos. I doubt they pay that much for General MacArthur.") Eventually, the lovers are united, but the reunion becomes strained because the wife—thinking her spouse long dead—latched onto a new beau. Finally, an oceanfront battle with Japanese forces reconciles the lovers, and in a typical ride-off-into-the-sunset ending, the twosome paddle out to a waiting U.S. submarine, leaving their conjugal problems behind on the bloody beach.

The Battle of Neretva

Republic, Directed by Valjko Brilajic, Released 1971

A typical Yugoslavian action yarn glorifying the Balkans' guerrilla warfare, with famous Hollywood stars peppered into a convoluted script, akin to the popular 1940s B-pictures. Here, Yul Brynner—a seasoned partisan thwarting the Nazis—blows up numerous bridges, while a German general (Curt Jurgens) bellows orders to his many subordinates. Eventually, the decisive battle of Neretva brings victory to the freedom fighters and death to Orson Welles, the turncoat supervising the Chetnik forces (Welles, plotting the defeat of the nationals "Let them destroy themselves.") Replete with many stock scenes—including the fight to the finish, the heroic female soldier, and the traitor in the midst—the photoplay heaps dollops of praise on Marshal Tito, the renegade Communist widely revered by his countrymen.

The Battle of the Bulge

Cinerama Productions Corporation, Directed by Ken Annakin, Released 1965

An elaborate, overstated, and fuzzy adaptation of the Germany army's desperate efforts to halt the Allied eastward advance in December 1944, when after weeks of seesaw fighting, the American forces, with superior airpower, overran the *Wehrmacht* in the frigid Belgian forest. Using an array of impressive stars—including Henry Fonda, Robert Ryan, Dana Andrews, Robert Shaw, and Telly Savalas—this wide-angled, 165-minute, pseudo-travelogue ignores most historical events and, instead, provides a stylized, soap-opera account of a pivotal U.S. victory. (Nazi tank commander Robert Shaw, explaining facetiously why his side can win: "Germans are still the best toy makers in the world.") With one inaccuracy after another, including a Belgian "Alps" aerial reconnaissance and a back-and-forth tank duel, this fiction-as-fact screenplay at time resembles a galloping Hollywood Western, complete with a rousing, cavalry-to-the-rescue ending.

Battleground

MGM, Directed by William A. Wellman, Released 1949

A finely crafted black-and-white testimony to the men of the 101st Airborne Division—the Screaming Eagles—who brought the *Wehrmacht* to an abrupt halt during their protracted Battle of the Bulge. Van Johnson, John Hodiak, and James Whitmore star as worn-out GIs, whose squad must spend Christmas week 1944 at Bastogne, dodging Nazi infiltrators during one of the War's coldest periods. Lacking adequate supplies and cut off from their own lines, the dogfaces maintain a shaky sense of humor (PFC Johnson and fellow GI, kibitzing over the password: "Hello Joe, what do you know? Just got back from a vaudeville show.") Modeled after the classical propaganda genre, the storyline preserves the hopes, aspirations, fears, and frustrations of a small but cohesive group of men, highlighting their eclectic backgrounds as they fight their way out of the Belgian woodlands.

Beach Red

Theodora Productions, Directed by Cornel Wilde, Released 1967

A strong, antiwar statement—based on the novel by Peter Bowman—that downplays heroics and, instead, focuses on the folly and egomania associated with battle. Now a marine officer, Cornel Wilde cautiously guides his men through the uncharted jungles of some unnamed South Pacific island, only to witness violent death at every turn, while his psychopathic top sergeant (Rip Torn) rants and raves about everything (Sergeant Torn to Captain Wilde: "I'm a Marine! Who gives a damn about this dead Jap now? He's nothing, he's worth nothing!") Heavy-laden with numerous flashbacks depicting wholesome family life, as well as some Eisenstein-type montage, the storyline portrays both Japanese and Americans as peaceful individuals longing for their wives, children, and hearths. Eventually, large numbers of marines and Japanese perish in a gory, allegorical end-of-the-film battle, allowing Cornel Wilde another opportunity to expatiate about war's absurdity.

Beachhead

United Artists, Directed by Stuart Heisler, Released 1954

A taut, watch-your-back, steamy jungle trek involving a four-man marine reconnaissance team operating behind enemy lines to disrupt Japanese logistics hours before a major U.S. offensive at the strategic island of Bougainville. Hard-talking Frank Lovejoy, an experienced noncom, moves cautiously, guiding his small squad from one skirmish to another, while a younger leatherneck, Tony Curtis, carps about military life. (Loudmouth Curtis to his sergeant: "What did all those years in the Marine Corps do to you? Burn your nerves out?") Eventually, the devil dogs rescue a French scientist and his daughter, and—after another arduous journey—return safely to their command post. Funniest scene: Corporal Tony Curtis, crawling through the jungle with a knife in his mouth, ready to pounce upon an unsuspecting Japanese soldier hiding in the underbrush.

The Beginning or the End

MGM, Directed by Norman Taurog, Released 1947

Another B-homily that ponders atomic energy's future in the postwar period. Employing a narrative, documentary format, the photoplay traces the Manhattan Project, starting with Einstein's warning to President Roosevelt, up to the *Enola Gay*'s early morning mission over Japan. Here the flamboyant scientist, Dr. J. Robert Oppenheimer, played by Hume Cronyn, offers a conservative interpretation while Brian Donlevy—portraying General Lester Groves—keeps his military staff on their toes with his demand for expediency. (Army major, Robert Walker, working with a physicist: "Just get us that bomb and get it before Hitler and the Japs.") One scene—depicting the Los Alamos implosion—seems macabre: Oppenheimer and his staff, unaware of nuclear energy's potential, rub suntan lotion on their skin as protection against the blast from this first atomic test.

The Best Years of Our Lives

MGM, Directed by William Wyler, Released 1946

A wonderful 171-minute Academy Award epic—one of the greatest films ever made—that amalgamates the joys, sorrows, and self-realizations of three combat veterans when they return to their thriving, mid-American city months after the war has ended. Dana Andrews is outstanding as a decorated B-17 bombardier, who discovers the postwar boom has no room for the men who dropped their explosives on German targets, while Fredric March, a former sergeant back from the Pacific island fighting, begrudgingly returns to his executive banking position. (March to wife: "Last year it was kill Japs; and this year it's make money.") Harold Russell, a young sailor who lost both hands when his ship was attacked, steals the show as a shy, sensitive, Norman Rockwell–type hometown boy hoping for a modicum of normalcy. Heavy with acerbic social criticisms that blast draft-dodgers, war profiteering, unfaithful wives, America-First committees, and short memories, the film's tempo—based on the free-verse poem by MacKinlay Kantor—reiterates the various modes of opportunism that existed on the home front and calls to task the important job of helping every returning serviceman.

Betrayed

MGM, Directed by Gottfried Reinhardt, Released 1954

Another spy-versus-spy melodrama that plunges a Dutch officer (Clark Gable) into a deadly cat-and-mouse game with a Resistance traitor (Victor Mature) during the final days of the spring 1944 Holland occupation, as monocled Gestapo officers routinely unravel Allied sabotage information prior to the Market Garden offensive. Unable to ferret out the German plant, the hard-nosed Gable scrutinizes his entire staff. (Major Gable, rationalizing his skepticism: "It's my job to look for the worst in people, suspect them, mistrust them, everyone.") After some comic-book adventures—including an elaborate pseudo-double-agent infiltration into a German hospital ward to rescue an underground fighter—Gable exposes the turncoat. Funniest scene: straight-faced Lana Turner, also an Allied agent, parachutes from an American C-47, wearing a mushroom-shaped helmet that resembles mission-to-Mars headgear.

Between Heaven and Hell

Twentieth Century–Fox, Directed by Richard Fleischer, Released 1956

A strong antimilitary CinemaScope proclamation—based on the novel by Francis Gwaltney—that accuses some American officers stationed on a Pacific island in 1945, labeling them irrational, pusillanimous, and fascist. Once a combat sergeant—now busted to slick-sleeved private—Robert Wagner harbors deep resentment against the army caste system. (Private Wagner explaining his reduction in rank: "Assaulting an officer under combat conditions.") Reassigned to a dangerous forward unit, he confronts Captain Broderick Crawford, a psychopathic tyrant known simply as "Waco," who sends him off to a precarious lookout station. After a Japanese attack, the good-looking Wagner manages to warn his unit, saving the lives of many soldiers. In a typical Hollywood happy-ending format, the deranged captain falls victim to a sniper shot, and the army command, now cognizant of its personnel shortcomings, places capable, intelligent men back in command.

The Big Red One

United Artists, Directed by Samuel Fuller, Released 1980

A stand-up-and-shout tribute to the GIs of the First Infantry Division—the fighting men who wear the big, red, number one emblazoned on their left shoulder—highlighting their many combat accomplishments. Lee Marvin—a battle-hardened sergeant from the Great War—serves as a father figure to his eclectic squad, from their initial assault landing in North Africa and subsequent campaigns in Sicily, Normandy Beach, the Battle of the Bulge and, finally, to the liberation of a Czechoslovakian concentration camp. Along the way, the foot soldiers—with a diverse collection of American youthful values—share tragedy, pathos, dreams, and an occasional female with their noncom, illustrating the importance of squad unity. (GI to buddy: "You said the U.S. Army is made up of the First Division and ten main replacements.")

Bitter Victory

Columbia, Directed by Nicholas Ray, Released 1957

Another parched, black-and-white, CinemaScope, Sahara Desert adventure yarn, detailing the training, planning, and implementation of a precarious British commando raid against an isolated Libyan outpost to steal General Rommel's offensive orders. Under the command of Major Curt Jurgens, the squad reaches its target, destroys the enemy camp, takes the documents, but, after some unforeseen events, becomes stranded in an abandoned tenth-century waterhole village. Off to the side, a disillusioned colleague, Captain Richard Burton, a former archeologist, disparages the mission's usefulness. (Captain Burton's tirade: "The fine line between war and murder is distance.") After a series of mishaps—including a deadly scorpion's sting, a long, hot march, and, as always, the stereotypical sandstorm—a British rescue team reaches the beleaguered group. Acclaimed a hero, Major Jurgens, in a nod to a gentleman's sensibilities, pins his recently awarded medal on a mannequin, a gesture of war's anonymity.

Black Brigade

ABC, Directed by George McCowan, Released 1970

Another campy, pseudo-blaxploitation, seventy-minute potboiler about the feats of an all-black infantry squad picked for a dangerous assignment to seize a strategic German dam in 1944. Headed by a redneck, southern officer, Stephen Boyd, this search-and-hold mission stands on shaky ground as the Georgia-born captain, annoyed by the unit's homogeneity, offers one taunt after another. (Captain Boyd to Lieutenant Robert Hooks: "This isn't a company, it's a circus.") Eventually, seven men sneak behind enemy lines, and—after some Marx Brothers antics—reach their objective, battle the Germans, and hold the roadway, allowing thousands of American troops easy passage for their eastern offensive (Lieutenant Hooks, explaining his unit's bravery: "Every one of those men volunteered to fight—to die for his country.") With numerous speech, sartorial, hirsute, and geographical anachronisms, the made-for-television screenplay, originally titled *Carter's Army*, offers low-budget praise for African American soldiers. Worst casting: well-known comedian Richard Pryor as an inept GI unable to understand simple instructions or comprehend military time.

Born to Ride

Warner Bros., Directed by Graham Baker, Released 1991

A far-fetched, made-for-adolescents hodgepodge about the unlikely adventures of the U.S. Army's first motorcycle squadron, highlighting some of their Looney Tunes escapades against the Gestapo during the closing months of 1939. Here, John Stamos, a one-time teenage idol, portrays a smart-aleck army corporal who constantly snubs military regulations, but is allowed some impunity because of his extraordinary riding skills (base commander Slobodan Dimitrijevic to Stamos: "I need somebody to train my men how to ride these machines—you're the man who can do that.") Soon, the good-looking motorcyclist winds up in Franco's Spain and—with his unit—rescues an American atomic physicist from the *Schutzstaffel*. Matured and exonerated from his foolish past, Corporal Stamos receives some military kudos plus a big kiss from the colonel's daughter. Laden with implausible situations, the whole shooting match resembles the cliffhanger serials popularized during the 1940s' Saturday-afternoon matinees.

The Boys from Brazil

Twentieth Century–Fox, Directed by Franklin J. Schaffner, Released 1978

An off-the-wall, science-fictional, à la Frankenstein fish story, claiming that the führer's chromosomes are alive and well in South America. Gregory Peck portrays the infamous mad scientist, Dr. Josef Mengele, who in 1978—using unspecified body specimens—has cloned dozens of young Adolf Hitlers, who eventually will create the Fourth Reich. (Dr. Peck, explaining his screwball plan: "Ninety-three boys are exact genetic duplicates of him [Hitler], bred entirely from his cells" while another former Third Reich officer, James Mason, smiles sardonically.) Meanwhile, a doddering, world-renowned Nazi hunter, Laurence Olivier, gets wind of this plan and, after a series of cat-and-mouse travel episodes, exposes everything. Based on Ira Levin's best seller, this popular motion picture continues the fringe conspiracy theory whose advocates preach Hitler did not perish in the Berlin bunker but, instead, is roaming around various South American countries, plotting a return to power.

Breakthrough

Warner Bros., Directed by Lewis Seiler, Released 1950

A let's-go, move-up, keep-low tribute to the GIs who landed at Omaha Beach, raced to the seawall, and, eventually, routed the Nazis from their strongholds, paving the way for a dramatic Allied breakthrough miles away at Saint Lô. Dodging many bullets and explosives, Sergeant Frank Lovejoy guides his chain-smoking squad from the Normandy coast into the arduous, inland hedgerow fighting, and, finally, on the road to Paris. (Sergeant Lovejoy explaining his unit's combat experiences: "Nobody walked across Normandy, they crawled.") Along the way this small, eclectic group—that included a green lieutenant, a dog lover, a future politician, a prankster, and a teenager—bond into a cohesive unit, protecting each other. With numerous newsreel inserts (some anachronistic), much of the photodrama reiterates that the American fighting man—when pushed to his limits—fights both arduously and bravely.

Breakthrough

Maverick International, Directed by Andrew V. McLaglen, Released 1978

A West German production (using the same title as a 1950 World War II motion picture) that continues the legendary exploits of a recalcitrant *Wehrmacht* soldier, Sergeant Steiner (of *Cross of Iron* fame) and his ongoing battle against sadistic, inhuman Nazi officers who issue a fight-to-the-death decree during the July 1944 Normandy retreat. Richard Burton seems miscast as the Third Reich noncommissioned officer who nonchalantly tells an American colonel (Robert Mitchum) about an upcoming German coup, hoping his information will force a truce. (Sergeant Burton to Mitchum: "The time for laughing at Adolf Hitler is passed. In a matter of hours, we shall hear that he is dead.") After the plot fails, an American general (Rod Steiger) orders a frontal tank assault and—following some minor skirmishes—the GIs, aided by Sergeant Burton, enter a French town and secure their position. With frequent antiwar, anti-Hitler, and anti-Gestapo references, this screenplay portrays the common German soldier as a kind-hearted innocent imprisoned by a rabid military system.

The Bridge at Remagen

United Artists, Directed by John Guillermin, Released 1968

A blatant antimilitary, antiofficer, and antiwar indictment, detailing the Allied attack of a strategic Rhine installation, the Ludendorff Bridge, and the Nazi's futile March 1945 defense. E. G. Marshall radiates as a Machiavellian U.S. Army general determined to take his objectives regardless of the human cost. (Marshall to subordinates: "We're risking 100 but we may save 10,000, even 50,000! What you got to do is throw your men across!) But a battle-hardened lieutenant (George Segal) and his sergeant (Ben Gazzara) display only scorn and contempt for their senior officers, while over in the German camp a Nazi major (Robert Vaughn) and his general (Peter Van Eyck) become casualties of their superior's unique cruelty. Containing numerous examples of leadership failure, the storyline lambastes the command system found in both armies.

The Bridge on the River Kwai

Columbia, Directed by David Lean, Released 1957

A 161-minute blockbuster—winner of seven Academy Awards—that describes the ordeal of some British POW's building a Japanese railway bridge in the Malaysian jungle and the efforts of a small Allied raiding team to destroy this important military target. Basically an antiwar picture with numerous box-office stars—including William Holden, Alec Guinness, Jack Hawkins, and Sessue Hayakawa—the story line questions the efficacy of heroics, megalomania, the officer caste system, Oriental fanaticism, and death before dishonor. (Commander William Holden badmouthing his superior: "You and that Colonel Nicholson, you're two of a kind! Crazy with courage, for what? How to die like a gentleman, how to die by the rules?") One of the most controversial scenes:

Alec Guinness, a ramrod British soldier, inadvertently drops his makeshift swagger stick into the river, a faux pas unthinkable for an English officer.

A Bridge Too Far

United Artists, Directed by Richard Attenborough, Released 1977

A puffed-up, we-can-win, flag-waving, 176-minute tribute to the Allied forces and their ambitious but ill-fated attempt to seize four strategic bridges during a daring Dutch offensive—code-named Market Garden—in September 1944. Using an array of impressive motion-picture stars portraying important military luminaries, the storyline, based on the book by Cornelius Ryan, weaves in and out of various British, American, and German command posts and battle sites, expostulating how the nine-day, seesaw fighting was really a combination of unrealistic planning, logistical screwups, and ineluctable serendipity. (Dirk Bogarde, portraying General Frederick "Boy" Browning, explaining why his side will win: "We're going to fly 35,000 men 3,000 miles and drop them behind enemy lines—it will be the largest airborne operation ever mounted!) Finally, after suffering numerous losses, the Allies capitulate, leaving behind many dead and wounded soldiers. (General Dirk Bogarde, rationalizing the defeat: "Well, as you know, I always thought that we tried to go a bridge too far.")

The Caine Mutiny

Columbia, Directed by Edward Dmytryk, Released 1954

Another critical jab at military life—from the Pulitzer prize novel by Herman Wouk—that depicts the fictional 1944 account of a half-crazed ship commander aboard a U.S. Navy minesweeper in the Pacific theater and his subsequent removal by junior officers, culminating with a court-martial to decide if such actions constitute a mutiny. Humphrey Bogart's portrayal of a demented captain convinces his staff that he is unfit for duty (Lieutenant Fred MacMurray to Lieutenant Van Johnson: "Captain Queeg has every symptom of acute paranoia—just a question of time before he goes over the line.") Eventually, Bogart's trial-room comportment—rolling three steel balls incessantly in his palm—exonerates the accused, even though their defense attorney (José Ferrer), feeling he has maligned the wrong man, heaves champagne into a celebrant's face.

Captain Corelli's Mandolin

Universal, Directed by John Madden, Released 2001

Another saccharine, 1940s wartime, romantic saga that proves, once again, the heart is a lonely hunter. Happy-go-lucky Nicolas Cage portrays an Italian mandolin-playing artillery officer, whose ill-disciplined unit occupies an idyllic Greek island, Cephallonia, while a German commandant politely ignores the lackadaisical nature of his subordinates. (Captain Corelli, explaining his nation's attitude about hostilities: "We're Italian, famous for singing, eating, making love.") Soon, the opera-singing Romeo catches the eye of a local beauty (Penélope Cruz), who—after some off-again, on-again flirtations—capitulates to the strumming musician. But Mussolini's 1943 escape changes everything as Italians and Germans, now enemies, fight their private battles, culminating in a gory end-of-the-film atrocity scene that separates the lovers. Two years later, however, they are united. Funniest scene: Captain Cage, marching in formation, in a manner that resembles the typical awkwardness exhibited by clumsy recruits during their first hours of basic training.

Captain Newman, M.D.

Universal, Directed by David Miller, Released 1963

A tricky blend of pathos, tragedy, and comedy depicting the psychiatric treatment of some American servicemen convalescing at an Arizona military hospital, circa 1943, where anxious commanders order their subordinates to make on-the-spot evaluations, employ fast treatment, and quickly return patients to their overseas fighting units. Soft-spoken Gregory Peck radiates as Josiah Newman, an army medical officer whose daily encounters with red tape, shell-shocked GIs, insufficient supplies, ambitious superiors, Italian prisoners-of-war, plus a locked-up ward of psychotic patients provide a continuous flow of humor, sadness, renewal, and optimism. (Captain Newman, explaining his laid-back philosophy: "We say 'Roger' quite a bit around here—makes us feel like heroes," while off to the side, his pretty nurse (Angie Dickinson), downplaying her maternal instincts, smiles gleefully.) With Tony Curtis as the preeminent goldbricking corporal holding an endless array of midnight-requisitioned materials, the whole shebang—complete with anachronistic haircuts, uniforms, aircraft, and jargon—could easily be titled, "The Three Stooges Get Drafted."

Captive Hearts

MGM, Directed by Paul Almond, Released 1987

Another implausible, love-conquers-all fairy tale that purports an Army Air Corps pilot (Chris Makepeace), along with his gunner, bail out of a crippled B-25 over northern Japan during December 1944. Quickly captured by frightened farmers, the two officers are first imprisoned in a mountainous village, but, after some roundabout events, are released to make needed household repairs. (Lieutenant Makepeace to his sergeant: "We better start planning our way out of here.") As the locals warm up to the young flyer, the ongoing war seems far away when a pretty Japanese widow (Mari Soto) catches his eye. Now, the twosome tiptoe around, hoping their mutual affection will not upset the proverbial applecart. When Japanese troops arrive, the town patriarch (Pat Morita) acts decisively, leading the lovers to the Sea of Japan. Ensconced in a small boat heading for the Chinese mainland, the Air Corps pilot waves a tender goodbye to his newfound sweetheart, promising that someday, when the birds are singing, he will return. Most unresolved question: what was a B-25, a two-engine bomber — with a limited range — doing in northern Japan?

Carmen Jones

Twentieth Century–Fox, Directed by Otto Preminger, Released 1954

A high-powered CinemaScope musical extravaganza updating George Bizet's famous opera, *Carmen*, to a black training base in the rural South sometime during the middle of the war. Harry Belafonte stars as a clean-cut army corporal — selected for flight-training school — who only wants to marry the innocent girl of his dreams. (Belafonte to sweetheart: "There's no use in waiting till the war's over for us to get married, not when I have a twenty-four-hour pass. We can have our honeymoon tonight.") Hours before his conjugal ceremony, the naive Belafonte capitulates to the charms of the post's femme fatale (Dorothy Dandridge), and after a series of musical adventures, the twosome flee to Chicago, barely escaping the authorities. Eventually, the strain of AWOL turns the good-looking Belafonte from a straight-arrow soldier to a jealous murderer. In its own simplistic way, the storyline denounces the segregated lifestyle of the African American GIs, a situation mandated by military regulations.

Casablanca Express

Globe, Directed by Sergio Martino, Released 1989

A preposterous Italian production — modeled after the spaghetti Westerns — that purports Winston Churchill's double duped the Nazis into attacking a local train heading for Casablanca during the early days of the 1942 North African campaign, while the real prime minister rendezvoused with President Roosevelt. Here, a two-star American general, seventy-three-year-old Glenn Ford, oversees this cloak-and-dagger mission while his British colleague (Donald Pleasence) — unaware of the ruse — plans an elaborate rescue mission. (Pleasence to staff: "We can't let Hitler fly our prime minister to

Berlin—I'm sure he'd rather die!") Soon Allied forces, firing anachronistic weapons, rout the Germans in a cavalry-to-the-rescue ending while another hero (Jason Connery) rides off into the sunset with his newfound girlfriend. Lacking any synchronized dialogue, the photoplay suffers from numerous revisionist inconsistencies, including a wild claim that Winston Churchill, aware of the impending Pearl Harbor attack, did not notify the White House.

Castle Keep

Columbia, Directed by Sydney Pollack, Released 1969

A lyrical, ontological, and mystical look at war's absurdity—based on the novel by William Eastlake—employing various forms of symbolism, spiritualism, and rationalism during the precarious 1944 Battle of the Bulge. As a one-eyed army major straddling a white thoroughbred, Burt Lancaster's laconic talk seems obtuse to his seven charges seeking refuge in a baroque castle in the Belgian forest, while his host (Jean-Pierre Aumont) explains the Freudian concept of destruction endemic to both sides. (Count Aumont, expatiating on military futility: "They planned this war because there was something they hadn't yet smashed.") Eventually both Allied and Nazi forces clash in a ritualistic Götterdämmerung, and the castle's ruins offer ignominious testimony to mankind's folly. Replete with numerous juxtapositions, including Peter Falk's portrayal of a soldier-turned-baker and Patrick O'Neal's obsession as an art historian, the convoluted story line is a classical retelling of the beauty and the beast fable.

Catch-22

Paramount, Directed by Mike Nichols, Released 1970

A heavy-handed, madcap, off-the-wall, black comedy—based on Joseph Heller's runaway best-selling first novel—that fires off both barrels at the lunacy of military life, blasting away at the nepotism, opportunism, goldbricking, and megalomania found during wartime. Alan Arkin is outstanding as an Army Air Corps bombardier, stationed on an unnamed Mediterranean island, whose daily attack missions have pushed him over the edge. Pleading mental instability, the acid-tongued Arkin discovers that military regulations forbid reassigning airmen who claim psychosis. (Captain Arkin, learning the intricacies of Catch-22: "In order to be grounded, I got to be crazy and I must be crazy to keep flying. But, if I ask to be grounded that means I'm not crazy anymore and I have to keep flying.") With an all-star cast that includes Jon Voight, Richard Benjamin, Art Garfunkel, Martin Balsam, Martin Sheen, Bob Newhart, and Orson Welles, no aspect of military life escapes lampooning.

Funniest scene: the flyers bomb their own base in a surrealistic, quid pro quo deal with the Germans involving some surplus cotton.

China Doll

Romina Productions, Directed by Frank Borzage, Released 1958

An easygoing, heart-tugging story about the antics of some Air Corps Hump pilots, who in 1943 routinely traverse the danger-prone Himalaya air route, and the misadventures of their senior pilot when he innocently "buys" a young Chinese girl, a bond servant, from her obliging father for a three-month period. Unable to extract himself from this ambiguous arrangement, hard-talking Captain Victor Mature initially ignores the pretty adolescent until the moment of truth, when infatuation ends and the heart takes over. (Captain Mature's declaration: "I guess I fell in love with you right from the beginning," culminating in marriage and a baby daughter.) Months later, a Japanese aircraft kill both parents, and, after years of orphanage life and U.S. red tape, a kindly priest finally unites the teenage girl with her father's close friends in a heartwarming, happy ending.

Code Name: Emerald

MGM, Directed by Jonathan Sanger, Released 1985

Another fictionalized, B-potboiler highlighting the secrecy surrounding the Operation Overlord logistics and the Allies' determination to keep the Nazi spy machine ignorant of the landing site and date. Based on the novel by Ronald Bass, the photodrama purports that a captured twenty-one-year-old U.S. Army first lieutenant—privy to this information—eschews Gestapo interrogation until good-looking American double-agent Ed Harris can parachute into France. There, Harris seduces a comely resistance worker, and with the assistance of a benign Nazi colonel (Max Von Sydow), smooth-talks his way past the German jailers to rescue the frail-looking American. (Double-agent Ed Harris to frightened officer, Eric Stoltz: "I'm with OSS—the Nazis think I'm working for them.) Funniest scene: clean-cut Ed Harris strutting around in a meticulously tailored Gestapo uniform, bellowing reprisal threats to everyone within hearing range.

Come See the Paradise

Twentieth Century–Fox, Directed by Alan Parker, Released 1990

A strongly worded, no-holds barred, revisionist indictment of Executive Law 9066—quickly passed after the Pearl Harbor attack—that sent thousands of

West Coast Japanese American citizens to barren internment centers for the war's duration. Here, an outspoken, leftist labor organizer (Dennis Quaid), married to a Japanese American, watches helplessly as federal agents—brandishing newly printed warrants—round up his wife and in-laws, claiming these soft-spoken family members represent a threat to America's security. (Quaid to Army official: "It's unconstitutional. They had their rights taken away from them. The nisei, who were born here, are American citizens!") Laden with many examples depicting the indignities heaped upon a hapless minority, scene after scene denounces the hysteria, racism, and opportunism responsible for their illegal confinement.

Command Decision

MGM, Directed by Sam Wood, Released 1948

A microscopic examination of the Eighth Air Corps' controversial 1943 precision daylight bombing raids over Germany that destroyed many strategic targets but caused a high casualty rate for the American airmen. Clark Gable is outstanding as the ramrod general who must send out dozens of aircraft each day on such perilous but tactical missions. (Gable to General Walter Pidgeon: "It was my decision to make, Sir, and I made it.") With Van Johnson, Brian Donlevy, Charles Bickford, and John Hodiak in supporting roles, the storyline—based on the Broadway play by William Wister Haines—takes numerous digs at American politicians, past and present, who, naively, deprecate airpower but now control the purse for all appropriations. With many actual aerial scenes, the film realistically captures the fright and discomfort found in the European air war.

Commandos

Heritage Enterprises, Directed by Armando Crispino, Released 1968

Another no-one-can-stop-us, get-out-of-the-way, B-yarn about a wily team of Italian-speaking American GIs, led by a chisel-face sergeant (Lee Van Cleef), who, in October 1942, don Italian uniforms, slither into a North African oasis, stab, strangle, and shoot fascist troops, dupe some Third Reich supply officers, and kill escaping prisoners, only to learn that their operation offers no military value. (Sergeant Van Cleef, explaining his mission: "This ain't no Halloween party.") Eventually attacked by some Panzers, both Americans and Germans—after an intricate back-and-forth struggle—perish in an elaborate, gory battle that insinuates war's futility. Most cerebral scene: *Wehrmacht* and U.S. officers discuss the nuances of Goethe's *Faust*, emphasizing the eighteenth-century poet's well-known chariots of destiny passage.

The Counterfeit Traitor

Paramount, Directed by George Seaton, Released 1962

A glowing testimony to the heroic Swedish oil broker, Eric Erickson, the man who posed as a Nazi sympathizer to learn important production information that resulted in many Allied bombing missions. William Holden portrays the American-born businessman, now a naturalized Swedish citizen, and his slow transformation from ardent capitalist to deft spy. (British Intelligence officer Hugh Griffith explaining the dangerous assignment: "You'll be hated for a while, there's no doubt about that. You'll be a quisling and you'll just have to live with that.") Based on the book by Alexander Klein, the storyline details numerous close calls inside the Fatherland—including clandestine meetings with underground workers, a love affair with a German contact, plus imprisonment and flight—before he reaches Stockholm an acclaimed hero. Funniest scenes: Holden, wearing a perfectly knotted necktie while sleeping in a cellar jail or dashing from captors, while his pudgy Gestapo nemesis, oblivious to firearm safety procedures, carries a Luger in the back pocket of his trousers.

Cross of Iron

EMI Films, Directed by Sam Peckinpah, Released 1977

Another revisionist tract—from the book by Willi Heinrich—that tones down Nazi bestiality by portraying individual members of the *Wehrmacht* as decent, honorable soldiers, mere pawns in an out-of-control, maddening war machine. James Coburn is convincing as a recalcitrant sergeant who must battle both his officers and the Russians as the German army slowly retreats from the Taman Peninsula in 1943. (Coburn, expressing his rage at the command structure "I hate all officers—all the Stranskys, all the Triebigs, all the Iron Cross scavengers in the whole German army," while his superiors [James Mason and Maximillan Schell] plan his death.) Basically a caustic, violent, and riveting salvo against the Prussian caste system that allows deranged, megalomaniac German officers unlimited authority, the screenplay—employing numerous surrealist concepts—suggests that World War II was fought only on the Eastern Front, expostulating that the Red Army, not the Nazis, were the real enemy.

Darby's Rangers

Warner Bros., Directed by William Wellman, Released 1957

A fuzzy (and distorted) paean to Colonel William Darby, the founder of the army's Ranger battalions that spearheaded important 1943 victories in North Africa and Italy. Looking firm and resolved, James Garner portrays the

Arkansas-raised officer as a hell-bent fighter, who leads his tip-of-the-javelin combat soldiers into many difficult battles against Nazi forces. (Colonel Garner, explaining his military strategy: "We're kind of a mustang outfit. We use the book, but occasionally a page or two gets mislaid.") Off to the side, his loyal sergeant (Jack Warden) rationalizes most problems with succinct Yiddish phrases. When not fighting their German adversaries, the enlisted men generally seduce vulnerable woman or visit immaculate Scottish homes, while a West Point lieutenant (Edward Byrnes) sports an Elvis-style coiffure and, after ten minutes of serious thought, marries a forlorn Italian so that the bleached-blond signorina may obtain some free GI penicillin.

Day One

Aaron Spelling Productions, Directed by Joseph Sargent, Released 1989

A made-for-television docudrama that traces the development of the atom bomb beginning with Albert Einstein's historical letter to President Roosevelt and culminating with the Japanese surrender. Laden with famous names from the 1940s, the storyline proffers a quaint mixture of fact and fiction about the complex Manhattan Project. Brian Dennehy coruscates as the hard-nosed, nononsense, military boss General Leslie Groves, who serves as foil, friend, and tormentor to the noted physicist, J. Robert Oppenheimer, played by David Strathairn. In this version, the controversial leftist suggests a moderate position. (Strathairn to colleagues, regarding the implementation of their new weapon: "Without the bomb, they have to invade Japan—a million American casualties.") Replete with many ambiguous moral questions, the photoplay eventually fizzles down to late 1945 as Oppenheimer, dismayed by the carnage of Hiroshima and Nagasaki, ponders his uncertain future.

D-Day: The Sixth of June

Twentieth Century–Fox, Directed by Henry Koster, Released 1956

Another hearts-and-flowers soap opera that peripherally uses the Normandy invasion as the backdrop for an American junior officer's adulterous affair with an insecure, love-stricken British social worker, who still pines for her missing-in-action boyfriend. As a London-based combat veteran assigned to Operation Overlord, Captain Robert Taylor lauds the fighting man preparing for the historic assault. (Taylor, praising an errant airman: "He'll conduct himself like soldier right in the gun turret of his B-17, flying over Germany in broad daylight.") But Taylor turns to mush every time Dana Wynter mentions his wife's name. Finally, on June 6 an elite Ranger squad assaults a German stronghold and—after a series of rope-climbing adventures—the enemy capitulates. Wounded in this daring raid, Robert Taylor—now convalescing in a London hospital—relinquishes his English lover and, in a saccharine fade-out, reluctantly returns to his stateside spouse.

Deadly Mission

Film Concorde, Directed by Enzo Castellari, Released 1977

Another B-copycat version of *The Dirty Dozen* in which five American soldiers, heading for stockade imprisonment, escape their captors in the French countryside and begin a 165-mile trek to the Swiss border. Along the way they rout some German troops and, eventually, stumble into a Resistance camp. There, following more convoluted events, they agree to storm a Third Reich stronghold, gather information, board a high-security Nazi train, and steal a secret gyroscope. With Bo Svenson in charge of this volatile mishmash, much of the screenplay resembles a Road Runner cartoon—these escapees shoot, strangle, punch, kick, stab, throw, push, burn, knee, and ram many Germans until, finally, an Army colonel (Ian Bannen) grabs the important wheeled instrument, proving once more that American troops, no matter how heinous their crimes, remain loyal to the old red, white, and blue. (Bo Svenson, explaining the rationale: "I think it's about time we got started with this war.") Funniest scene: six-foot-two Bo Svenson walking with his five-foot-eight colonel in a manner resembling a Mutt and Jeff cartoon.

Death of a Soldier

Suatu Film Management, Directed by Philip Mora, Released 1986

A strong indictment against the U.S. Army's military justice system that in 1942 ordered the hanging of a mentally deranged American GI for murdering four Australian women. As expected, James Coburn radiates as the military lawyer appointed to defend the psychotic soldier. Soon, he realizes the futility of any arguments when his superiors—eager to cement the relationship with their Aussie ally—censor all his courtroom motions. (Coburn to girlfriend: "If we allow this to happen without protest, we're nothing more than judiciaries, killers, Nazis. That's what the Nazis do, isn't it?") With many scenes depicting American officers as alcoholics, degenerates, or fascists, the storyline takes numerous potshots against General MacArthur (Jon Sidney), denouncing the four-star commander as insensitive, opportunistic, and autocratic.

One unsettling scene—highlighting the whitewashing of a shooting incident between Australian and American troops—demonstrates MacArthur's dictatorial power to silence any critic.

December

I.R.S. Media, Directed by Gabe Torres, Released 1991

A psychological examination of the anger experienced by some male adolescents—residing in an exclusive Vermont preparatory school—as news of the Pearl Harbor attack blares from their radios. Soon, a clean-cut senior (Wil Wheaton) repudiates the mock heroics espoused by his roommates and, contrary to the sophomoric flag-waving atmosphere, refuses to enlist. After hours of back-and-forth arguments, the young loner produces a copy of the 1939 National Book Award title—Dalton Trumbo's *Johnny Got His Gun*—citing reasons how this novel altered his perception of patriotism. (Wheaton to friends: "This book! It made me see how crazy war is.") Eventually, with the administration's blessing, a busload of upperclassmen embark for their induction center, leaving the taciturn Wheaton to his private ruminations. Strongest scene: the headmaster burns Trumbo's book, fearful that other students will read this antiwar tract.

Decision before Dawn

Fox, Directed by Anatole Litvak, Released 1951

A well-crafted, espionage thriller—based on George Howe's novel, *Call It Treason*—that follows the thorny path some *Wehrmacht* POWs follow after agreeing to become Allied agents in their homeland, hoping such service can bring the war to a quick end and spare their townspeople total obliteration. Here, a hard-nosed American commander (Gary Merrill) wants quick results and accurate information. (Colonel Merrill, laying down the law while another officer (Richard Basehart) watches cautiously: "If we found you've betrayed us, whether you're a double agent or a plain crook, you'll wind up in front of a firing squad.") Soon, a twenty-year-old corporal (Oskar Werner) reaches his hometown and, after a series of close calls—that include meeting an old family friend, becoming friendly with a lady of the evening, falling in with a black marketeer, and, finally, posing as a medic—learns the location of troop movements. As a minor revisionist work filmed on location in Wurzberg, a bombed-out town, the screenplay suggests that not all Germans were Hitler-worshipping belligerents but, instead, decent people caught up in unfortunate circumstances.

The Desert Fox

Twentieth Century–Fox, Directed by Henry Hathaway, Released 1951

A meticulously worded, subtly distorted, revisionist whitewash that heaps dollops of praise upon one of Hitler's successful generals, Erwin Rommel, the acclaimed, hands-on officer whose North African victories earned him the sobriquet, "The Desert Fox." James Mason's precise English enunciation sounds anomalous coming from the Teutonic field marshal who—after witnessing the führer's accelerated primitivism—reluctantly joins the unsuccessful conspiratorial movement, hoping to salvage some dignity for his nation. Eventually discovered, he chooses death before dishonor (Rommel, venting his frustration: "Those hoodlums again, those thieves and crooks and murderers, those toy soldiers, those dummy generals with their books and charts and maps and posters.") With many prominent English actors in supporting roles, the photodrama often resembles a British cabinet meeting, except, this time, the participants wear swastikas and Iron Crosses instead of Savile Row morning coats.

The Desert Rats

Twentieth Century–Fox, Directed by Robert Wise, Released 1953

An all-male, hard-as-nails, flag-waving, we-can-do-it, semidocumentary tribute to the fighting men of the Ninth Australian Division. Those worn-out, down-under soldiers emerge, like desert rats, from their Libyan sand trenches to attack the *Wehrmacht* troops, disrupting Field Marshal Erwin Rommel's July 1941 Suez Canal offensive. Lt. Colonel Richard Burton bellows many orders to his noncommissioned officers, determined to keep his green charges from harm's way during the 242-day defense of Tobruk. (Colonel Burton, praising the enlisted man: "Being an infantryman is the toughest job in the Army.") Over in the German camp, James Mason portrays the field marshal as a likable bon vivant enjoying gourmet meals, bespoke uniforms, and attentive military valets. Best scene: Colonel Burton meets his old schoolmaster in the enlisted-men's ranks and—in an awkward reversal of fortunes—proffers gratitude for those formative years.

The Devil's Brigade

United Artists, Directed by Andrew McLagen, Released 1968

Another rip-roaring, go-in-headfirst commando photodrama that highlights the amalgamation of some ill-disciplined American GIs—along with a group of straight-arrow Canadian soldiers—into a well-honed fighting unit dubbed the Devil's Brigade. In this anomalous outfit, tough-talking Lt. Colonel William Holden makes no bones about his assignment, while off to the side, Major Cliff Robertson grins sardonically. (Holden to troops: " . . . I want men that are tough, love to fight, fight to win, and would rather die than quit.") Eventually, these fighters reach Italy and in a few days capture a hilltop town with dozens of German prisoners and then storm a mountain stronghold to topple a strategic Nazi observation post. Loosely based on historical facts, this screenplay—from the book by Robert H. Adleman and George Walton—offers strong testimony to this highly decorated unit and its many European victories, proving, once again, that when pushed to the limit, the Allied soldier accepts the call to colors.

The Dirty Dozen

MGM, Directed by Robert Aldrich, Released 1967

A fast-moving adventure story—based on the book by E. M. Nathanson—that takes some nasty swipes at the U.S. Army officer caste system and its harsh penal code against enlisted men. Lee Marvin sparkles as a recalcitrant combat major who must recruit, discipline, and train twelve military prisoners—misfit GIs facing execution or long prison terms—and lead them on a suicide mission behind German lines hours before the D-Day invasion. (Hard-talking Major Marvin, venting his frustration: "I didn't pick these men—the army did! Remember? And I didn't pick this assignment either!") Eventually, this oddball unit—dubbed the Dirty Dozen—parachutes into France and, after some zany comic-strip adventures, blows up a renaissance chateau, killing many high-ranking Nazi officers. Top-heavy with Hollywood stars—including Donald Sutherland, Charles Bronson, Telly Savalas, Robert Ryan, Clint Walker, and John Cassavetes—the storyline caricatures American officers as either cynical, hard-nosed, or adipose, while citing the average foot solder, regardless of his faults, as loyal, patriotic, and sacrificial.

Don't Go Near the Water

MGM, Directed by Charles Walters, Released 1957

A plush, thick-vegetation, blue-water, CinemaScope college-freshmen comedy—from William Brinkley's acclaimed novel—that suggests the 1944 South Pacific American offensive resembles the dozens of shenanigans often associated with playful fraternity life. Smooth-talking Glenn Ford radiates as a frustrated public-relations naval lieutenant working for a pettifogging commander, while off to the side, most of his colleagues concoct intricate plans to avoid combat. (Lieutenant Ford to pals: "The public relations outfit is a collection of oddballs and freaks.") Numerous subplots include blackmailing an obnoxious war correspondent, arranging a romantic tryst between an enlisted tar and a pretty nurse, building an officer's club with inexperienced maintenance people, allowing a voluptuous reporter aboard a combat destroyer, providing a school building for the native children, and, finally, in a Pygmalion nod, grooming a foul-mouth sailor into a refined speaker capable of addressing the Admiral's staff. The whole kit and caboodle downplays the carnage of this combat zone and, instead, suggests that World War II was, in reality, all fun and games.

The Eagle Has Landed

Associated General Films, Directed by John Sturges, Released 1977

A fictionalized suspense tale—from the best-selling novel by Jack Higgins— that purports in 1944 an elite Nazi commando group secretly parachuted into eastern England and, after a series of close calls, assassinated Winston Churchill. Michael Caine's Cockney accent seems strange, coming from a highly decorated Nazi who finally reaches the prime minister's countryside verandah, while his commander, one-eyed Robert Duvall—spouting aphorisms from Carl Jung's synchronicity theory—issues cryptic orders from the Fatherland. As the American officer who discovers the German plot, Captain Treat Williams finally guns down the Axis agent only to discover the "prime minister" was an impostor. Saturated with glowing references to Third Reich humanitarianism, the story line sugarcoats every aspect of Hitlerism. (Nazi colonel, Michael Caine, rationalizing his capture: "I thought the plot failed because one of my men died saving the little girl up there.")

Eight Iron Men

Columbia, Directed by Edward Dmytryk, Released 1952

Another B-story that examines the stress and frustration a small American squad endures when confined to a bombed-out French house during the war's last months, as Nazi snipers take an occasional potshot at their invaders. Here, Lee Marvin, a senior NCO in charge of the eight iron men holed up in this temporary shelter, keeps a tight rein on his charges while exasperated by the lack of tangible information. (Sergeant Marvin to Corporal Richard Kiley: "That's the trouble with this war—a lousy patrol war—crawl on your belly in the mud, stick a knife in some guy, always in the dark!") Eventually, the GIs rout their adversaries and—acclaimed as heroes—return to their rear lines. Replete with hackneyed dialogue, this B-picture contains one visual cliché after another, including the lone GI who tosses a hand grenade with deadly accuracy into a German pillbox, while offering an incantation to his baseball idol Bob Feller.

The Enemy Below

Twentieth Century–Fox, Directed by Dick Powell, Released 1957

Another deep-six, CinemaScope underwater operational narrative—based on the novel by D. A. Rayners—that pits a crafty American destroyer captain against a U-boat commander in a convoluted cat-and-mouse mission during the final days of the South Atlantic hostilities. Robert Mitchum's Yankee intransigence forces worn-out German officer Curt Jurgens to reevaluate Nazi fealty, as his submarine dives deeper to avoid American depth-charge detonations. (Commander Jurgens to aide: "I'm sick of this war—it's not a good war.") Finally the U-boat surfaces, and in an outlandish Götterdämmerung, both ships—now heavily damaged—sink ignominiously to the sea's bottom. With one pithy observation after another, the all-male storyline pooh-poohs the dangers of naval combat, suggesting that conflict is a romantic and chivalrous undertaking.

Ensign Pulver

Warner Bros., Directed by Joshua Logan, Released 1964

A lackluster, watered-down sequel to *Mister Roberts* (1955) that continues the madcap, South Pacific confrontation between a U.S. Navy cargo ship's crew and their loose-cannon commander, Burl Ives, while on the starboard side, the ship's laundry officer, Ensign Pulver (Robert Walker Jr.) keeps the pot boiling with his many sophomoric pranks. Eventually, the captain's unknown past emerges and—following some minor concessions—everyone reconciles their differences. (Robert Walker Jr. explaining Burl Ives sudden reassignment: " . . . He's saying thank you now, by leaving the ship he loves.") Most amazing feat: the makeshift medical operation where Ensign Pulver—in an astonishing six minutes—makes an incision, removes the appendix, cauterizes the stem, and, without missing a beat, sutures the patient while his medical pal, Walter Matthau, relays instructions via ship-to-shore phone.

Escape to Athene

Pimlico Films, Directed by George P. Cosmatos, Released 1979

A half-spoof, half-serious take about the Nazi occupation of an antique-laden Greek island circa 1944. This time, Roger Moore portrays a jaded German

POW commandant who keeps one step ahead of his Gestapo superiors, while Allied prisoners David Niven, Elliott Gould, Richard Roundtree, and Sonny Bono constantly upset the applecart with their recalcitrant antics. (Gould, kibitzing with his captor about his terpsichorean skills: "I can teach dancing to the men—help limber them up after all that goose-stepping.") Eventually, a serendipitous breakout frees the prisoners, destroys the Axis armament, routs the *Wehrmacht* forces, and returns the island to local control. Replete with many anachronistic weapons, language, scuba gear, and even a New York Yankees baseball cap, this part-Western, part-make-believe photodrama shuns all verisimilitude and, instead, portrays this dark page of World War II history as nothing more than a walk in the park. Funniest scene: Nazi troops, guarding a rocket station, wearing specially designed Buck Rogers uniforms.

The Extraordinary Seaman

MGM, Directed by John Frankenheimer, Released 1969

An E-for-Easy, lighthearted, oddball frolic that traces the exploits of three shipwrecked U.S. sailors who reach a Pacific island, where they discover a dilapidated vessel, HMS *Curmudgeon*. A spiffily dressed British officer, David Niven, cajoles the tars into making the ship seaworthy. Soon, these gallants take to the open waters, but the blue jackets, much to their chagrin, learn that their English host is, in fact, a ghost destined, à la Ancient Mariner, to roam the ocean until one good deed redeems him. (Commander Niven, explaining his predicament: "I have been in the Royal Navy for forty-three years; granted since my death, I have been somewhat inactive.") After a few cheery mishaps, this do-it-yourself crew destroys a Japanese vessel, allowing the wraith passage to the hereafter. Funniest scenes: Commander Niven's empty whisky glass automatically refills, allowing unlimited imbibitions.

Eye of the Needle

United Artists, Directed by Richard Marquand, Released 1981

A high-powered spy thriller—adapted from the best-selling book by Ken Follett—that traces the sub-rosa activities of a Nazi plant in war-torn London that sends coded messages about the D-Day operations to Berlin. As a rabid devotee of Hitlerism, Donald Sutherland oozes villainy in every frame, obsessed with his own megalomania. (Axis cohort to stony-faced Sutherland: "You must deliver them personally to the führer.") When his cover falls apart, the German spy eludes British officialdom, takes a twining northern escape route, and reaches a remote Scottish island inhabited by a small, caretaker family.

Attempting to make a U-boat rendezvous, the Machiavellian agent commits two murders. He is finally thwarted by a simple English woman with a handgun in a gory end-of-the-film death scene, allowing General Eisenhower's invasion to proceed as scheduled.

The Fallen

Anthem Pictures, Directed by Ari Taub, Released 2006

An off-centered combat tale—borrowing generously from the synchronistic format of *The Young Lions* with a nod to Chaplin's *The Cure*. The story traces the comings and goings of a U.S. quartermaster platoon, a retreating Nazi squad, a disarrayed Italian reinforcement group, and a gang of angry partisans during the October 1944 Northern Italy campaign and their eventual hillside Götterdämmerung. With numerous Freudian, Sartrean, and Jungian overtones, the entire screenplay—using an impressive array of unknown actors—   •
depicts the common soldier, regardless of nationality, as a frustrated, hungry, and overburdened individual, a mere pawn on a chessboard, led erratically toward an inglorious death by uncaring and, occasionally, inept officers. (Sergeant John McVay, explaining the ground pounder's plight: "Those infantry boys get killed every day of the week.") With numerous allegorical, symbolic, and ontological scenes, this 2004 screenplay, arriving almost sixty years after war's end, equates the European battlefield with Polonius's view of sixteenth-century drama: tragical-comical-historical-pastoral.

Farewell to the King

Orion Pictures, Directed by John Milius, Released 1989

An offbeat, discursive allegory that juxtaposes war's absurdity with the virtues of the Noble Savage. Nick Nolte shines as an American GI who, in 1942, deserts his Bataan post, reaches Borneo's northern coast, and—after a series of make-believe adventures—becomes king of a local headhunter tribe. Three years later, British paratroopers locate his isolated village, and soon the blue-eyed sergeant's serene world evaporates as a fleeing, ragtag Japanese army forces a deadly confrontation. With numerous antimilitary swipes, this fictional drama—based on the book by Pierre Schoendoerffer—excoriates English brutality while downplaying American heroism. (Discalced ruler Nolte, explaining his motives: "Just before the fall of Corregidor—when MacArthur skipped out—some of us figured it was time to go too.") Drollest scene: longhaired Nick Nolte's linguistic skills, articulating an esoteric native dialect to wide-mouthed, British botanist-turned-major, Nigel Havers.

Fat Man and Little Boy

Paramount, Directed by Roland Joffe, Released 1989

Another revisionist point-of-view examination of the designing, building, and implementing of the atomic bomb, emphasizing the logistical, monetary, and moral issues associated with the Manhattan Project. Paul Newman's trim waistline offers minor distraction in his tough portrayal of the outspoken, pudgy military commander, General Leslie Groves, while Dwight Schultz sparkles as the leftist physicist, J. Robert Oppenheimer. Frequently at odds with each other, the dominant General Newman finally convinces the temperamental scientist to bring an end to the Pacific war. (Newman to Schultz: "You want to sit on your hands, polish your conscience—while we might be able to end this whole thing with one shot?") Burdened with ongoing philosophical arguments, the motion picture offers strong rationalizations regarding the thorny issue of obliterating the two Japanese cities.

Fatherland

HBO Pictures, Directed by Christopher Menaul, Released 1994

A convoluted "What if?" made-for-television, fictionalized social commentary—based on the book by Robert Harris—that suggests an off-the-wall ending to World War II. In 1944 the Allied Forces—after being pushed into the sea at the abortive Normandy invasion—create a separate peace with the führer. One year later, the Americans detonate two atomic bombs on Japanese cities, forcing that nation's capitulation. Russia, now standing alone, still fights an eastern front war with Germany. By 1964 King Edward and Queen Wallis govern England, Joseph Kennedy Sr. is the U.S. president, and Hitler—still ruling Germany—remains a frail seventy-five-year-old dictator, while his nemesis, Joseph Stalin, now eighty-five, stealthily puffs his pipe. With Rutger Hauer and Miranda Richardson in starring roles, the storyline meanders from one illogical point to another as German nationals struggle to find normalcy in their troubled lives. (Nonplussed Miss Richardson, asking a naive question: "What does Final Solution mean? What happened at Auschwitz?)

The Final Countdown

United Artists, Directed by Don Taylor, Released 1980

A high-flying, science fiction kaleidoscope that shows off the U.S. Navy's modern carrier power in a manner usually found in the eerie scripts that made the popular television series, *The Twilight Zone*, a household word. Kirk Douglas stars as the captain of the USS *Nimitz*, a flattop cruising west of the Hawaiian Islands in late 1979, while Martin Sheen, a civilian observer, studies military protocol. Soon, a phantasmagoric sea storm transposes the ship back into a late-1941 time zone where the F-15s spot the Japanese armada. (Douglas to officers: "Every man on this ship knows that we have radar and visual contact with the Japanese fleet approaching Pearl Harbor on December 6, 1941.") Unable to upset the course of history, the carrier reluctantly returns to the present, allowing the sneak attack to culminate. Replete with pithy hindsight observations, this offbeat tale glamorizes every facet of life aboard an electronically operated navy fighting ship.

Fireball Forward

Twentieth Century–Fox, Directed by Marvin Chomsky, Released 1972

Another made-for-television fabrication that suggests the 1944 Normandy breakout campaign was hampered by the espionage activities of a turncoat Resistance fighter, who radios Nazi artillerists strategic Allied positions. As a former combat sergeant promoted to major general, Ben Gazzara takes command of a hard-luck outfit with a high casualty rate and, using a low-key approach, gains the respect of the enlisted men, while calling for unerring standards from his officers. (General Gazzara chiding his old pal, Colonel Eddie Albert, about military discipline: "Now you either cut the mustard or I send you back! I'd hang my brother if he screwed up a combat assignment.") Eventually, American intelligence agents eliminate the spy, and within minutes a successful frontal attack routs the Axis forces, opening the road to Paris.

Five Fingers

Twentieth Century–Fox, Directed by Joseph Mankiewicz, Released 1952

Another sub-rosa espionage thriller—based on the memoirs of a high-ranking Nazi, L. C. Moyzisch—that claims the Third Reich obtained secret information from an Albanian valet working in the British Embassy in neutral Turkey during the early months of 1944. James Mason is superb as the servant-turned-bon-vivant, whose passion for fine food, *grand cru* wines, and pretty women transforms him into a master spy photographing Allied war plans for the Axis. (Mason, explaining his deception skills: "I usually just photographed everything in sight that's stamped secret, most secret, and top secret.") Soon his luck runs out, and after taking an intricate escape route from Ankara to Istanbul, and then Rio de Janeiro, he begins a lavish lifestyle that abruptly terminates when Brazilian officials—puzzled by the thousands of British pounds being spent—discover his banknotes are nothing more than counterfeit currency, a method of payment frequently employed by the Germans.

Five for Hell

Filmstar, Directed by Gianfranco Parolini, Released 1968

Another low-budget, made-in-Italy, strictly-for-fun, B-frolic that borrowed many ideas from *The Dirty Dozen* and *Where Eagles Dare*. This one is about some oddball GIs, recruited to infiltrate an Italian villa and steal a secret Nazi plan. (General Bill Vanders, explaining the mission: "Fifty thousand of our men will fall into a death trap, unless we can find out about Plan K, proposed by the führer.") Under the leadership of a gung-ho, baseball-aficionado officer (John Garko), this diverse group—including both a safecracker and trampoline ace—finally reach their target and proceed to dupe, exasperate, somersault, shoot, stab, strangle, flip, push, and foil many Germans before extracting the needed information. While basically a frisky, picaresque story, punctuated with a snazzy musical score, the whole nine yards resembles a typical 1960s spaghetti Western in which numerous shoot-outs and elaborate pyrotechnics punctuate most scenes. Funniest casting: sinister-looking SS officer (Klaus Kinski), ranting and raving about the Third Reich's achievements. (Kinski to subordinate: "It's not for you to judge the orders of our führer.")

Flags of Our Fathers

DreamWorks, Directed by Clint Eastwood, Released 2006

A high-powered, digitally enhanced retelling of the historic Iwo Jima flag-raising photograph—snapped by Joe Rosenthal on February 23, 1945—and the bittersweet fame thrust upon three surviving members by jingoistic, oleaginous, public-relations officials intent on exploiting the elation this black-and-white picture inspired. Based on James Brady's best-selling book (his father is the sailor in the picture), the photodrama vacillates between the bloody island fighting, where U.S. casualties skyrocket (Marine officer explaining the enemy's tenacious defense: "This is Japanese soil, sacred ground—they will not leave politely") and the psychological difficulties experienced by the three men on their stateside tour, their discharge, and the eventual alcohol-related death of one leatherneck, Ira Hayes (Adam Beach), the Pima Indian who experiences heartfelt praise on the one hand, while the other receives vicious racial slurs on the nationwide bond-selling drive. Most discouraging scene: a young Marine, horsing around on a transport ship, falls into the ocean and, owing to warfare's exigencies, is left to fend for himself, while a disillusioned sailor observes, "So much for no man left behind."

Flat Top

Monogram Pictures, Directed by Lesley Selander, Released 1952

A high-flying, do-not-ignore-the-wave-off-flag, aircraft carrier, B-saga that details the training and eventual combat success of a fighter squadron during the 1944 Philippine invasion. Barking numerous orders from the ready room, Commander Sterling Hayden demands complete adherence to navy regulations, while his executive officer (Richard Carlson) suggests a relaxed approach. (Stone-faced Hayden to airmen: "Keep your noses clean, fly straight, and we're all going to get along just fine.") Produced by an original poverty-row studio—noted for cutting any conceivable corner—this attack-them-from-the-air tale often contains anachronistic newsreel or documentary footage. Typical budget-cutting insert: U.S. fighter pilots head off to dogfight advancing Japanese planes in torpedo-laden aircraft.

Flying Leathernecks

RKO, Directed by Nicholas Ray, Released 1951

Another rip-roaring, red-white-and-blue, John Wayne, blast-them-from-the-skies, action story that glorifies the volant adventures of a Marine Corps fighter squadron hard at work during the 1942 Guadalcanal campaign. Once more the commander of a close ground-support unit, Major John Wayne, with the help of Captain Robert Ryan, routs the Japanese force at every turn, demonstrating unequivocally the semper fidelis credo. (Duke Wayne to colleague: " . . . this is where we separate the men from the boys.") Replete with many documentary newsreel inserts, the photoplay depicts the heavy American losses spent for this island victory. Most risqué scene: John Wayne, home on stateside leave, kisses his wife and then—in an atypical moment—spirits her into the bedroom.

Force of Arms

Warner Bros., Directed by Michael Curtiz, Released 1951

A drawn-out hearts-and-flowers soap opera—based on a short story by Richard Tregaskis—that uses the 1943 Italian winter offensive as the backdrop for some heavy-handed romance within the officer cadre. Here, a battlefield-commissioned lieutenant (William Holden) and his dogface squad spend many days fighting the Nazis sequestered in the Roman hills. Back on leave, the good-looking Holden meets a Pollyanna Wac (Nancy Olson), and after a whirlwind courtship, the twosome marry, briefly enjoying a makeshift honeymoon. (Lieutenant Holden to Lieutenant Olson: " . . . I'm going to live forever because of you.") Returning to their units, the newlyweds' joy shatters when the husband is reported missing in action. After a protracted search, Lieutenant Olson finds her spouse convalescing in a military hospital. Reunited, the two officers—in a sudsy fade-out—swear eternal devotion.

The Frogmen

Twentieth Century–Fox, Directed by Lloyd Bacon, Released 1951

A fast-paced adventure tale glamorizing the high-risk assignments of the navy's underwater demolition teams—the frogmen—as they swim in the danger-laden waters off the Japanese homeland during the war's closing months. Leading a handpicked squad, Richard Widmark obeys all military directives punctiliously. (Commander Widmark to crew: "We're ordered to blow up the only known Jap submarine pen south of the home islands.") Chief Petty Officer Dana Andrews's approach is less authoritative or caustic. With an array of ocean action scenes, the story line highlights the elaborate training and strong camaraderie that keeps this all-volunteer outfit fine-tuned. Best scene: the frogmen's retrieval from the ocean using a small lariat, rubber lifeboat, and precision teamwork.

From Hell to Victory

Wardway, Directed by Hank Milestone, Released 1979

Another French-Italian-Spanish, dubbed-into-English production that proves once again that ineluctable, serendipitous events mold human emotions. On August 24, 1939, six close friends—two Americans, two French, one English, and one German—celebrate summer's end at a festive Paris party, vowing to make this happy occasion an annual event. But one week later, with the invasion of Poland, these plans dissolve as each person becomes involved with the ongoing global conflict. Over the years, the six lives intertwine, and in one macabre scene, the Frenchman—now a Resistance fighter—unknowingly kills his German friend, a *Wehrmacht* officer. With George Peppard and George Hamilton in starring roles, the photodrama spends much time examining lost love or missed opportunities. (American war correspondent (Sam Wanamaker) reflecting on the snows of yesterday: "It's hard to believe that kind of happiness ever existed.")

From Here to Eternity

Columbia, Directed by Fred Zinnemann, Released 1953

A strong indictment of the fascist-type mentality—that includes favoritism, bullying, torture, and death—at a U.S. Army base, a few miles from Pearl Harbor, as reported in the highly acclaimed first novel by James Jones. Burt Lancaster stars as a straight-arrow top sergeant, whose sangfroid demeanor slowly erodes when he falls for his commander's wife. (Sergeant Lancaster's view of the military hierarchy: "I hate officers—I always hated officers!") Montgomery Clift likewise shines as the lowly recluse who refuses to join a regimental boxing squad to expedite a promotion, while Private Frank Sinatra—in an Academy Award role—becomes a victim of a sadistic stockade sergeant. When the Japanese attack their outpost on December 7, all differences are quickly reconciled as the troops prepare to defend their island. Much of the photoplay depicts the negative side of army life, highlighting the abusive qualities of authority.

Gallant Bess

MGM, Directed by Andrew Marton, Released 1946

A gee-whiz, golly, Pollyannaish testimony to the nation's farmland youth, those get-up-early, hard-working lads who leave rural America and, using their homespun skills, serve in the armed forces. Marshall Thompson is wonderful as a sixteen-year-old orphan, who fudges his age, enlists in the Navy, and because of his tractor skills, joins the Seabees (Young Thompson, explaining his reasons: "You have to go, even if you have to lie to go.") Days before shipping overseas his favorite foal contracts pneumonia and quickly expires. Grief-stricken, the tar returns to his outfit and eventually lands on a Pacific island, where Japanese soldiers fight a rearguard action. Deep in the jungle he stumbles upon a wounded mare and, using common sense, nurses the horse to recovery. In a matter of days she becomes the outfit's mascot. At war's end, navy officials, pleased by this wholesome, symbiotic relationship, look the other way as feisty Gallant Bess leaps onto a cargo ship, offers the brass a few happy neighs, and joins her bluejacket admirers for the voyage home.

The Gallant Hours

United Artists, Directed by Robert Montgomery, Released 1960

A fine-tuned, quasi-documentary hagiography of Fleet Admiral William F. Halsey, the tough-talking sailor whose Kill Japs! Kill Japs!, Kill More Japs! credo, combined with some good luck, routed the Japanese invaders during the precarious 1942 Solomon Islands campaign. Former song-and-dance man James Cagney downplays the four-star officer's well-known belligerency and, conversely, portrays a soft-spoken, introspective man with a messianic plan for victory. (Bull Halsey to his command staff: "If we lose Guadalcanal, there will be nothing to stop them to go all the way down to Australia.") With fighter-pilot Dennis Weaver serving as foil, much of the storyline highlights the intricate cat-and-mouse game between Japanese general Isoroku Yamamoto and Halsey's intelligence section—and the culminating moment when the Japanese code, now broken, allows an American triumph. Using numerous religious messages, including a Roger Wagner Chorale soundtrack that constantly blares patriotic dirges, this film reiterates the righteousness of America's cause in the brutal Pacific theater.

Go for Broke!

MGM, Directed by Robert Pirosh, Released 1951

A down-to-earth testimony honoring the Japanese American GIs who formed the highly decorated 442nd Combat Team. Portraying a youthful Texas shave-tail supervising a squad of nisei soldiers, Van Johnson—after a shaky start—witnesses the bravery of these tightly knit GIs as they rout the *Wehrmacht* in Italy and France. (Lieutenant Johnson, mocking a captured Nazi officer who cannot understand why Japanese men are wearing U.S. uniforms: "Didn't Hitler tell you? Japan surrendered and they're fighting on our side now!") Replete with many stock scenes, including the GI with the girl back home, the college graduate who eschews a commission, and the malcontent who eventually learns the value of teamwork, the storyline is the Wake Island saga told in reverse (this time, the Americans win). Best scene: President Truman decorates this unit at an elaborate White House ceremony.

Golden Earrings

Paramount, Directed by Mitchell Leisen, Released 1947

Another lighthearted, desultory melodrama where a vain Gestapo officer chases a British colonel during the last week of August 1939 in the Black Forest town of Freiburg. Here Ray Milland, an English undercover agent, escapes from a Nazi stronghold and, after some precarious moments, meets a sensual gypsy, Marlene Dietrich, who agrees to disguise the good-looking fugitive as a clan member. (Sultry Dietrich, applying facial make-up to Milland: "I can make a gypsy out of log of wood.") Based on the novel by Yolanda Foldes, the screenplay blatantly ignores the Third Reich's persecution of gypsies and suggests that this subculture rollicked around small Bavarian towns eking out a paltry living by palmistry, while a foreign agent—operating right under the *Schutzstaffel's* nose—unobtrusively filches a German poison gas formula and escapes to his homeland. Silliest scene: Ray Milland reading the palm of a *Wehrmacht* youth, promising the soldier good fortune and amatory adventures.

The Good German

Warner Bros., Directed by Steven Soderbergh, Released 2007

An offbeat, black-and-white, stylized, film noir homage to the 1940s spy-versus-spy melodramas produced in the same chiaroscuro, voice-over format made during that long-ago decade. Easygoing George Clooney radiates as an American journalist, who arrives in Berlin to cover the July 1945 Potsdam Conference. He is quickly enmeshed in international intrigue—black market activities, former girlfriend, and Nazi rocket scientists—while off to the side, his military driver explains the sub rosa opportunities. (Corporal Tobey Maguire to his passenger: "The war is the best thing that ever happened to me.") With scene after scene lifted from such classics as *The Third Man*, *The Blue Dahlia*, and *Murder, My Sweet*, this contemporary production lauds Hollywood's golden age, when movies were made on studio sets without special effects. Best scene: the airport ending, a wonderful copycat tribute to Humphrey Bogart and Ingrid Bergman's sudsy farewell in *Casablanca*.

The Good War

Bauer Martinez Studios, Directed by Giorgio Serafini, Released 2005

An off-the-wall allegory—supposedly based on a true story—that details the frustrations of Italian prisoners interned in Hereford, Texas, when American military officials demand the inmates sign an antifascist statement before repatriating them. Here, a seventy-two-year-old bird colonel (Roy Scheider) hobbles throughout the compound, perturbed that a combat injury has given him this stateside assignment. (Colonel Scheider, bemoaning his fate: "I've been put out to pasture.") In a strange twist of fate, as a quick-thinking Neapolitan (Luca Zingaretti) plots his escape, the camp unexpectedly closes, stranding the commander and his charge. Now in a precarious situation, the two men, with little food, put aside their differences and, for the next few agonizing days, claw at each other, dissecting war's futility. As a twenty-first century morality tale, the screenplay, ping-ponging from one solipsistic point to another, rationalizes why former allies are now enemies and former enemies are newfound allies.

The Great Escape

United Artists, Directed by John Sturges, Released 1963

Another elaborate 173-minute kaleidoscope—based on the book by Paul Brickhill—that details the planning, implementation, and eventual escape of seventy British officers from a closely guarded stalag, deep inside the Fatherland, to their freedom, capture, or death. As the only American POW in this otherwise homogeneous group, Steve McQueen sparkles with Yankee intransigence, determined to free himself from Nazi captivity. (Captain McQueen to English colleagues: "By morning, I'm going to be so far away you couldn't hear it if they were shooting at me with howitzers.") Using an all-star cast—including James Garner, Richard Attenborough, Charles Bronson, James Coburn, and Donald Pleasence—this edge-of-your-seat action yarn contains a myriad of subplots, as the captive Allies use their ingenuity to elude the Nazis. Best scene: Steve McQueen, on his motorcycle, approaching the Swiss Alps.

The Guns of Navarone

Columbia, Directed by J. Lee Thompson, Released 1961

An action-packed CinemaScope production—based on Alistair MacLean's novel—that traces the 1943 high-powered adventures of some Allied saboteurs sent onto a small Greek island, who after many close calls, destroy two massive German guns poised to attack a British rescue convoy. Appointed leader of this well-honed team, Gregory Peck, with linguistic and mountain-climbing skills plus his sangfroid, thwarts the Nazis at every turn. (Peck to colleague: "The only way to win a war is to be just as nasty as the enemy.") With Anthony Quayle, David Niven, Anthony Quinn, and Stanley Baker in supporting roles, the screenplay contains the knife-wielding marksman, the explosives expert, the traitor in the midst, the loyalty of numerous underground fighters, and the "I'll-kill-you-after-the-war" malcontent. Also included are some random antiwar scenes that—in strong, unequivocal language—lambaste the mock heroics of combat.

The Gypsy Warriors

Universal, Directed by Theo James, Released 1978

Another frivolous, made-for-television B-mumbo jumbo that suggests that World War II was an ongoing Mack Sennett two-reeler devoid of any horror or mayhem. James Whitmore Jr. and Tom Selleck portray two wisenheimer

American officers who, in June 1940, parachute into France on an espionage mission involving the ubiquitous secret Nazi chemical-weapons factory. After some Saturday-matinee heroics—coupled with a little romantic digression involving a comely gypsy (Lina Raymond)—the German production plant is rendered inoperative even though some of the military tactics resemble a Daffy Duck cartoon. (Bedazzled Captain James Whitmore Jr. to his fellow saboteur, easygoing Captain Tom Selleck: "Your West Point ring! We're on an undercover operation and you're wearing a West Point ring!") Originally titled *Deadly Wine*, this photoplay became the basis for a television series that—after eight weeks of low ratings—was yanked off the airwaves.

Halls of Montezuma

Twentieth Century–Fox, Directed by Lewis Milestone, Released 1950

A high-powered, hit-the beaches, dig-in, go-get-'em glorification of the U.S. Marines and their many Pacific island victories. Squad lieutenant Richard Widmark steps lively leading his leathernecks from a beachhead invasion, through dangerous marshlands, and finally, to heavily fortified caves, where his men—the best of American prowess—capture enemy prisoners and, eventually, locate a strategic Japanese rocket-launching site. With Jack Palance, Robert Wagner, and Karl Malden as dyed-in-the-wool fighters, the marines, after many hardships, battle their way back to their command post much to the acclaim of Major Richard Boone. Best scene: the squad honors a fallen comrade. (Sergeant Jack Webb—paraphrasing John Donne's poetry—eulogizes a friend's sacrifice: "Now we are part of the world, the world is part of us. If any part suffers, all suffer; if any part loses freedom, all will lose it.")

Hanover Street

Columbia, Directed by Peter Hyams, Released 1979

This hearts-and-flowers melodrama proves that true love conquers all. Good-looking Harrison Ford—a B-25 American pilot stationed outside of London in 1943—stumbles into a complex romance with a married woman, bright-eyed Lesley-Ann Down. After a series of serendipitous events, the dashing airman is unknowingly paired with her husband, Christopher Plummer, to infiltrate Gestapo Headquarters in northern France. Soon the two men steal an important codebook, and their escape route—back to England—resembles one implausible B-adventure after another as Resistance fighters thwart the Nazi war machine at every turn. Now in London, the noble-minded officer quietly utters his sudsy good-bye. (Lieutenant Ford whispering his swan song to Miss Downs: "I love you enough to let you go, which is more than I've ever loved anything or anybody in my life.")

Hart's War

MGM, Directed by Gregory Hoblit, Released 2002

A unimaginative bricolage of stock scenes plucked from *Battleground*, *Stalag 17*, *Slaughterhouse-Five*, *The Great Escape*, *The Caine Mutiny*, *The Tuskegee Airmen*, *A Few Good Men*, and *To Kill a Mockingbird* that details the comings and goings of a large contingent of American GIs jammed into a German POW compound during winter 1945. Bespectacled Bruce Willis seems miscast as a full bird colonel who orchestrates a U.S. court-martial as a ruse to destroy a nearby munitions factory. Lieutenant Colin Farrell, a naive Yale graduate, works assiduously to defend his charge, a black Air Corps pilot, from the lynch-mob mentality of the makeshift trial barracks. (Lieutenant Farrell to Colonel Willis: "I'm just trying to protect my client.") Eventually, as a redemptive symbol, Colonel Willis—exhorting his honor, duty, and country doctrine—sacrifices himself in a bizarre exchange of one life for many, demonstrating once again that in war, the end justifies the means.

Heaven Knows, Mr. Allison

Twentieth Century–Fox, Directed by John Huston, Released 1957

A modern reworking of the Robinson Crusoe fable—from the novel by Charles Shaw—where a sinewy marine corporal (Robert Mitchum), adrift for days in the South Pacific, finally reaches a small island that is inhabited solely by a Roman Catholic nun (Deborah Kerr). Soon, the twosome form a polite friendship while honing their survival skills. (Mitchum to nun, explaining the improbability of a U.S. rescue: "The brass planned to bypass a lot of these islands on the way to Tokyo, at least that's the scuttlebutt.") After a series of arduous events—that include eluding Japanese patrols, recovering from illness, and sidestepping a love declaration—the twosome are saved by tough-fighting U.S. forces. With many allegorical references, the screenplay's motif— the dignity of religious institutions—restates the wholesome nature of America's participation in the global conflict.

Hell in the Pacific

Selmur Pictures, Directed by John Boorman, Released 1968

A complex parable that in an esoteric way offers insight about survival, friendship, and tolerance. As a Japanese officer marooned on a remote South

Pacific atoll during the war's closing months, Toshiro Mifune's solitary existence in such a harsh environment requires discipline. Eventually, a naval pilot (Lee Marvin) washes ashore, and the two men—initially hostile to each other and unable to communicate verbally—concede a shaky truce. Realizing the futility of remaining in their barren location, they construct a raft and finally reach another deserted coral island, only to perish from an explosion. Using many theological symbols—including a crucifixion scene—this modern-day Bible story contains many religious themes. (Captain Marvin to his Japanese companion: "How come you guys don't believe in God?")

Hell Is for Heroes

Paramount, Directed by Don Siegel, Released 1962

Another we're-all-in-this-together drama of an isolated six-man army infantry squad that must halt a *Wehrmacht* attack on the hilly Siegfried line during the perilous 1944 offensive. Here a tight-lipped, psychotic, recalcitrant private (Steve McQueen) glowers menacingly at both American and German forces. (Private McQueen, threatening a seventeen-year-old Polish orderly: "You show up on the line, I'll blow your head off.") Another private (Bobby Darin) takes a more realistic approach to combat. (Darin to replacement: "Look, up here, this gun is your life.") Soon, the refractory McQueen—unable to accept any military regulations—starts a private war by charging uphill and destroying a strategic Nazi pillbox, only to perish at his moment of glory. As a coda, the screenplay acknowledges that the U.S. Armed Forces contain a fair share of deranged individuals whose violent and excessive temperaments frequently undermine everyone's welfare.

Hell to Eternity

Atlantic Pictures, Directed by Phil Karlson, Released 1960

A B-grade, fictional account—supposedly based on a true incident—about an orphaned Los Angeles boy who was raised by a Japanese American family during the 1930s, and after Pearl Harbor enlisted as Marine Corps interpreter. Jeffrey Hunter portrays a clean-cut leatherneck who slowly learns military rudiments under the tutelage of his combat sergeant (David Janssen). When their unit hits the beach at Saipan, the twosome encounter many close calls, culminating with Private Hunter's capture of a Japanese general. (Hunter explaining to a Japanese officer that he understands his language: "I understood that double-crossing speech! These men died without any reason.") Appalled by the Japanese civilian casualties on this Pacific island, Private Hunter uses his linguistic skills to rescue many nationals before they commit a ritualistic suicide. One scene—the surrender of dozens of haggard enemy soldiers to a lone marine—is a copycat version of the closing minutes of Warner Bros.' 1940 classic, *Sergeant York*.

Hellcats of the Navy

Columbia, Directed by Nathan Juran, Released 1957

Another humdrum, seafaring melodrama bemoaning the inner loneliness a naval commander endures after he sacrifices an officer's life to preserve the safety of his submarine. Here, Ronald Reagan—the skipper of an underwater Hellcat working the precarious Japanese straits—stands by his decision to lose one lieutenant rather than allow his vessel to perish. (Commander Reagan to colleagues: "Did you think I enjoy letting men drown?") Exonerated by his senior staff and encouraged by his girlfriend (Nancy Davis), the soft-spoken Reagan takes to the seas again and—in a stereotypical confrontational scene—destroys many enemy vessels, much to the acclaim of his crew and former detractors. Introduced by the famous war hero Admiral Chester W. Nimitz, this battle story glorifies every facet of Pacific theater naval operations.

The Heroes of Telemark

Columbia, Directed by Anthony Mann, Released 1965

A high-powered adventure tale glamorizing the planning and implementation of a daring British-Norwegian raid that destroyed the Nazi heavy-water plant operating on the Scandinavian peninsula. As a scientist turned saboteur, Kirk Douglas guides a handful of commandos into the German factory that is manufacturing Hitler's untried atomic weapon. (Kirk Douglas, explaining his motives to his ex-wife: "We're working for the Resistance.") With Richard Harris at his side, the raiders sneak into the plant and—with a little gravitational help from Mother Nature—obliterate this military threat. Loosely based on actual events, this historical reconstruction—reminiscent of some 1940s propaganda films—praises Norwegian intransigence toward their Axis captors.

Hiroshima: Out of the Ashes

Hallmark Home Entertainment, Directed by Koreyoshi Kurahara and Roger Spottiswoode, Released 1995

Another fiftieth-anniversary, made-for-television, let's-tell-both-sides-of-the-story, 185-minute disquisition that sifts through the moral, logistical, political, and military complexities responsible for the dropping of the first atomic bomb. Kenneth Welsh radiates as President Harry S. Truman—who along with numerous aides and advisers—must decide the most pragmatic method to end World War II. (General Lesley Groves, played by Richard Masur, demanding an immediate deployment of the weapon: "Now we got the bomb and a chance to use it. For Jesus' sake, let's use it where the Japs will feel it the most!") Using a quasi-documentary format, this in-depth screenplay depicts the numerous egos—American, English, Russian, and Japanese—responsible for the first nuclear attack.

Hitler

Warner Bros., Directed by Stuart Heisler, Released 1962

An overstated B-production that chronicles national socialism's early days, beginning with the publication of *Mein Kampf* and culminating with the Poland blitzkrieg invasion. As the domineering führer demanding blind obedience from his swastika-wearing followers, Richard Basehart suffers from an oedipal complex as he balances his emerging dictatorship with a puppylove crush on his young niece. When the romance turns sour, the infatuated Hitler turns his amatory attentions toward Eva Braun, with a grandiose promise of a New Order. (Richard Basehart to his Nazi charges: "In that hour, I was responsible for the fate of Germany and, thereby, I became the supreme judge of the German people.") Replete with one distortion after another, the photoplay closely resembles the ad hominem format of the anti-Hitler films produced during the war.

Hitler's SS: Portrait in Evil

Metromedia Productions, Directed by Jim Goddard, Released 1985

An elaborate, 150-minute, made-for-TV analysis of the infamous *Schutzstaffel* (the SS) as viewed through the eyes of two German brothers from the early 1931 Stuggart beer-hall meetings to the Third Reich's 1945 Berlin collapse. During this unprecedented period, the older son (Bill Nighy) joins Heinrich Himmler's Gestapo, rationalizing that the reform policies will benefit the nation, while his younger brother (John Shea) prefers the Storm Troopers. Hitler's June 30, 1934, Night of the Long Knives massacre changes everything when their ideological differences openly clash. (SS Officer Nighy, venting his anger: ". . . if you have any idea what they're doing to tens of thousands of people. . . .") Eventually, the elder brother realizes his misguided loyalties and watches—with cynical resignation—the New Order's capitulation. With stellar performances from David Warner, Tony Randall, Carroll Baker, and José Ferrer, this historical storyline depicts much of the ruination caused by this dreaded organization.

Homecoming

MGM, Directed by Mervyn LeRoy, Released 1948

Another hearts-and-flowers soap opera—overflowing with oleaginous wartime-separation sentimentality—about a materialistic surgeon, who treats well-to-do patients respectfully, while ignoring backyard urban problems. In another stereotypical, he-man role, Clark Gable sparkles as a married, bon vivant doctor, who, after Pearl Harbor, joins the medical corps, completes basic training, and arrives in the European combat zone. For the next three years he lives and works with injured frontline GIs, while slowly falling for his outspoken nurse (Lana Turner). Unable to reconcile his dilemma, the smooth-talking Gable balks at any commitment until, in a typical 1940s Hollywood marriage-is-sacred, divorce-is-impossible ending, the pretty nurse dies from combat injuries, allowing her sweetheart an easy out. (Lieutenant Turner's deathbed coda to Colonel Gable: "When a soldier leaves his outfit, all debts and friendships are cancelled.") Funniest scenes: groups of doctors, gathered at various functions, smoking one cigarette after another, oblivious to any injurious health risks.

Hornet's Nest

United Artists, Directed by Phil Karlson, Released 1970

A far-fetched, high-jinks yarn describing the heroics of an American soldier who parachutes into Nazi-occupied Italy. With a motley gang of native children—plus a comely German doctor—he eludes Gestapo forces and eventually blows up a strategic dam, allowing Allied troops a counterattack. Rock Hudson—a lone GI stranded behind enemy lines—offers numerous shibboleths regarding his underground mission, while his young charges whistle esoteric warning codes. (Hudson to some Italian adolescents: "We'll kill over 10,000 Nazis by blowing up that dam.") Since the film is a joint Italian-American production, the entire plot mimics the numerous spaghetti Westerns of this period, parodying such stock scenes as the fistfight, the shoot-out, and the hero riding off into the sunset, only this time the handsome American leading man, lacking any equestrian support, sits in a dilapidated military truck.

Imitation General

MGM, Directed by George Marshall, Released 1958

An offbeat, fast-talking, quasi-slapstick screenplay that spotlights the afternoon antics of a combat-experienced master sergeant, who—following a series of comic misunderstandings—assumes the role of a dead, one-star army officer in the French countryside, weeks after the Normandy invasion. As always, Glenn Ford sparkles as a "general" who quickly musters some inexperienced soldiers, plans an outlandish offensive, blasts an enemy observation post, and knocks out some German tanks snared in a ditch. His wisecracking pal, Corporal Red Buttons, eggs him on and, back in the farmhouse, vivacious Taina Elg, unable to speak English, smiles approvingly. (Sergeant Ford, explaining why this ruse is necessary: "Unusual situations call for unusual solutions.") With frequent nods to Charlie Chaplin's silent one-reelers, this mistaken-identity storyline combines wartime drama with military frivolity.

In Enemy Hands

Artisan Entertainment, Directed by Tony Giglio, Released 2004

Another implausible, hot-air, three-dollar-bill fairy tale that claims a benevolent Nazi U-boat commander—acting contrary to Hitler's take-no-prisoners edict—places a group of American sailors in their cramped submarine rather than allow the bluejackets to perish on the ocean. (Nazi officer Thomas Kretschmann to Chief Petty Officer William Macy: "Do you know why I picked up your men? I'm tired of this war.") But in a few hours, meningitis strikes more than half of the German crew, and soon both sides combine their manpower for basic survival. (First Officer Kretschmann to everyone: "We are now on the same side.") Soon, the U-boat is attacked by Nazi and Allied vessels, and as a token of friendship, Chief Macy allows the German captain to destroy the valuable ENIGMA code box before an American destroyer rescues everyone. As a revisionist tract this far-fetched undersea yarn, saturated with Pollyanna dialogue, downplays the Third Reich's open-seas brutality and, instead, suggests that beneath their gold-plated swastikas, Nazi commanders are compassionate and noble individuals.

In Harm's Way

Paramount, Directed by Otto Preminger, Released 1965

A powerful, 180-minute tribute to the naval officer corps where innovative planning, strong leadership, and precision coordination obliterate a Japanese armada threatening the Pacific theater. Standing on the bridge, Rear Admiral John Wayne must lose two ships, his left leg, and his estranged son before winning a major sea battle, while his girlfriend, easygoing Patricia Neal, x-rays his fractured right arm. Based on the novel by James Bassett, the storyline amalgamates numerous plots, including Executive Officer Kirk Douglas's fall from grace and sacrificial redemption. (Kirk Douglas, shouting his jubilation over the Pearl Harbor attack: "O Rock of Ages. We got ourselves another war—a gut-busting, mother-loving navy war.") With an all-star cast that uses Henry Fonda, Burgess Meredith, Dana Andrews, and Franchot Tone in high-ranking roles, every aspect of naval life—from the mundane to the complex—seems orderly and glamorous.

In Love and War

Twentieth Century–Fox, Directed by Philip Dunne, Released 1958

Another glorified CinemaScope paean to the fighting men of the U.S. Marine Corps—based on the novel by Anton Myrer—that emphasizes the male bonding found in love and war. Jeffrey Hunter, Robert Wagner, and Bradford Dillman star as hardened gyrenes who put aside their social-class differences to fight the Japanese in a vicious 1944 Pacific island battle. Back in sunny California, their three women—from diverse backgrounds—stoically wait, each hoping her man's name will not appear in the newspaper's casualty reports. Eventually, the Marines secure their island, but one combat private cannot fathom his unit's savagery toward the enemy. (Private Dillman, shouting his disgust: "We're all butchers! Just kill and kill and kill and nobody cares why.") Best action scene: Sergeant Jeffrey Hunter blows up a Japanese tank.

The Incredible Mr. Limpet

Warner Bros., Directed by Arthur Lubin, Released 1964

A lighthearted, whimsical, just-for-fun, family-oriented romp that intersperses a conventional photodrama with animated cartoons. Timid, 4-F Don Knotts illuminates as bespectacled Mr. Limpet, an amateur ichthyologist who frequently fantasizes about piscatorial life. (Knotts, during a typical daydreaming session: "I wish I were a fish. Fish have a better life than people.") Eventually, the Flatbush bookkeeper's wish comes true and—after a series of flitting, underwater belly laughs—he teams up with a navy petty officer (Jack Weston) to pinpoint Nazi submarines operating in the North Atlantic. Acclaimed a hero after V-J Day, Mr. Limpet begins a new mission, enlisting porpoises for Cold War military assignments. Best scene: Mr. Limpet, using a little pelagic know-how, redirects German torpedoes in a 360-degree arc and smiles gleefully as the explosives detonate in their original firing tubes.

Is Paris Burning?

Paramount, Directed by René Clement, Released 1965

A detailed look at the political, social, and military events occurring in the French capital during the turbulent month of August 1944. As Allied forces prepare to liberate the City of Lights from its four years of occupation, a Nazi commandant—under strict orders from the führer—plans to demolish every building, monument, and bridge. Based on the best-selling book by Larry Collins and Dominique Lapierre, the black-and-white screenplay contains an array of impressive stars—including Kirk Douglas, Anthony Perkins, Charles Boyer, Jean-Paul Belmondo, Glenn Ford, Robert Stack, and Yves Montand—to portray famous personages, Resistance fighters, plus French, German, and American forces. Finally, the Third Reich general responsible for destroying Paris (Gert Froebe) capitulates to his humanistic values and surrenders his army. (Swedish ambassador Orson Welles praising the German's decision: "History will be grateful to you for having saved a very beautiful city.")

Judgment at Nuremberg

United Artists, Directed by Stanley Kramer, Released 1961

An in-depth examination of the controversial Allied war-crimes tribunal responsible for the onerous task of assigning guilt to dozens of high-ranking Nazis. Spencer Tracy demonstrates the best of New England jurisprudence as he spends eight months sifting through reams of ambiguous evidence, ever mindful of the political Cold War ramifications of his verdict. (Judge Tracy to colleague: "I'm a rock-ribbed Republican, who thought that Franklin Roosevelt was a great man.") Replete with intricate subplots—and a cast that includes Burt Lancaster, Judy Garland, Montgomery Clift, Richard Widmark, Marlene Dietrich, and Maximilian Schell—the *j'accuse* finger vacillates from scene to scene. Personages, laws, and loyalties are indicted for a long list of bestial crimes. Eventually, many Nazi followers must answer for their wartime activities, but their life-imprisonment sentences, considered severe by German nationals, are eventually abrogated as American statesmen—mindful of hostile Russo-American relations—seek support from their former enemy against the new Stalinism threat.

Kelly's Heroes

MGM, Directed by Brian G. Hutton, Released 1970

A heavy-handed, half-spoof account of some enterprising GIs who—after a series of Looney Tunes adventures—loot $16 million in gold bullion from a local bank behind German lines during the 1945 offensive. Clint Eastwood's deadpan smile reassures his buddies of the screwball plan's efficacy, while Top Sergeant Telly Savalas bellows numerous orders to the "heroes." Unaware of the ground pounders' impending peculation, General Carroll O'-Connor lavishly awards medals to men in his command, including a dysfunctional tank driver (Donald Sutherland). (GI Sutherland, enunciating the psychological attributes of heroism: "To a New Yorker like you, a hero is some type of weird sandwich.") Funniest scene: three GIs, satirizing the classic Hollywood Western shoot-out, lithely approach a Nazi tank, while over in his bedroom, Carroll O'Connor pins two stars onto his pajama's epaulets.

King Rat

Columbia, Directed by Bryan Forbes, Released 1965

A dreary, tiresome, pseudo-allegorical morality tale—from James Clavell's book—depicting the hardships that British, American, and Australian prisoners-of-war endure in a Japanese camp on the Malay Peninsula in 1945. George Segal scowls as Corporal King, a streetwise American soldier who manipulates both Allied officers and Japanese guards with numerous scams and black-market deals. His nemesis, British lieutenant Tom Courtenay, proffers one blowhard threat after another. (Provost Officer Courtenay to King Rat: "Like all criminals, you're greedy.") Finally liberated, the smooth-talking American, realizing his power niche is over, rationalizes his behavior. (Corporal Segal to rescue official: "There's no harm in looking after your clothes?") Most ponderous scene: Segal and his minions enjoy a mystery meal that consists of dog meat, a recipe frequently prepared in Asian culture.

Kings Go Forth

United Artists, Directed by Delmer Daves, Released 1958

Another combat-related soap opera, based on the novel by Joe David Brown, highlighting the military pursuits of a squad leader (Frank Sinatra) as he leads his army patrol into battle against German forces in the southern France theater during the June 1944 advance. In his spare time, he woos a carefree Riviera belle (Natalie Wood). (Lieutenant Sinatra philosophizing about the vagaries of war: "Some days we drink champagne, courtesy of the French, and some days we eat dirt, courtesy of the Germans.") Inevitably, a good-looking, slick-talking infantry corporal (Tony Curtis) horns in on his officer's girlfriend and, after a series of lies, innuendoes, and broken promises, wins the heart of the French lass, only to drop her like the proverbial hot potato. As retribution for his perfidy, the corporal dies in a nighttime skirmish while Frank Sinatra, now a captain and minus his right arm, returns to his lost love and the twosome, in a gooey Hollywood ending, pledge eternal devotion.

The Last Day of the War

Sagittarius Production, Directed by Juan Antonio Bardew, Released 1969

A B-for-Budget, cliché-ridden travesty about a tight American infantry squad assigned to rescue an important German scientist before a demented Gestapo officer—ignoring the formal V-E Day mandate—locates this turncoat, who is squirreled away in an Austrian hamlet. U.S. sergeant George Maharis (of *Route 66* fame) fights, stabs, and shoots many Nazi soldiers before rescuing his charge, while pulchritudinous Maria Perschy, wearing fancy high-heeled shoes during her Alpine ascent, smiles approvingly. Produced as a joint Italian, Spanish, and American venture, the storyline—borrowing heavily from the 1930s Hollywood oaters—contains one implausible situation after another. (Sergeant Maharis, explaining his secret mission, "We're looking for someone—a German scientist, civilian kraut, because the SS is looking for him, we gotta get there first.")

The Last Drop

Carnaby International, Directed by Colin Teague, Released 2005

An offbeat, part-spoof, part–Road Runner, three-tier romp about the comings and goings of a British paratroop squad, two Nazi renegades, and a loose-cannon American colonel. In September 1944 they roam around the Dutch countryside looking for Berlin-bound art treasures, while nearby, Axis and Allied forces fight the decisive Market Garden battle. As part of the English team, glider pilot Billy Zane seems confused about their mission. (British Tommy, offering a personal observation: "This ain't no cloak-and-dagger job.") When they reach a farmhouse cellar loaded with plunder, a U.S. officer (Michael Madsen) ponders his future. (German opportunist [Steve Speirs], suggesting a deal: "Surely if the spoils of wars should just happen to fall into the brave hands of such men as yourselves.") With one improbable comic-book, hodgepodge, shoot-out scene after another, much of the plot resembles a Saturday-morning cartoon. Best impersonation: Michael Madsen as Colonel J. T. Colt, a General George S. Patton wannabe.

The Last Tyrant

Group One, Directed by Carlo Lizzani, Released 1974

Another European-made docudrama outlining the final days of Benito Mussolini, the Italian dictator who created a fascist state, aligned his nation with Hitler, declared war on the Allied Forces, and, subsequently, met an ignominious death during the April 1945 uprising. As American GIs approach Milan and Nazi troops falter into the Fatherland, only glabrous Rod Steiger could mimic the egomaniacal traits of the ruler—now facing ruin—negotiating an escape to Switzerland. (*Il Duce's* aspirations: "Once the war is over, we must have our share of the glory and the reward.") An influential Roman Catholic cleric (Henry Fonda) also realizes the futility of the autocrat's reign. (Cardinal Fonda's exasperation: "This was the man who thought he was another Caesar.") Eventually, some quick-moving partisans thwart his retreat and summarily execute the leader who brought devastation to their country, even though the trains, following his edict, ran on time.

The Last Warrior

Pathfinder Pictures, Directed by Martin Wragge, Released 1989

Another B-mishmash that lifts a few scenes from *The Last Samurai, Hell in the Pacific*, and *Heaven Knows, Mr. Allison* to form a convoluted action yarn about a U.S. Marine sergeant (Gary Graham) stranded on a remote Pacific island with a Roman Catholic nun (Maria Holvoe) and their harrowing adventures when a sword-wielding Japanese officer (Cary-Hiroyuki Tagawa), obsessed with his Bushido philosophy, forces his American foe into an elaborate duel-to-the-death contest. After many setbacks, including an unremitting jujitsu beating, the leatherneck rallies, forges ahead, and in a gory finale kills his Oriental nemesis. (Tagawa, expatiating on defeat: "One to one, you are no match for us, except when you fight us with your machines.") With some pseudo-religious overtones, this low-cost storyline—using minimal dialogue—reaffirms the maxim that in wartime, a spiritual presence always guides the victor.

Letters from Iwo Jima

DreamWorks, Directed by Clint Eastwood, Released 2006

An overblown, simplistic, distorted, there-are-two-sides-to-every-story sugarcoating of the bloody February 1945 Iwo Jima invasion as seen through the eyes of hapless Japanese soldiers, pawns of sadistic, Emperor-worshipping officers who insist they fight until the death. (Japanese general Ken Watanabe's draconian instructions: "Not one of you is allowed to die until you have killed ten enemy soldiers.") Eventually, U.S. Marines storm this lava-encrusted island and, after fierce fighting, decimate the outnumbered defenders. With defeat a certainty, most Japanese either join suicidal banzai charges or explode grenades on their chests. As a revisionist interpretation, much of the screenplay ignores the brutal and sadistic reign of Japanese aggression and, instead, purports the common soldier's virtues—kindness, sensitivity, and nonbelligerency—come forth in poignant letters sent to their mainland families. Most contrived scene: various American officials at a plush 1929 Washington, D.C., reception first present their Oriental guest with a crafted pearl-handled revolver then, at the dinner table, taunt him about his Bushido beliefs.

The Longest Day

Twentieth Century–Fox, Directed by Ken Annakin, Andrew Marton, Gerd Oswald, and Bernhard Wicki, Released 1962

An elaborate 175-minute black-and-white blockbuster—based on the best-selling book by Cornelius Ryan—that documents the historical Normandy invasion as witnessed by Allied and Axis forces at numerous battle sites and command headquarters. Using a large contingent of famous stars—including John Wayne, Robert Mitchum, Richard Burton, Curt Jurgens, Rod Steiger, and Robert Wagner—the screenplay details the successes, good fortune, tragedy, and dumb luck that both sides experience during this longest of days. Utilizing many subplots juxtaposed against the larger issue of Allied determination to gain a foothold on Fortress Europe (tough-talking Colonel John Wayne to his taut American paratroopers: "Your assignment tonight is strategic. You can't give the enemy a break, send them to hell!"), the film offers a subtle justification for the many casualties necessary for this important victory.

MacArthur

Universal, Directed by Joseph Sargent, Released 1977

A gargantuan, I-am-in-charge, do-not-question-my-orders testimony to the five-star general whose clarion I-Shall-Return promise became an inspiring catchword throughout the Pacific theater. Hard-talking Gregory Peck depicts the many frustrations, defeats, and achievements General Douglas MacArthur experienced, including the Corregidor withdrawal, Australian regrouping, island-hopping strategies, Philippines retaking, V-J Day celebration, Japanese rehabilitation, presidential hopeful, Inchon invasion, executive dismissal, and, finally, congressional "Old Soldiers Never Die" speech. References to his low casualty rate are numerous. (MacArthur, explaining his policy: "Good commanders do not turn in heavy losses.") This hagiographical storyline reiterates MacArthur's dictum, "In war there can be no substitute for victory." Best scene: in a reflective mood, a somber General MacArthur visits the Bataan Death March survivors.

Malaya

MGM, Directed by Richard Thorpe, Released 1949

A farfetched, implausible absurdity about two American mercenaries who in 1942 surreptitiously enter this Japanese-controlled Southeast Asian country and—after a series of make-believe adventures—smuggle all the raw rubber onto the deck of a hidden U.S. Navy transport. Spencer Tracy and Jimmy Stewart portray this unlikely dyad who organize a small raiding party of modern-day buccaneers, while corpulent Sydney Greenstreet—interested in the gold bullion his fellow countrymen carry—aids in the peculation. (Stewart explaining the need for this vital raw material: "We're organized to get the rubber out without the knowledge of the Japs.") As the Japanese officer in charge of the occupation forces, Richard Loo adds another stereotypical villain role in his long career as the slimy Oriental nemesis who can bend but never break a captor's will.

The Man Who Never Was

Twentieth Century–Fox, Directed by Ronald Neame, Released 1955

An elaborate CinemaScope production that purports the 1943 Allied Sicily invasion succeeded because an intricate British intelligence operation hoodwinked the Germans into deploying their defensive forces to Greece. As a naval commander, Clifton Webb selects a cadaver, creates a detailed, bogus military identification pattern, and sends the body adrift off the Iberian Peninsula until it reaches a Spanish fishing village. Here, a Nazi agent procures his "classified" information and—after a cursory London undercover examination by Third Reich spy Stephen Boyd—the Germans accept this plan hook, line, and sinker. Supposedly based on actual events, the photoplay restates the quiet heroism of the United Kingdom. (Commander Webb to the deceased's father: "I can assure you that this is an opportunity for your son to do a great thing for England.")

The McKenzie Break

MGM, Directed by Lamont Johnson, Released 1970

Another revisionist tract depicting the numerous stratagems some bright, agile, resourceful German prisoners of war employ to escape from a British camp located in Western Scotland. Burly Brian Keith radiates as an intelligence officer assigned to prevent a rumored breakout, while his nemesis, U-boat Commander Helmut Griem, smiles sardonically at military directives. (Captain Keith, explaining his task: "I got sent up here to do a job—I'm supposed to find out what's behind that break.") After punctilious planning, including clandestine radio messages, elaborate tunnel boring, and synchronized crowd diversions, the Germans slither from their confinement. Later—following some *Mission Impossible* adventures—they reach a Nazi submarine but, in a surprising denouement, watch incredulously as their commander, just yards from freedom, surrenders unceremoniously to his English captors.

Memphis Belle

Warner Bros., Directed by Michael Caton-Jones, Released 1990

An elaborate testimony to the first crew in the Eighth Air Force to fly the coveted twenty-fifth mission, a feat allowing each man stateside duty. Youthful Matthew Modine shines as a B-17 captain who lifts his aircraft from the quiet plains of southern England to the German port of Bremen to bomb the city's industrial area on May 17, 1943. (Modine to airmen: "We were sent here to bomb a factory. If we don't do it, someone's going to have to come back and do it for us.") Constantly under attack by Luftwaffe fighters or ack-ack bursts, the bomber—damaged in its critical landing section—limps back to its home base, much to the acclaim of elated senior officers and public-relations staff. While the storyline is pure Hollywood fiction, it is, nevertheless, a paean to William Wyler's 1944 aerial documentary *The Memphis Belle*, a film that glorified this landmark crossing.

Merrill's Marauders

Warner Bros., Directed by Samuel Fuller, Released 1962

An all-male, nothing-can-stop-us, 200-mile, India-to-Burma trek by three thousand army volunteers, dubbed "marauders," to destroy Japanese strongholds in this strategic southeastern peninsula. Here, in the dense, swampy terrain, one-star General Frank Merrill (Jeff Chandler) rallies his weary men from one dangerous area to another, while his commanding officer General "Vinegar" Joe Stillwell (John Hoyt) warns everyone about the price of failure. (General Stillwell to officers: "Your job is to keep the Japanese out of India—keep them from linking up with the Germans.") Based on the book by former marauder Charlton Ogburn, this Technicolor adaptation graphically recalls the humid climate, hostile vegetation, numerous diseases, and enemy offensives these GIs endured during their three-month march, a feat responsible for expunging most Japanese forces from Burma. Strangest scenes: in numerous battle encounters, the Japanese soldiers fall to their deaths in an exaggerated, terpsichorean manner resembling dance students auditioning for ballet school.

A Midnight Clear

Beacon, Directed by Keith Gordon, Released 1992

A caustic, surrealistic, ontological look at war, death, and friendship—from the book by William Wharton—that demeans the caste system separating enlisted men from their officers. Ethan Hawke sparkles as a young, pensive sergeant who, along with five other GIs from an intelligence and reconnaissance squad, squirrel themselves in the Ardennes Forest during the Christmas 1944 German offensive. Here they come face to face with their adversaries in a symbolic snowball fight, and soon both sides realize the futility of conflict. (Sergeant Hawke, lamenting his conscription: "We want to make it clear we're not actually part of this army.") Eventually, the GIs accept the Germans' surrender offer, but in a Kafkaesque turn of events, the Americans inadvertently kill their new friends. Packed with numerous religious, allegorical, and atonement references, the photoplay labels U.S. officers as fascists, responsible for destroying the innocence of youth.

Midway

Universal Pictures, Directed by Jack Smight, Released 1976

A rousing, fly-off-the-deck, flag-waving, Sensurround extravaganza explaining the meticulous logistics, warrior determination, and old-fashioned good luck that enabled U.S. forces to defeat a large Japanese convoy at the decisive June 1942 Battle of Midway. Here, Henry Fonda portrays Admiral Chester Nimitz, the naval hero who relied on instinct to send his outnumbered ships into combat. (Admiral Fonda, stressing his perilous situation: "Our three carriers and our escorts are all that stands between the enemy fleet and the American coastline.") Off to the side, Captain Charlton Heston proffers needed advice. Basically an all-male docudrama, this 132-minute screenplay—laden with actual (and occasionally anachronistic) newsreel footage—details the heavy American pilot losses in this decisive victory. (Japanese Admiral Yamamoto [Toshiro Mifune] ruminating about lost youth: "They sacrificed themselves like samurais, these Americans.")

The Misfit Brigade

Panorama, Directed by Gordon Hessler, Released 1987

A low-budget, heavy-handed, quasi-revisionist B-spoof of American World War II screenplays, containing one mock-heroic after another. This time the easygoing, salt-of-the-earth German soldier, the traditional Hollywood villain, takes center stage as a kind-hearted, frolic-loving individual. Over on the Russian front, good-looking Bruce Davison commands a penal tank crew, composed of assorted misfits on a suicide mission to blow up a Russian train in exchange for freedom. (SS Colonel David Carradine explaining the rules: "The sacrifice of your wretched lives will bring glory to the führer."). After many Keystone Kops adventures—include leading a brothel romp, posing as Red Army fighters, and uncovering a joint German/Russian resort (complete with nude swimming)—these recalcitrants destroy the target, return to base and, as predicted, are double-crossed by General Oliver Reed. However, in a make-believe ending, U.S. fighter planes attack the base and, in a twist of fate, the misfits kill the SS officers, proving once again the righteousness of the *Wehrmacht* soldier.

Mission of the Shark

Fries Entertainment, Directed by Robert Iscove, Released 1991

A gripping, harrowing, and frightening photodrama that depicts the torpedoing of the USS *Indianapolis* on July 29, 1945 and the crew's unbearable four-day ordeal as they bobble helplessly in the South Pacific. Stacy Keach is superb as Captain Charles McVay, who can only watch in terror as marauding sharks attack his men, while back in command headquarters the cruiser's destruction has gone unnoticed. Eventually, the men are rescued, but the casualty rate became the greatest naval loss in World War II. (Captain Keach, dumbfounded by the statistics: "880 men are dead, that's a fact, a terrible fact.") As a made-for-television movie, the screenplay blasts high-ranking naval officials for their poor management and callous handling—including a kangaroo court-martial—of this terrible incident.

Mission to Death

Independent-International Pictures, Directed by Kenneth W. Richardson, Released 1966

A seventy-one-minute, B-for-bottom-of-the-barrel potboiler, produced by a cost-cutting company known for rehashing the same unknown actors, utilizing amateur photography equipment, and failing to synchronize any sound track. Jim Brewer "stars" as a tough-talking sergeant leading a platoon of U.S. soldiers to attack a Nazi radar station in Northern France during the January 1945 offensive. (Brewer, explaining his raison d'être: "I'm doing the best I can for one reason—and that's to get the job done and go home.") After destroying their first target, the GIs run into some bad luck and, in a gory, end-of-the-film shoot-out, all perish while a voice-over coda expatiates on the folly of war. Most serendipitous event: the GIs, while fighting a January war in a damp, frigid region of France, always travel in warm, sunny weather without any winter clothing.

Mister Roberts

Warner Bros., Directed by John Ford and Mervyn LeRoy, Released 1955

Another CinemaScope performance—based on the novel by Thomas Heggen—depicting a naval captain as an irrational, sadistic buffoon, who bullies his crew aboard a supply vessel on duty in the noncombatant South Pacific during the spring of 1945. As a pettifogging martinet, James Cagney is no match for his executive officer, Mr. Roberts (Henry Fonda), an easygoing ensign constantly at odds with his superior. (Fonda to Cagney: "How did you ever get command of a ship? I realize in wartime they have to scrape the bottom of the barrel, but where did they ever scrape you up?") With Jack Lemmon and William Powell in supporting roles, the storyline sustains some comical moments of pelagic life interspersed with numerous uncomplimentary remarks about the officer-privilege system, especially Captain Cagney's obsession with maintaining a palm tree on the ship's forward deck.

Morituri

Twentieth Century–Fox, Directed by Bernhard Wicki, Released 1965

A stylized, antiwar, cat-and-mouse thriller that pits an anti-Nazi national, reluctantly working as a British agent, against Gestapo officers on a German freighter delivering needed cargo to the Fatherland. Marlon Brando's Teutonic accent proffers one shibboleth after another as he surreptitiously slopes around the vessel—commanded by Captain Yul Brynner—defusing all explosives while occasionally expatiating his own brand of nihilism. (Brando to a female prisoner: "All wars are idiotic, one is not different from the other.") After a series of drawn-out events that include slinking between an Allied convoy, a rendezvous with a Japanese submarine, an abortive change-of-command plot, and, finally, detonating some dynamite to scuttle the ship, the Mozart-loving Brando, standing stoically on the damaged bridge, ponders the Roman gladiator's salute to Caesar, *morituri te salutant*—we who are about to die salute you—as he awaits rescue by the American navy.

The Mountain Road

Columbia, Directed by Daniel Mann, Released 1960

A low-grade, B-potboiler—closely akin to the 1940s sagebrush Westerns—spotlighting the heroics of an Army demolition team assigned to blow up some Chinese roadways during a strategic 1944 Allied retreat from encroaching Japanese forces. Jimmy Stewart seems miscast as an engineering major, frustrated by the anarchy that has enveloped most of the fleeing refugees. (Major Stewart to Oriental girlfriend: "I got to believe that what I'm doing means something.") Along with Sergeant Harry Morgan, the Americans escape from local bandits, destroy their objectives, and reach the safety of their command post. One scene in particular—the indiscriminate strafing of a peasant village by Major Stewart's men—shows the Caucasians as flagrant racists exhibiting strong hatred toward all Chinese. With so much Sinophobic dialogue, the storyline suggests that the Chinese, not the Japanese invaders, are the real adversaries.

Murphy's War

Paramount, Directed by Peter Yates, Released 1971

Another war-is-futile tract that pits the demonic forces of Nazism against a monomaniacal, revenge-obsessed Irish merchant seaman's rage. Peter O'-Toole's blue eyes sparkle as the lone survivor of a German U-boat attack in Caribbean waters during the first week of May 1945. Rescued by a French oil engineer (Philippe Noiret), he hastily repairs a dilapidated biplane and—armed with some homemade Molotov cocktails—makes a low-level pass, damaging the Axis ship hidden in a nearby estuary. Eventually, the submarine heads for open waters, where Seaman O'Toole—now commanding a rickety steel barge—continues the fight that culminates in a watery Götterdämmerung, destroying both friend and foe. Based on the novel by Max Catto, most scenes indict the seafaring Third Reich for their savage show-no-mercy warfare. (O'Toole venting his anger: "They shot the entire crew in the water.")

My Foolish Heart

Warner Bros., Directed by Mark Robson, Released 1949

A hearts-and-flowers soap opera—from a short story by J. D. Salinger—that traces the loneliness of a distraught coed whose army sweetheart accidentally dies in a stateside training mission, a few months after the War has started, and her subsequent rebound marriage to the wrong man. Susan Hayward glows as a caustic dipsomaniac whose school-days memories of her deceased boyfriend (Dana Andrews) only brings bitterness and unhappiness to her current husband (Kent Smith). Eventually, the stoic Miss Hayward comes to terms with the human cost of the war and agrees to an amicable divorce, allowing her best friend to walk away with her spouse. As social commentary, the storyline reiterates the nation's fears, confusion, and humor during the early months of 1942. (Character actor Robert Keith, poking fun at Private Dana Andrews' ill-fitting uniform: "Well, I must say, you are the sorriest-looking Casanova I've ever seen.")

The Naked and the Dead

RKO, Directed by Raoul Walsh, Released 1958

An elaborate adaptation of Norman Mailer's controversial novel that takes an assailing look at some of the troubled personalities in the U.S. Army leadership corps as they advance inland on a South Pacific Japanese-held island during the 1943 offensive. As a fascist-minded one-star general, Raymond Massey reiterates his Nietzschean absolutism philosophy, while his sadistic platoon sergeant, Aldo Ray, shoots Japanese prisoners to extract the gold fillings from their mouths. (General Massey to Lieutenant Cliff Robertson: "The only way you can generate the proper attitude of awe and obedience is by immense and disproportionate power.") With numerous references to unfaithful wives, the million-dollar wound, the officer/enlisted man schism, and the sexually active 4-Fs, much of the screenplay reaffirms the frustration each foot soldier endures in his jungle-fighting microcosm.

Never So Few

MGM, Directed by John Sturges, Released 1959

Another high-jinks Far Eastern adventure tale—based on the novel by Tom T. Chamales— belaboring the rough-and-tumble antics of Captain Frank Sinatra routing the Japanese during the 1944 Burma invasion campaign. With Peter Lawford, Steve McQueen, and Philip Ahn as members of a motley, behind-the-lines commando team, Old Blue Eyes—after blasting his Oriental enemies out of the jungle bush—takes a respite from combat to woo flirtatious Gina Lollobrigida. (Captain Sinatra to his shapely Italian girlfriend: "I'm going to miss you! Where I'm going, nobody smells of soap.") Eventually, the storyline takes a macabre twist when Sinatra's team crosses the Chinese border, attacks a renegade warlord's camp, and—in a highly charged scene—executes their prisoners in a manner reminiscent of the Japanese atrocities commonly found in the 1940s Hollywood propaganda films. Funniest scene: Frank Sinatra wearing a pasted-on goatee.

A Night in Casablanca

United Artists, Directed by Archie Mayo, Released 1946

An eighty-five-minute gem—featuring the wacky Marx Brothers—that parodies Michael Curtiz's 1943 Academy Award–winner *Casablanca* and, as a bonus, takes a quick swipe at Howard Hawks's 1944 war film *To Have and to Have Not*. Fast-talking Groucho Marx, now a hotel manager in postwar Casablanca, romps his way through numerous misadventures as foreign intrigue, Nazi agents, and secret treasures emerge everywhere, and Chico and Harpo create their own form of mayhem. Soon, a chief inspector bellows orders to "round up the usual suspects," while ensconced in another room, Groucho spoofs both the famous roulette game scene and the Bogart and Bergman airport farewell. (Groucho, now flying the airplane: "We have to keep going until we run out of gas.") In its own simplistic way, this photo-drama signaled the end of Hollywood propaganda pictures, allowing directors to create new themes, ideas, and motifs about the global conflict.

Night of the Fox

Dove Incorporated Production, Directed by Charles Jarrott, Released 1990

Another Yugoslavian-made adventure yarn—based on the popular novel by Jack Higgins—that employs big-name Hollywood stars in roles incompatible with their ages and acting skills. As a senior British general who orders the rescue of an American officer stranded on the Nazi-occupied island of Jersey, eighty-two-year-old John Mills reminds his subordinate, George Peppard, that the fate of the D-Day invasion rests solely on his shoulders. Soon, the pudgy American major infiltrates Gestapo headquarters, dupes numerous

German officers, and after some Saturday-afternoon cartoon adventures, rescues his man, only to learn of his commander's double-dealing. (Peppard to Mills: "Sometimes I wonder who the enemy is!") Most unrealistic scene: sixty-two-year-old George Peppard climbing down a rainspout, a feat difficult for a man forty years younger.

The Night of the Generals

Columbia, Directed by Anatole Litvak, Released 1967

Another pro-German, revisionist homily that suggests most Nazi generals were noble, high-minded, and kind individuals—interested only in assassinating Hitler—while, occasionally, one rotten officer turns up to spoil the barrel. Peter O'Toole portrays a psychopathic general whose brutal murders of local prostitutes remain unnoticed until his colleague, Colonel Omar Sharif, relentlessly investigates these mutilations. (Nazi intelligence officer Omar Sharif, explaining his obsession: "I'm interested in just one general who killed a girl and thought because he was a general he could play God in bed as well as in battle.") Eventually O'Toole's crimes are brought to justice, and his impromptu suicide serves as the coda to expiate all misdeeds. With many famous actors—including Tom Courtenay, Donald Pleasence, Philip Noiret, and Christopher Plummer—this fictional thriller whitewashes much of the horror associated with the Third Reich's occupation policies.

No Man Is an Island

Universal, Directed by John Monks Jr. and Richard Goldstone, Released 1962

A long-winded, I-will-fight-the-Japanese-from-the-hills, Pacific island action tale, loosely based on the exploits of Seaman George Tweed, a thirty-two-year-old bluejacket stranded behind enemy lines on Guam, whose three-year hit-and-miss forays frustrated the Japanese occupation forces. Good-looking Jeffrey Hunter endures many close calls as he slides in and out of different hideaways, aided by local natives. (Seaman Hunter explaining his predicament to a local Catholic priest: "You see, there were five of us. I was in charge, I'm the only one left.") Eventually, an American ship appears on the horizon, and using his Morse code skills, the quick-thinking sailor guides this destroyer out of harm's way. Acclaimed a hero and reunited with his Chamoru sweetheart, an older and wiser serviceman now understands the mystical lines of John Donne's metaphysical poem.

None but the Brave

Warner Bros., Directed by Frank Sinatra, Released 1965

A low-key, antiwar parable about some stranded Marines and abandoned Japanese soldiers on an uncharted Solomon island, circa 1943, who originally battle each other but eventually discover the futility of killing and call a truce. Now a chief navy corpsman, Frank Sinatra treats friend and foe equally. (The Voice, proffering a humanist position after amputating the leg of a Japanese soldier: "I didn't save that kid's life to see him get shot.") Meanwhile, his superior (Clint Walker), must convince his glory-hungry lieutenant the lesson of tolerance and understanding. Soon, this harmony dissipates when a U.S. rescue ship approaches—causing a resumption of hostilities—and the carnage that follows only restates the storyline's pacifist motif. Best scene: Sinatra enters the Japanese military camp to perform a lifesaving operation using only rudimentary instruments plus the omnipresent whiskey bottle.

Okinawa

Columbia, Directed by Leigh Jason, Released 1952

Another slow-moving B-potboiler describing the adventures of a five-man gunnery crew aboard a U.S. Navy destroyer during the spring 1945 Okinawa offensive, where dozens of Japanese suicide pilots—the kamikazes—aim their aircraft at American warships. The ship's captain, pudgy Pat O'Brien, fully understands the dangers of Japanese fanaticism. (O'Brien to command staff: "The most effective weapon the Japs have—kamikaze!") When Seaman Cameron Mitchell and his fellow jacktars, personifying the best of Yankee intransigence, line up the bandits in their crosshairs, most of the enemy airpower is blasted out of the sky, crashing violently into the sea. Using a generous supply of documentary footage—from both sides—the storyline details the ferocity of this final island victory.

Once before I Die

F8 Productions, Directed by John Derek, Released 1965

A high-jinx, shoot-'em-from-the-hip, equestrian yarn—akin to the Saturday-matinee B-oaters—that traces the hoofprints of some polo-playing U.S. Army cavalrymen, who galloped away from an aerial attack near their Philippine base during the early hours of December 7. Traveling west toward Manila, this spirited group, led by jodhpurs-wearing Major John Derek, statuesque Ursula Andress, and glabrous Lieutenant Richard Jaeckel, endure an array of make-believe adventures that include attacking a Japanese tank with fallen trees and burning bushes, plus a benevolent sexual experience proffered by Miss Andress to a neophyte GI so that the lad may experience coitus "once before he dies." Most prophetic scene: Major John Derek expostulates on Japanese expansionism. (Derek explaining the Greater East Asia Co-Prosperity Pact to the politically uninformed Andress: "They bombed Pearl Harbor; obviously, they're planning something big.")

Onionhead

Warner Bros., Directed by Norman Taurog, Released 1958

A low-budget comedy-melodrama that blends some Laurel and Hardy slapstick, a femme fatale's psychosis, a corrupt mess officer's duplicity, a ship's captain's morality, and a submarine attack in an eighty-four-minute screenplay that jumps from one genre to another. After joining the Coast Guard in spring 1941, a happy-go-lucky Oklahoma college student (Andy Griffith) laughs his way through basic training, receives a chief petty officer's rank, becomes a cook and, after more shenanigans, finds a Boston sweetheart. Soon, the girlfriend drops him, marries another sailor, and after her new husband sails off to Greenland, seduces the confused hayseed. Back in his kitchen, he acts decisively when he eventually discovers a theft operation that, literally, takes good food from sailors' mouths. (Chief Griffith to his staff: "As long as I'm the head cook, I'm running this galley.") Acclaimed a hero after some fancy machine-gun-firing against a U-boat, he runs into an old hometown flame and, after a quick courtship—much to the acclaim of his pals and officers—marries the pretty maiden, proving, once again, that true love comes to those who wait.

Operation Bikini

American International Pictures, Directed by Anthony Carras, Released 1963

Another cost-cutting, use-lots-of-newsreel-footage, B-for-bad, seventy-seven-minute train wreck that traces the comings and goings of a Navy demolition team assigned to destroy a U.S. submarine, lying ignominiously at the bottom of a South Pacific atoll, before Japanese forces, lurking nearby, find this vessel and retrieve important intelligence codes. Anemic-looking Tab Hunter seems apathetic about his directive while his bosun mate, Jim Backus (the voice of the popular cartoon character, Mr. Magoo), listens apprehensively. (Lieutenant Hunter, explaining the mission:

"We're here to find the sub that was sunk in the channel last month.") After a few comic-strip adventures, the unit, spearheaded by teen idol Frankie Avalon, swims many fathoms underwater, sets the charges, and, after a few close calls, demolishes the ship, much to the relief of its commanding officers. Funniest juxtaposition: Frankie Avalon's daydreaming fantasies, where, twice, he croons romantic songs to bikini-clad girlfriends, who, shaking their scantily clad bodies, offer tangible evidence of the American man's why-we-fight credo.

Operation Crossbow

MGM, Directed by Michael Anderson, Released 1965

A fabricated action tale glamorizing the sub-rosa world of some Allied agents, who in 1943 parachute into the Fatherland and—after some cat-and-mouse escapades with the Gestapo—destroy the underground factory that manufactures the V-2 rocket. Working as an American spy speaking flawless German, George Peppard sweet-talks his way out of most predicaments until starry-eyed Sophia Loren learns about the mission. Unable to trust the Italian widow, Peppard approves her execution and likewise sacrifices Tom Courteney to a Nazi firing squad. Infused with many examples of ambiguous loyalties, the storyline reiterates the aphoristic concept that all's fair in love and war. (British citizen Anthony Quayle, now aligned with the Third Reich, rationalizing his perfidy: "Before Hitler came to power we were nothing. Now, we're the greatest nation in the world—the most feared and most respected.")

Operation Pacific

Warner Bros., Directed by George Waggner, Released 1951

A straightforward, below-the-waves, blast-the-enemy adventure detailing the perilous missions that Silent Service members routinely experienced in their war against Japan. As always, John Wayne is superb as the captain of the USS *Thunder*, a submarine destroying Japanese vessels in the Pacific waters, while rescuing many downed American airmen. (Wayne, bellowing orders after torpedoing another enemy ship: "Take her down, fast and deep—rig for depth charge, rig for silent running.") With many references to the "I'm-just-an-ordinary-guy-not-a-hero" sailor, the photodrama quietly reaffirms the importance of every man's role in the combat zone and honors the many sacrifices needed for victory. (Wayne, eulogizing the *Thunder*'s chief petty officer: "Chiefs have been taking care of this man's navy for a long time.")

Operation Petticoat

Universal International, Directed by Blake Edwards, Released 1959

A pleasant, easygoing, and harmless comedy that sidesteps the horror and brutality of World War II and, instead, spoofs the global conflict as a series of wisecracking, double-entendre events. Here, suave Cary Grant radiates as the skipper of a damaged American submarine that limps out of harbor following a Japanese air attack in December 1941, while his junior officer (Tony Curtis) smooth-talks everyone for needed parts to keep the underwater vessel operational. (Commander Grant, rationalizing such behavior: "To paraphrase Mr. Churchill, never have so few stolen so much from so many.") Once on the high seas, the crew experiences an array of zany adventures that include a busty nurse blocking a narrow walkway, a voodoo blessing from a local witch doctor, two village women giving birth in the forward cabin, an askew torpedo attack that blows up a Japanese truck, and—as the pièce de résistance—the unintentional priming of the ship's outer surface that dries a bright pink.

O.S.S.

Paramount, Directed by Irving Pichel, Released 1946

An elaborate now-it-can-be-told tribute to Wild Bill Donovan's acclaimed cloak-and-dagger organization—the Office of Strategic Services—an undercover group responsible for many covert, worldwide operations that disrupted numerous Axis offensives. (Colonel Donovan to charges: "Learn how to kill—quickly, silently!") After intense stateside training, good-looking Alan Ladd moves stealthily through the Brittany back roads. There—after some smooth talking, close calls, and unexpected luck—he destroys an important Nazi railroad tunnel necessary for the Allied D-Day invasion, while his girlfriend (Geraldine Fitzgerald) maneuvers their escape. Soon, the twosome sneak across the Rhine to facilitate the U.S. Army's advance into the Fatherland where, again, they slip in and out of dangerous situations. Finally, their luck falters, and as a farewell expiation, the pretty Miss Fitzgerald sacrifices her life for a mission's success. (Tough-talking Alan Ladd, ruminating about his lost love: "I didn't even know her real name.")

Pacific Inferno

Nathaniel Productions. Directed by Rolf Bayer, Released 1979

A totally distorted and tasteless photodrama using the infamous Bataan Death March—an historical event where hundreds of emaciated American

GIs perished from Japanese savagery—as the backdrop for a preposterous underwater search-for-silver travesty. Former football running back Jim Brown, "stars" as a U.S. Navy diver, who along with other bluejackets, surrenders to the Japanese when Corregidor capitulates. Soon, these prisoners receive good food, hearty beverages, and clean housing and are put to work retrieving sunken treasure. (Imperial officer to sailors: "I bring you pleasurable food and drink. This number-one best Japan wine.") In his evening hours, Seaman Brown hooks up with some guerrillas and, after some comic-book adventures, removes the prized bullion, swims to a nearby village, and, in a gory finale, blows up a barge, kills many Japanese, and—in a nod to contemporary American racism—accepts a martyr's death. Replete with anachronistic haircuts, eyeglasses, slang, attitudes, and music, the entire production depicts POW life as nothing but a series of minor irritations.

Paratroop Command

American-International Pictures, Directed by William Witney, Released 1959

A B-for-bottom-of-the-barrel, jump-out-of-the-plane, stand-up-and-shoot yawn describing the comings and goings of some paratroopers during the 1943 Italian campaign. Here, an airborne soldier (Richard Bakalyan), unaware of an offensive ruse, accidentally kills a squad member, and soon everyone turns against him. (Corporal Bakalyan, explaining the misunderstanding: "I swear, Lieutenant, when I shot, so help me, I never knew it was the Cowboy.") Unable to shake this stigma, the downtrodden Bakalyan—hoping for redemption—zigzags across a minefield, steps on an explosive, but lives long enough to deliver a needed radio. With numerous scenes of documentary footage interspersed in the storyline, this seventy-one-minute quickie—from a production company noted for using unknown actors, watered-downed scripts, and a seven-day shooting schedule—explains the war as nothing more than a comic-book scenario.

Paratrooper

Columbia, Directed by Terence Young, Released 1953

Another unlikely airborne story glamorizing the recruitment, training, and combat assignment of some British paratroopers who distinguish themselves in a 1942 North African raid. Here, tough-guy Alan Ladd plays a former U.S. Air Corps pilot who joins the Royal Army as an enlisted man to forget some unpleasant stateside experiences. Soon, this stereotypical loner refuses any leadership assignment. (Major Leo Genn berating Private Ladd: "One fine day—whether you're wearing three stars or three stripes or nothing at all—the men are going to look to you.") Eventually, the blond-haired American, with the help of a kindly English girlfriend, realizes his folly, and in a formula film ending, accepts his wartime responsibility, much to the glee of his pals and superiors.

Patton

Twentieth Century–Fox, Directed by Franklin J. Schaffner, Released 1970

An elaborate 171-minute hagiography to the unorthodox, flamboyant, and controversial four-star general known to his men as Blood-and-Guts, the larger-than-life egocentric officer responsible for many important battlefield victories. In an Academy Award performance, George C. Scott captures the idiosyncrasies of the unconventional George S. Patton—from his Bible-quoting oratory down to his ivory-handled revolver—beginning with his 1943 North African campaign until his triumphant 1945 entry into the German capital, while his commander, General Omar Bradley (Karl Malden) spends many hours cautioning his charge about military propriety. Frequently obsessed with megalomania, the outspoken general seems hoisted by his own petard with his many diatribes. (Patton to hospital doctors, regarding admittance procedures: "Battle fatigue is a free ride—yellow bellies' ticket to the hospital. I'm not going to subsidize cowardice.")

Pearl Harbor

Touchstone Pictures, Directed by Michael Bay, Released 2001

An over-the-top, computer-enhanced, *Weekly Reader*, special-effects retelling of the December 7 attack as seen through the eyes of two Tennessee-born pals, their shared girlfriend, plus an entourage of noted 1941 personalities. These include President Roosevelt, whose famous residence, the White House, anachronistically sports central-air-conditioning ducts on the rooftop. At a Hawaiian air base, two Air Corps pilots (Ben Affleck and Josh Hartnett) chase after a pretty woman (Kate Beckinsale), while on the high seas, the Imperial Japanese fleet steams closer to their Sunday-morning target. While the love triangle reaches a discomfited stalemate, enemy air squadrons attack Pearl Harbor, destroying most of the Pacific fleet and killing thousands of civilians and servicemen. (Colonel James Doolittle, played by Alec Baldwin, assessing the damage: "You know at Pearl they hit us with a sledgehammer.") Eventually, the U.S. forces reorganize and, in a stunning coup de main, bomb

Tokyo. With numerous examples of dramatic license, much of this soap-opera-laden storyline implies that Japan attacked Pearl Harbor for the sole purpose of resolving an awkward ménage à trois.

The Pigeon That Took Rome

Paramount, Directed by Melville Shavelson, Released 1962

A lighthearted spoof that japes military bureaucracy, Prussian discipline, and Italian family life in an offbeat manner that resembles the classical farce. Here, in 1944, two Army spies—Charlton Heston and Harry Guardino—working undercover in Rome must rely on carrier pigeons to convey messages, while keeping a low profile in the Nazi-occupied city. After a series of sidestepping misadventures, that include wooing comely lasses, sweet-talking German soldiers, inadvertently eating their prized homing birds at a gala Easter dinner, and sending the wrong instructions to Allied command, the duo are acclaimed heroes as the city capitulates to the attacking Americans. Completely nonplussed by the turn of events, Captain Heston waxes philosophical. (Heston to pal: "This is no war—it's an insane asylum!") With numerous potshots at opportunistic officers, this laid-back, antiwar photodrama quips the conflict as a happy-go-lucky child's game supervised by goofy, out-of-it adults.

Play Dirty

United Artists, Directed by André Detoth, Released 1969

A cynical reappraisal of the British North African campaign where senior staff officers—perched safely behind their oversized desks—dispatch a small attack team behind enemy lines, fully aware that these Tommies will perish in the hot desert fighting. Here, the leader of this motley squad (Michael Caine) slowly realizes the sacrificial nature of his assignment as his men capitulate to the heat, terrain, and Nazi offensives. Back in headquarters, Harry Andrews—in another brash commander role—manipulates their deaths into a well-orchestrated propaganda coup, culminating with an English counterattack. Laced with strong Machiavellian overtones, the storyline depicts the worst of British forces, stressing their primordial needs. (Michael Caine, expatiating his moral code: "I want to survive here—I watch, I listen, and I say nothing.")

The Plot to Kill Hitler

Warner Bros., Directed by Lawrence Schiller, Released 1990

A pie-in-the-sky, puffed-up, made-for-television, revisionist paean to the Nazi officers, who—hoping to save their country from continued Allied bombings—

masterminded the assassination attempt of their führer. After some detailed logistics, a briefcase containing an explosive is placed next to Hitler at a July 20, 1944, staff meeting. However, the Nazi leader survives the detonation, much to the plotters' dismay. (Brad Davis as General Claus von Stauffenberg: "I set off a bomb during my conference with the führer. I saw the blast myself. No one who was in that room can still be alive.") Soon, top-ranking officers endure their own terror as Hitler—played by Mike Gwilym—orders brutal reprisals for anyone remotely associated with this plot. With numerous heroic actions, this sugarcoated photoplay suggests that most top-ranking Nazis were astute, magnanimous, and nonbelligerent nationals who could care less about lebensraum.

Proud

Castle Hill, Directed by Mary Pat Kelly, Released 2004

A heart-warming, Norman Rockwell, factual story that honors the 160 African American sailors who manned an escort destroyer, the USS *Mason*, on many dangerous North Atlantic crossings during the height of wolf-pack attacks. Ossie Davis radiates as the real-life Seaman Lorenzo Dufau, who along with his shipmates, performs laudably in an Eleanor Roosevelt experiment to determine the efficacy of black seamen. (Senior citizen Davis, explaining why African Americans fought in World War II: "The only colors that count are red, white, and blue.") During one perilous crossing, the vessel—ignoring the ocean dangers—dramatically forges ahead in high, windy, seas, providing their convoy needed support. Best scenes: a 1994 admiral's reception for these men, awarding medals—long overdue because of wartime racial policies—plus President Clinton's 2003 tribute, citing these sailors for their "Magnificent, magnificent effort!"

The Proud and the Profane

Paramount, Directed by George Seaton, Released 1956

An overblown tribute to the men of the Marine Corps—from Lucy Herndon Crockett's novel *The Magnificent Bastards*—who fought the Japanese in the South Pacific campaign and then returned to the peaceful French island of New Caledonia for training and medical care. Here a martinet battle commander (William Holden) hones his youthful charges razor sharp, disdaining any weakness or emotion. (Colonel Holden, dressing down a naive chaplain: "I want my men to be superstitious about only one thing—when they come face-to-face with a Jap in the bush, I want them to consider it very bad luck not to kill him first.") Eventually, the sangfroid colonel capitulates to the warmth of a Red Cross worker (Deborah Kerr), and following an off-again, on-again romance, the twosome are united in a saccharine end-of-the-movie fade-out. One scene in particular—Deborah Kerr placing flowers at the military cemetery—restates the high casualty rate sustained in the island-hopping warfare and, subliminally, deifies all fallen members of the Corps.

PT 109

Warner Bros., Directed by Leslie H. Martinson, Released 1962

A glamorized version of President John F. Kennedy's 1943 South Seas combat experiences—based on the book by Robert J. Donovan—that portrays the youthful naval lieutenant (j.g.) as intelligent, versatile, and resourceful. Assigned to a mosquito-boat command, good-looking Cliff Robertson quickly learns the rudiments of seamanship and, along with a fine-tuned crew, attacks a Japanese island to rescue some stranded marines. Later, an enemy ship rams their plywood hull, and following a series of close calls—including an arduous ocean swim, ducking from Japanese forces, and functioning without food or medical supplies—the sailors are rescued after Lieutenant Kennedy dispatches his famous message-inscribed coconut. (Lieutenant Kennedy, reassuring the tars: "We're getting out of here if we have to get in the water and drag this damn island back with us!")

Racing with the Moon

Paramount, Directed by Richard Benjamin, Released 1984

A wonderful, joyous, coming-of-age fulfillment that limns the hopes, aspirations, and uncertainties of two Californian youths who—in the 1942 winter—are counting the days before their Marine Corps induction. Sean Penn and Nicolas Cage portray lifelong friends eager to leave their pin-boy jobs, become leathernecks, and rout America's enemies. (Cage to Penn: "The only future we got is Germans and Japs.") As their days dwindle down, the twosome enjoy some last-minute shenanigans that include chasing after girls, drinking whiskey, and hustling some bluejackets in a pool game. Finally, the magic date arrives, and much to the acclaim of family and friends, the boys, now eighteen years old, jump on the train, confident their enlistment will bring an end to the global conflict.

The Raiders of Leyte Gulf

Hemisphere Pictures, Directed by Eddie Romero, Released 1963

A cut-to-the-bone, jerky, shoot-at-everyone, B-for-Bad soap opera that peripherally depicts the Philippines resistance movement weeks before General

MacArthur's historic "I-Shall-Return" pageantry. On a remote Malay archipelago, Lieutenant Michael Parsons leads an attack team against a Japanese stronghold to rescue an American prisoner. (Lieutenant Parsons to group, "We're still in the middle of a war.") Off to the side, his native girlfriend (Liza Moreno) whispers sweet nothings into his ear. (Liza to sweetheart: "Is it true that most Americans are afraid of lizards?) Soon, machine-gun bullets rebound, hand grenades explode, and the Japanese forces are routed, but in a sudsy fade-out, the two lovers—reconciled to any anomaly—bid a saccharine farewell, promising to unite at war's end.

The Ravagers

Hemisphere, Directed by Eddie Romero, Released 1965

Another low-light, terse-dialogue, B-quickie from a shoestring production company known for hacking out one war title after another. Unshaven John Saxon moves slowly as a U.S. Army captain leading a motley Filipino guerrilla team dodging a retreating Japanese patrol during the closing summer days of World War II. Finally, the Japanese soldiers commandeer a Roman Catholic convent but are promptly routed by the jungle fighters. (Major Saxon, explaining his offensive strategy: "If we don't lose our heads, we got a fighting chance.") Meanwhile, his subordinate (Fernando Poe Jr.), after killing many banzai-spouting soldiers, pauses to make eyes at Bronwyn FitzSimons, a disheveled American damsel in distress.

The Red Ball Express

Universal, Directed by Budd Boetticher, Released 1952

A fast-driving, no-road-too-difficult, no-trip-too-arduous tribute to the men of the Army Transportation Corps, the GIs who drove overpacked trucks hundreds of miles to supply General Patton's tanks with gasoline and ammunition during the July 1944 Normandy breakout. As always, Lieutenant Jeff Chandler takes charge of a diverse group of soldiers, quickly molds them into a tight unit, and leads them down many a hazardous thoroughfare to deliver needed matériel. (Lieutenant Chandler, explaining their mission: "The line of trucks between here and the front is almost continuous—a load of supplies will be dropping behind Patton every minute, day and night.") With Sidney Poitier as a young corporal espousing some racial harmony, the fast-moving storyline (using many grainy newsreel inserts) highlights the heroic work of the many African American GIs who served in this important outfit.

Reign of the Gargoyles

Concrete Productions, Directed by Ayton Davis, Released 2006

Another black-magic, they're-everywhere, airborne comic-strip romp detailing a mad Nazi scientist, who during the winter 1945 defensive brings to life—à la Frankenstein—hundreds of gargoyles that fill the French skies to destroy Allied bombers. (U.S. crew member, radioing his superiors: "They're slaughtering us in the air, on the ground!") Eventually, some downed airmen, led by Joe Penny and Wes Ramsey, team up with British commandos and Resistance members and, after a series of make-believe adventures, hop into a German airplane, turn a few switches, fly into a gaggle of gargoyles, and then ram a sacred spear into the "heart" of the primary monster, rendering all others ineffective. With many references to medieval sorcery, this harmless, make-believe yarn offers the same vicarious thrills found in noisy video-game arcades.

Run Silent, Run Deep

United Artists, Directed by Robert Wise, Released 1958

Another all-male, I-want-revenge, Silent Service potboiler—based on the novel by Edward L. Beach—that juxtaposes the loneliness-of-command theme against the larger issue of destroying Japanese seafaring vessels during a 1943 offensive. Clark Gable shines as an obdurate U.S. Navy submarine captain patrolling the South Pacific theater, secretly searching for the enemy ship that blasted him out of the water a year ago. When confronted by his second-in-command (Burt Lancaster) about the efficacy of a one-man show, Gable pooh-poohs his executive officer. (Gable to Lancaster: "A captain can redefine orders if he feels he has an advantage.") Eventually the Japanese vessel is spotted and—in a typical climax—sunk by some deft bowshot torpedoing. As a coda, Gable's underwater death, an expiation for disobeying military directives, deifies the men of the submarine command.

Saints and Soldiers

Go Films, Directed by Ryan Little, Released 2003

A quiet remembrance of the dozens of American prisoners murdered by German forces in the Belgian forest near the small town of Malmedy during the December 1944 Battle of the Bulge. During this infamous massacre, four GIs run into the woods, flee their captors, forage for weapons, and eventually team up with an English pilot carrying logistical information. After numerous close calls—including ducking into a cellar while Nazis frolic overhead in the living room, hiding in a farmhouse, killing a Nazi to stop a rape, freeing a simple German soldier, and finally, driving through a *Wehrmacht*'s camp wearing their enemy's uniforms, the needed information reaches the Allied command post. Young, Bible-reading Corporal Corbin Allred sparkles as the group's marksman, whose simple but competent mannerisms frequently collide with his religious convictions. (Allred to pal: "Do you believe in a life after this one?") Off to the side, his sergeant keeps a watchful eye. Best scene: each man, in a moment of fraternal bonding, reveals intimate secrets: Corporal Corbin's confession: "I never kissed my wife till the day we were married."

Sands of Iwo Jima

Republic, Directed by Allan Dwan, Released 1949

The quintessential combat film of the postwar period that—in a quiet, dignified manner—honors the Marine Corps for their many island victories. Who else but John Wayne could portray a tough, gruff squad sergeant who teaches his young charges the meaning of loyalty, teamwork, and semper fidelis? (Straight-faced Sergeant Wayne to replacements: "Before I'm through with you, you're going to move like one man and think like one man—if you don't, you'll be dead!) Soon the marines assault Iwo Jima and, along with John Apgar and Forrest Tucker, push inland to witness the historic Mount Suribachi flag rising. Here, a Japanese sniper fells John Wayne, and after a short eulogy the gyrenes—mindful of their sergeant's sacrifice—continue their attack. Using three real-life members from the Joe Rosenthal photograph in the cast, the screenplay reaffirms the high human cost of the South Pacific fighting.

Saving Private Ryan

DreamWorks, Directed by Steven Spielberg, Released 1998

An overpowering, one-of-a-kind, flag-waving accolade to the U.S. forces that landed on Omaha Beach on June 6, 1944, fought their way inland, and finally secured the beachfront. Tom Hanks sparkles as a Ranger officer who leads his squad uphill, attacks German defenders, and, finally, seizes their strongholds. A few days later, his men journey into the French countryside to locate a young paratrooper (whose three older brothers recently died in combat) and bring the private back to the command post. After many difficulties, including fighting rearguard *Wehrmacht* soldiers, discovering the "wrong" Private Ryan, and ambushing a radar station, the Rangers find their charge but, in an unanticipated turn of events, must fight against an Axis attack. (Captain Miller's appraisal: "Things have taken a turn for the surreal.") Eventually, Private Ryan reaches safety, but Captain Miller perishes defending his position. Most harrowing scene: the first twenty-eight minutes, depicting the indescribable carnage U.S. forces experienced on the Normandy coast.

The Sea Chase

Warner Bros., Directed by John Farrow, Released 1955

Another hot-air, revisionist production purporting that most German nationals were noble, austere, and kindhearted, while only the degenerates embraced Hitler's world-domination policies. Here, John Wayne, as an anti-Nazi German sea captain, slips his steamer from an Australian harbor—after the 1939 Poland invasion—determined to reach home port. After months of ocean turmoil, including the ubiquitous sea storm, a shark attack, a suicide, and pursuit by a revenge-bearing British warship, Wayne finally reaches a Norwegian fjord, where in an ambiguous ending he disappears with mysterious, bleached-blond Lana Turner. (Captain Wayne, waxing philosophically: "Immortality has nothing to do with fame.") With obvious parallels to the *Odyssey* and the *Rime of the Ancient Mariner*, this screenplay retells the "long voyage home" saga as a World War II parable, only this time, the Germans are heroes.

The Sea Wolves

Paramount, Directed by Andrew V. McLaglen, Released 1980

A far-fetched fairy tale purporting that a motley group of over-the-hill British civilians living in Calcutta formed a high-powered commando team and destroyed three Nazi warships moored in nearby Goa, a Portuguese neutral port. David Niven moves cautiously as the leader of these former cavalrymen, while two English officers—Gregory Peck and Roger Moore—supply the covert military logistics necessary to coordinate this raid. A plethora of subplots—including the mysterious femme fatale, waterfront spies, cryptic code books, secret radio room, and the ship's engine that falters before starting—add to the fast-moving action that proves, once again, the indomitable force of English prowess. (David Niven, explaining his unit's determinism: "We're a little thin on top and thick in the middle, but I guarantee you, every one of these fellows would pull his own weight.")

Sealed Cargo

RKO, Directed by Alfred L. Werker, Released 1951

Another well-deserved pat on the back for those quiet-spoken fisherman on the northeastern Canadian coast who kept a sharp eye for Axis warships. As always, Dana Andrews keeps a steady course as a Nova Scotian fishing-boat skipper who answers a distress signal from a floundering ship and tows this vessel into a nearby village harbor. Suspicious of the captain's roundabout explanation, the quick-thinking Canadian slips on board and, after some fancy footwork, discovers a secret hull containing U-boat torpedoes. Soon, the Germans return to their ship. (Nazi captain Claude Rains, revealing his rank: "I am an officer of the German Navy. You do not think I would surrender a vessel under my command to a handful of fisherman.") But they are no match for the mariners, who overcome their enemies and deftly sail it out of the harbor, await the arrival of two Axis submarines and—after some tricky maneuvering—set off an explosive, destroying both U-boats.

The Secret of Santa Vittoria

United Artists, Directed by Stanley Kramer, Released 1969

A frivolous, distorted, and oversimplified view of the 1943 Italian campaign that implies only a few nationals supported *Il Duce*'s fascist policies, while most of the Nazis strut around a village square winking at the pulchritudinous locals. Anthony Quinn sparkles as a kindhearted, bumbling peasant, who—after some convoluted escapades—becomes the mayor of an isolated hilltop village, Santa Vittoria. When the German army arrives to confiscate the town's wine harvest—over a million bottles—the denizens move quickly to hide their prized possessions. (Quinn to council members: "Without our wine, we are nothing!") Much to their surprise, the ruse works, and the gullible Germans withdraw. Based on the book by Robert Crichton, the photoplay sugarcoats Mussolini's autocracy and suggests—in a roundabout way—that most Italians, sitting in their outdoor cafes sipping vino, detest their leader's wartime policies.

The Sharkfighters

United Artists, Directed by Jerry Hopper, Released 1956

A breezy tribute to a small but important coterie of U.S. naval scientists, stationed in Cuba circa 1944, who work long hours and endure numerous frustrations to perfect a shark repellent that will protect any servicemen abandoned in the ocean. Chain-smoking, hard-talking Victor Mature, a lieutenant commander and survivor of a Pacific shark attack, heads a meticulous laboratory experimenting with numerous chemicals. After weeks of testing, they stumble upon the perfect mixture. (Mature to crew: "We got a repellent that works.") Soon, he leaps into the hostile ocean and, immersed in this solution, proves its efficacy as one shark after another diverts from its fuliginous odor. Funniest scene: Victor Mature, anxious to start work, jumps onto the research ship, heading to a known breeding area, accoutered in full navy dress uniform—jacket, tie, and shined shoes—an outfit no tar would dream of wearing for such an assignment.

Shining Through

Twentieth–Century Fox, Directed by David Seltzer, Released 1992

Another boy-saves-girl spy melodrama—based on the novel by Susan Isaacs—that spotlights the peripatetic skills of an American O.S.S. agent (Michael Douglas) as he stealthily moves between European capitals, obtaining classified information during the shaky pre–Pearl Harbor days. After war is declared, his young bilingual secretary (Melanie Griffith), eager to help the Allied cause, joins this sub-rosa group, enters the Fatherland and—following a series of Nancy Drew adventures—photographs important military information. Eventually discovered, she experiences a few close calls until the good-looking Douglas literally carries her across the Swiss border. (Colonel Douglas, pronouncing his affection: "I don't want to lose you, I want to be with you always.") Best anachronistic scene: during the 1942 winter, Colonel Douglas wears the combat infantryman's badge, a medal not yet awarded to American GIs.

Ski Troop Attack

Filmgroup, Directed by Roger Corman, Released 1960

Another sixty-three-minute, B-quickie, from a director frequently called "King of the Drive-ins," whose trademark low-budget productions contain strident music, generous newsreel inserts, and skimpy lighting. This one is about a five-man U.S. ski patrol who in December 1944 reconnoiter parts of the Ardennes, while the nearby German high command plans a surprise offensive. Straight-arrow junior officer (Michael Forest) cautiously guides his squad from one snowy ridge to another, dodging the enemy. (Lieutenant Forest's directive: "As long as this weather says socked in, the ski troops are the division's only eyes behind the lines.") Eventually, the GIs stumble upon a trestle bridge and, after some fancy maneuvering with homemade explosives, destroy this strategic overpass, stymieing the Axis attack. Best special effects scene: the popular model-railroad-train set used during the final scene, emblazoned with the manufacturer's prominent logo.

Slaughterhouse-Five

Universal, Directed by George Roy Hill, Released 1972

A wide-eyed, off-the-wall, science fiction take—based on Kurt Vonnegut's acclaimed novel—that pokes fun at armed-service protocol, prisoner-of-war-camp life, interplanetary travel, and staid opticians, while calling into question the elaborate, February 1945 Dresden carpet-bombing attack. Michael Sacks radiates as a simple, nineteen-year-old, gawky American GI, Billy Pilgrim, who is captured at the Battle of the Bulge and sent to Dresden. There, along with his pals, he squirrels inside an abandoned slaughterhouse during the Allied air raid. Eventually liberated, he returns home, marries the boss's daughter, raises children, and sells many eyeglass frames while, unknown to friends and family, he time-trips between past and future. (Sacks, explaining his history: "Dresden, I was there.") Replete with numerous absurd situations that lampoon military folly, the screenplay echoes Vonnegut's contention that modern warfare—the creation of older men—is fought by unsuspecting children, who for the most part, understand nothing about conflict.

SS Doomtrooper

Combat Productions, Directed by David Flores, Released 2006

Another space-age, comic-book adventure about a mad Nazi scientist (Ben Cross), who in winter 1945 creates a defensive weapon against advancing Allied forces—an atomized, twenty-foot Hulk look-alike supermonster, impervious to every explosive. Soon, an American commando team— headed by Captain Corin Nemec—locates this laboratory-made leviathan. (Captain Nemec's warning: "The only thing standing between the First Army and that freak of nature is us.") Following a series of wide-eyed skirmishes in a stolen tank and jeep, the team finally hotwires the monster's circuitry, causing a meltdown. With numerous tonsorial and linguistic anachronisms, including a Vietnam reference about special ops and the Stone Age, this strictly for laughs, action-figure game never takes itself seriously. Best homage scene: a frustrated GI, Private Parker Lewis, blurts out, "I can't win," a reference to Fox's popular 1990 television comedy *Parker Lewis Can't Lose*, a three-year series that starred Corin Nemec.

Stalag 17

Paramount, Directed by Billy Wilder, Released 1953

A half-spoof, half-serious look at the problems some six hundred American prisoners of war encounter in a German camp—a stalag—during the closing days of 1944 that downplays the abhorrence of Nazi brutality. William Holden depicts a close-mouthed Air Corps sergeant whose daily wheeling and dealing with his captors affords him minimal comfort, much to the annoyance of his fellow GIs, while guttural-speaking Sig Rumann plods along in another cookie-cutter "Schultz" role. Eventually, the cynical noncom redeems himself by catching a smooth-talking plant and rescuing a trapped officer from the clutches of the *Schutzstaffel*. Frequently criticized for ignoring Nazi atrocities, the storyline constantly pokes fun at Hitlerism. (GI prisoner to his buddies: "Always remember, just because the Krauts are dumb doesn't mean they're stupid.")

The Steel Claw

Ponderey Productions, Directed by George Montgomery, Released 1961

A made-on-a-shoestring, ninety-three-minute, B-adventure-yarn aggrandizing the jungle-fighting exploits of a one-handed Marine captain—wearing a homemade steel claw—as he leads a motley guerrilla band into the Philippine interior to rescue a one-star general from his Japanese tormentors. Matinee idol George Montgomery fords fast-running streams, climbs steep hills, and slithers under thick underbrush before reaching the Japanese camp, where after some more shooting-from-the-hip exploits, he realizes that the freed U.S. "general" is really an opportunist staff sergeant who wanted better treatment from his captors. (Tough-talking Montgomery to imposter: "So, you decided to play General—why didn't you drop the act when we picked you up?") Undaunted by this setback, the fast-thinking marine officer, along with his wounded girlfriend (Charito Luna), treks his charges back to the American outpost, proving once again the never-say-die spirit of a fighting man.

Straight into Darkness

Silver Bullet, Directed by Jeff Burr, Released 2005

A tasteless, repulsive, twenty-first century, pseudo-artistic travesty that highlights sexual and scatological themes in a manner usually reserved for special-effects, let-the-blood-flow horror films. Scott MacDonald and Ryan Francis "star" as two Army deserters, who, in 1945, escape from confinement, crawl through a French minefield, and finally stumble into a forlorn warehouse with a valuable art collection stashed in the cellar. There, an eccentric caretaker (David Warner) oversees a handful of physically handicapped orphans, outcast children who, under his tutelage, are now expert killers. A gory battle ensues when a *Wehrmacht* squad arrives to remove the art. (Private Francis, analyzing his situation: "They're here for the paintings.") Most of the Germans die, while Private MacDonald, in an expiatory gesture, fights to the finish, allowing his friend and the children to escape. (Private MacDonald's final words: "Quit squawking and start walking.")

Submarine Seahawk

American International Pictures, Directed by Spencer Gordon Bennet, Released 1958

Another how-low-was-my-budget underwater potboiler that rehashes pelagic themes, standard clichés, and navy jargon found in most Silent Service B-photodramas. Now, in the dangerous, Japanese-laden Pacific waters, Captain John Bentley cautiously guides the USS *Seahawk* on a reconnaissance mission to pinpoint enemy positions, while off to the side, his all-Caucasian crew grumbles about missed opportunities. Eventually, their skipper locates an elaborate Japanese reserve force, and soon American aircraft blow this hostile armada out of the water, much to the acclaim of his seagoing doubting Thomases. (Bentley to men: "We gave the Jap carrier the deep six.") With many scenes of anachronistic, documentary footage, this eighty-three-minute, black-and-white film resembles the B-propaganda quickies made during the war.

The Tanks Are Coming

Warner Bros., Directed by Lewis Seiler, Released 1951

A low-budget, "let's get moving" adulation of the Army Tank Corps GIs, the men that spearheaded the perilous July 1944 Normandy breakout. Steve Cochran stands firm as a cocky, self-centered, chip-on-the-shoulder NCO, who—despite his obnoxious behavior and frequent solecisms—intelligently maneuvers his unit out of harm's way. (Sergeant Cochran, waxing eloquently about his leadership qualities: "I ain't getting nobody killed! Ninety-eight percent of the guys in cemeteries got there because they made mistakes, which I don't do.") Frequently shunned by his squad, the loudmouth Cochran, after rescuing a corporal, quickly becomes a hero and, much to the admiration of his men, leads the first tank squadron heading for Berlin. As with most B-flag-waving productions, this photodrama contains many newsreel scenes, hoping to add a little verisimilitude to a skimpy storyline.

Task Force

Warner Bros., Directed by Delmer Daves, Released 1949

A Fourth-of-July, flag-waving testimony to the navy pilots who attacked the Japanese fleet at Midway, winning a pivotal battle and altering the war's course. Gary Cooper—a longtime pioneer for aircraft-carrier superiority—sparkles as an aviation officer whose twenty-seven-year career recalls the rudimentary flying conditions that existed just after World War I. Frustrated by the isolationist movement to denigrate naval airpower, the quiet-spoken Cooper—along with character actor Walter Brennan—eventually creates a powerful flattop fleet that forces Japan's capitulation. (Commander Cooper lambasting a cynic's criticism of floating airfields: "If the country had followed that advice, our West Coast newspapers right now would be printed in Japanese.") Using many stock newsreel insertions, this quasi-documentary format restates the navy's heroism and sacrifices in a subtle but forceful manner.

The Thin Red Line

Twentieth Century–Fox, Directed by Terrence Malick, Released 1998

A 170-minute, pseudo-epistemological, what-is-the-meaning-of-war? allegory—based on James Jones' acclaimed novel—that uses the U.S. Army's 1942 Guadalcanal follow-up invasion as a metaphor for various ontological questions inherent in contemporary society. Nick Nolte is outstanding as a rough-and-ready infantry colonel. While his top sergeant (Sean Penn) cautiously ruminates, Nolte pushes his C-for-Charlie squad into the jungle's interior to rout diehard Japanese from their pillboxes. (Colonel Nolte to subordinate: "We're going straight up that hill there.") Caught in their own heart of darkness, this small fighting unit—an eclectic mixture of spiritualism, loneliness, insecurity, and atavism—experiences numerous existentialist dilemmas before the island is secure. Most dubious casting: John Travolta, as an opportunist one-star general, prancing aboard a ship in a manner suggestive of a disco dancer, and George Clooney, as a rearguard officer, badmouthing replacements with his bag-of-wind platitudes.

36 Hours

MGM, Directed by George Seaton, Released 1964

Another spy-versus-spy thriller using the D-Day invasion as the setting for psychological intrigue. James Garner stands tall as an American intelligence officer who is first drugged, then kidnapped, and finally flown to a bogus American hospital in Germany. There, a Nazi doctor (Rod Taylor) almost convinces his "patient" that five years have elapsed since the Allies defeated Hitler, that Henry Wallace is the U.S. president, and that American forces govern Third Reich territory. Slowly Major Garner unravels their scheme and, with a little help from a concentration camp victim (Eva Marie Saint), escapes into Switzerland. (Nurse Saint, offering her assistance: "I'll do anything to help you, believe me.") As a quasi-science-fictional tale, the screenplay—in an obvious nod to 1964 Cold War politics—tones down Nazi bestiality and indirectly suggests that most Germans were kind, noble, altruistic, and anti-Hitler.

The Tides of War

Arrow Releasing, Directed by Neil Rossati, Released 1990

A low-budget, plenty-of-sunshine, comic-book debacle describing the transformation of a unsmiling Austrian naval officer from killer commando to an anti–New Order, anti-Gestapo apostate, who singularly destroys a V-2 rocket station on a remote Bahamian island during the war's closing months. After landing surreptitiously, blond-haired David Soul rationalizes his assassination of innocent British nationals as a military necessity. (Captain Soul, justifying his actions: "I lost a wife and son to an English bombing raid.") Slowly, he becomes disheartened when he witnesses the *Schutzstaffel's* cruelty to the natives building a launching site. Soon he renounces Hitlerism, becomes a fugitive, and—with the help of a missionary school teacher (Yvette Heyden)—wreaks havoc on the Nazi scheme to fire a projectile at Washington, D.C. Acclaimed a hero of sorts, his prior misdeeds are conveniently forgotten by the Allied forces when they retake the island.

A Time of Destiny

Columbia, Directed by Gregory Nava, Released 1988

An offbeat gothic thriller using the 1944–1945 Italian campaign as the backdrop to a brooding, symbolic storyline that includes family dissension, delayed love, and obsessive revenge. Here, a morose American sergeant (William Hurt) spends most of his time stalking another GI (Timothy Hutton) to avenge his father's stateside car death. Eventually brought together in a combat situation, the psychopathic Hurt—temporarily putting aside his idée fixe—proffers friendship to the unsuspecting soldier. (Hutton to new buddy, William Hurt: "It's a deal, then, O.K. You and me, we're going to live through this war.") After a series of bizarre events—including a confrontation in an Italian village—the two men separate, only to reunite a few months later at a San Diego church tower in a horrific climax. As a combat film, the theme is a constant reiteration that the U.S. forces contain a fair share of the mentally deranged.

A Time to Love and a Time to Die

Universal, Directed by Douglas Sirk, Released 1958

Another elaborate CinemaScope production purporting that most German foot soldiers, fighting on Russian soil, were kind, understanding, and victims of their superior's wanton cruelty. Here a *Wehrmacht* private (John Gavin)— on a ten-day furlough during a late-winter 1944 Soviet offensive—arrives home and learns that his parents are missing, many residents are homeless, the Allied bombing is unrelenting, and Nazi opportunism and treachery are everywhere. Then, he meets an old school friend, frightened Liselotte Pulver, and after a two-day courtship, the couple marry. (Private Gavin, on his first date: "I've nearly two years combat pay with me and only two weeks to spend it.") Back on Russian soil—one week later—the lovesick bridegroom, repulsed by war's horror, dies at the hands of some disgruntled Soviet prisoners. Adapted from Erich Maria Remarque's novel, the storyline—told from the German viewpoint—rationalizes most of the Third Reich's Eastern Front brutality.

To Hell and Back

Universal International, Directed by Jesse Hibbs, Released 1955

A quiet, unobtrusive, uplifting recollection of America's most decorated World War II hero in a manner that downplays flag waving and, instead, offers muted testimony to the fears, hopes, bonding, and frustration every foot soldier experiences. Audie Murphy portrays himself as the shy, baby-faced, laid-back, sixteen-year-old rural Texan who, following the Pearl Harbor bombing, enlists in the Army and—after extensive infantry training—embarks for the North African invasion. Soon, his regiment is reassigned, and by war's end, the soft-spoken GI fought in seven major campaigns, earned a battlefield commission, and received the coveted Medal of Honor. Best scene: the recently appointed second lieutenant, mindful of his squad's safety, leaps on a disabled tank and repels a Nazi infantry attack. (Lieutenant Murphy, ordering his men to take cover: "I'm going to stay here and see if I can get some artillery working.")

Tobruk

Universal, Directed by Arthur Hiller, Released 1966

A fast-moving, fictional, African desert yarn that highlights the combined efforts of an American officer, some British Tommies, and a tough group of Jewish commandos as they infiltrate the Nazi stronghold in Libya and subsequently blow up the Third Reich's strategic oil supply. Here, a famous hit-and-run fighter, Major Rock Hudson, encounters numerous problems—including air strafing, the stereotypical traitor-in-the-midst, and native intransigence—before reaching the port city of Tobruk. (Major Hudson, explaining his survival philosophy: "I'd never consider dying for a cause—no matter how noble!") Replete with James Bond escapades, the photoplay contains one implausible situation after another, nullifying the plot to a copycat version of the popular 1940s Saturday-afternoon cliffhangers.

Too Late the Hero

Cinerama Productions Corporation, Directed by Robert Aldrich, Released 1970

A modern-day redemption parable about a goldbricking navy officer (Cliff Robertson) who, following a series of complicated events, becomes part of a British commando raid on a New Hebrides island in spring 1942. After some bad luck, most of the squad is either captured or killed, and—along with an English corporal (Michael Caine)—Lieutenant Robertson must retreat deeper into the jungle to avoid enemy forces. (Caine, reiterating the nature of Japanese cruelty: "Treat you all right? They'll chop your bloody head off—I saw what they did in the hospital in Singapore.") Eventually, the two men reach their command post's perimeter, but only Michael Caine survives a last-ditch run to safety. With many analogies to the Vietnam conflict, the screenplay depicts war as a sadistic outlet for those mentally deranged individuals whose craving for violence requires constant gratification.

Tora! Tora! Tora!

Twentieth Century–Fox, Directed by Richard Fleischer, Toshio Masuda, and Kinji Fukasaku, Released 1970

A quasi-documentary, both-sides-of-the-story, minuscule examination of the inexplicable events leading up to the Japanese attack on Pearl Harbor, blaming numerous U.S. officers for their failure to act decisively. With an array of Hollywood male stars—including Jason Robards, Joseph Cotton, and Martin

Balsam—the 144-minute storyline weaves between Japanese and American high commands as numerous personalities scrutinize or ignore the political events responsible for December 7. (Admiral Martin Balsam, explaining why Japanese torpedo planes are ineffective in the forty-foot waters of Pearl Harbor: "A torpedo dropped from a plane will plunge to a depth of seventy-five feet or more before it levels off.") As a revisionist tract, the photoplay humanizes the Japanese officers responsible for this day of infamy, almost suggesting that FDR's embargo policy forced this Oriental nation to act so determinedly.

Torpedo Run

MGM, Directed by Joseph Pevney, Released 1958

Another fictional, high-powered, CinemaScope story about life aboard a U.S. Navy submarine in the Pacific theater, the loneliness of command, and the moral dilemma reached when innocent noncombatants perish during wartime. Here, a skipper (Glenn Ford) on a search-and-destroy mission accidentally sinks a Japanese transport vessel carrying fourteen hundred American civilians, including his wife and child. (Navy buddy [Ernest Borgnine] cautioning his friend about firing the ill-fated torpedo: "This attack is more than routine.") With stoic resignation, he gradually puts this tragedy behind him and, in a gleeful finale, blows up the Japanese aircraft carrier responsible for launching the planes against Pearl Harbor. Feeling slightly repentant for this new victory, the good-looking commander—still pondering the efficacy of his earlier misdeed—moves out to sea, ready to fight more Japanese warships.

The Train

United Artists, Directed by John Frankenheimer, Released 1965

A solid, riding-the-rails, suspense meller that proves the French Resistance's mettle once again, as these *chemin de fer* workers move quickly to prevent the Nazis from transporting stolen national artworks to Germany during their hasty August 1944 Paris retreat. Fast-moving Burt Lancaster—now a Gallic stationmaster—quietly orchestrates subtle forms of sabotage that prevent a heavily fortified train's embarkation from a small, occupied village, while his nemesis, Third Reich Colonel Paul Scofield, an obsessive, monomaniacal art collector, fumes in frustration. (Hard-talking Lancaster, explaining his mission: "To hell with London. We started this whole thing for one reason—to stop the train.") With some unexpected help from screen idol Jeanne Moreau, the Nazis cannot muster enough steam to thwart French determination to save their historical paintings from destruction or pilferage.

The Tuskegee Airmen

HBO Pictures, Directed by Robert Markowitz, Released 1995

A wonderful, made-for-television, flag-waving tribute to the African American officers of the 332nd Fighter Group, the Tuskegee airmen who flew hundreds of European missions, protecting American bombers from Luftwaffe offenses. Andre Braugher coruscates as the legendary Colonel Benjamin O. Davis, the highly decorated commander who must fight both military racism and Nazi ack-ack blasts, while back in the nation's capital, a southern senator (John Lithgow) spouts hatred and virulence against these U.S. flyers. (Colonel Braugher, defending his unit: "A fair and impartial opportunity is all we ask.") With Cuba Gooding Jr. and Laurence Fishburne in the pilot's seat, every aspect of this famous air group's history—from their early Alabama training days to their hundreds of aerial citations—receives one accolade after another.

Twelve O'Clock High

Twentieth Century–Fox, Directed by Henry King, Released 1949

An elaborate testimony to the airmen who fly the dangerous B-17 attack missions from their English countryside bases deep inside the German border. Gregory Peck stars as a group commander who slowly transforms a hard-luck bombing outfit into a precision fighting unit, while his assistant (Dean Jagger) keeps a sharp administrative eye on military regulations. Nominated for four Academy Awards, the picture—based on the book by Beirne Lay Jr. and Sy Bartlett—contains detailed aerial combat scenes, restating the high human cost involved in the air war against the Luftwaffe. As a martinet leader, who gradually loosens his grip, Gregory Peck vacillates between villain and hero. (General Peck, chewing out a subordinate for a variety of offenses: "I'm going to get your head down in the mud and trample it; I'm going to make you wish you'd never been born.")

U-571

Universal, Directed by Oliver Wood, Released 2000

A fast-paced, no-holds-barred, up-periscope seafaring thriller that pits the nautical skills of a young U.S. submarine lieutenant against the resources of the German navy during a 1942 mid-Atlantic confrontation. Motivated by national security, quick-moving Matthew McConaughey, along with a sixty-one-year-old chief petty officer (Harvey Keitel), leads a raiding party that commandeers a floundering Axis U-boat, seizing its prized ENIGMA cipher machine. Soon, the American sailors man the derelict Nazi vessel and, after a series of depth-charge adventures, surface to send a beeline bow shot at a German destroyer. (Lieutenant McConaughey exhorting a frighten seaman: "You're going to go back down in that bilge and you're going to do your job, sailor.")

Under Ten Flags

Paramount, Directed by Duilio Coletti, Released 1960

Another revisionist high-seas tale glamorizing the "true" exploits of a supposedly benign Nazi naval commander who, after shelling or torpedoing numerous Allied merchant ships—killing seamen and passengers—treats the survivors with unusual benevolence. Here, a German officer (Van Heflin) pushes credibility to its limits with his Oklahoma accent, while his staff members—wearing spiffy white uniforms and behaving like eager cruise waiters—denigrate their captain's altruism. (Heflin to Nazi crew: "As long as I am in command of this ship there will be a minimum of bloodshed, a minimum of suffering.") Eventually, the British navy destroys its seagoing enemy, and in a corny formula ending, both Nazi and English officers salute each other, oblivious to the mayhem they created.

Until They Sail

MGM, Directed by Robert Wise, Released 1957

Another heart-warming, I-will-love-you-forever, CinemaScope drama, from a short story by James Michener. This story traces the romantic ups and downs of four New Zealand sisters who—from the safety of their ocean-view cottage—watch their Kiwi men march off to war, only to be replaced by U.S. Marines training for Pacific island offensives. Here, the matriarch (Jean Simmons), along with her three siblings, witness six years of separation, heartache, bereavement, perfidy, upheaval, and, finally, V-J Day. (Miss Simmons, venting her frustration: "American supermen with more money than they ever had before in their lives, dazzling little girls who are lonely.") Eventually—after months of soul-searching—the cautious Miss Simmons, realizing that all is fair in love and war, changes her tune and admits that a well-mannered, quasi-cynical marine major (Paul Newman) is really the man of her dreams.

Up Periscope

MGM, Directed by Gordon Douglas, Released 1959

Another "all ahead full, steady as she goes, right full rudder" potboiler that aggrandizes all facets of submarine life. While not lamenting the loneliness of command, pudgy Edmond O'Brien ponders the efficacy of obtaining a Japanese codebook, located on a lightly guarded enemy island, by sneaking a frogman ashore. (Captain O'Brien to volunteer: "If we can break that code first, we're going to save a lot of ships and a lot of men.") Eventually James Garner dons a wet suit, swims unobtrusively inland, and—in a series of Captain Marvel escapades—slithers through the jungle, creates a diversion, tiptoes into a radio hut, photographs the classified information, and without blinking an eye, breaststrokes back to the submarine. Using one cliché after another—including the malcontent, the fake oil slick, and numerous depth-charge attacks—the photodrama lavishes heavy praise on the Silent Service.

Varian's War

Showtime, Directed by Lionel Chetwynd, Released 2001

A wonderful testimony to the American humanitarian Varian Fry, who during the ambiguous pre–Pearl Harbor days pulled numerous strings, affected different roles, and endured some close calls to quietly smuggle hundreds of Jewish artists, intellectuals, and scientists (including Marc Chagall, Franz Werfel, Max Ernst, Hannah Arendt, and Heinrich Mann) from Nazi-occupied France to the United States. Utilizing his best foppish mannerisms, bespectacled William Hurt spends many hours arguing his noble cause, while his assistant (Julia Ormond) spouts her free-love credo. (Hurt to colleagues: "We all know that the Nazis have a particularly cold hatred for artists and intellectuals they consider degenerate.") As a made-for-cable motion picture, the storyline—mirroring many of the ideas found in *Schindler's List*—extols the New Englander's unrelenting determination to rescue any persecuted individual.

The Victors

Columbia, Directed by Carl Foreman, Released 1963

A caustic look at the everyday life of a rifle squad, where each man experiences fear, loneliness, uncertainty, and, occasionally, elation. Sergeant Eli Wallach bellows many orders to his squad as they advance through Sicily, France, and finally Germany, watching the Axis forces slowly capitulate.

Along the way, the foot soldiers drink unlimited bottles of vintage wine, smoke one cigarette after another, and chase local women in a frivolous manner resembling a Saturday-night college fraternity blast. (Corporal George Peppard's appraisal of Sicilian females: "The place is like a barnyard.") With George Hamilton and Peter Fonda in leading roles, this screenplay—replete with subtle antiwar strains—ignores heroics and instead offers muted praise to the average GI. Most harrowing scene: a young, frightened American soldier's ordeal, when taken to an empty field, tied to a post, blessed by a chaplain, and executed for desertion.

Victory

MGM, Directed by John Huston, Released 1981

Another prisoner-of-war-escape travesty that ignores the horrific living conditions found under Nazi subjugation but, instead, suggests that military confinement resembles the shenanigans found in intercollegiate sports rivalry. Here, an American POW (Sylvester Stallone) appears too well fed and muscular, while his British pal (Michael Caine), aided by a stereotypically benign German officer (Max von Sydow), organizes a soccer match between the captives and their masters. Soon, both teams square off in a Paris stadium, and with the help of Pelé (and other international football-players-turned-actors) the Allied team snatches the prize. (POW Stallone, explaining his philosophy: "You guys do what you want, but I'm leaving. I ain't going back to prison!")

The Wackiest Ship in the Army

Columbia, Directed by Richard Murphy, Released 1960

A lighthearted comedy (with a few somber moments) depicting the misadventures of an easygoing naval lieutenant (Jack Lemmon), who—along with teen idol Ensign Ricky Nelson—is hoodwinked into taking command of a rundown sailing vessel, the USS *Echo*, and gliding this ship into the Japanese-patrolled New Guinea waters to report enemy positions during the March 1943 Battle of the Bismarck Sea offensive. (Fast-maneuvering Jack Lemmon, escaping from some Nipponese coastal attacks: "Boatswain, stand by to make sail!") With numerous subplots, the storyline occasionally parodies the exaggerated Hollywood stereotypes found in many World War II action films, including the motor that does not start, the Japanese officer who graduated from UCLA, a hold-your-breath journey through an ocean minefield, and the titular use of the noun "army," while in fact, this branch of the service is never mentioned in this ninety-nine-minute photoplay.

The Walls of Hell

Independent-International Pictures, Directed by Gerardo De Leon and Eddie Romero, Released 1964

Another eighty-eight-minute, low-grade, B-for-bottom-of-the-barrel pot-boiler from a production company noted for grinding out World War II screenplays with unknown actors, sultry actresses, and nonexistent dialogue. Once more, Fernando Poe Jr., a U.S. Army noncom, shoots, stabs, and strangles many Japanese soldiers in the narrow streets of the Philippine walled city, Intramuros, during the February 1945 allied offensive. (Sergeant Poe, proffering advice: "You fight your war, I'll fight mine"). His commanding officer (Jock Mahoney) crawls through a narrow tunnel, dodges enemy bullets, and, after some hand-to-hand fighting, rescues his sweetheart (Cecilia Lopez) from a Japanese prison. Using a generous supply of newsreel footage, this budget photodrama depicts the Filipino guerrillas as stealthy fighters, determined to rout their Oriental adversary.

The War Lover

Columbia, Directed by Philip Leacock, Released 1962

A psychological evaluation of the airmen who, in 1943, left the safety of their English bases to attack enemy targets on the European mainland. As a mono-maniacal pilot, Captain Steve McQueen derives visceral satisfaction from the risks associated with combat flying, much to the confusion of his copilot, Lieutenant Robert Wagner, and girlfriend. (McQueen to comely Shirley Anne Field, hoping his braggadocio will result in a sexual conquest: "I'm going to stay until the last bomb is dropped and maybe I'll be the one that drops it!) Eventually, his luck falters when his B-17—riddled by bullets after a German raid—cannot maintain altitude on its homeward flight. With the White Cliffs of Dover in view, Captain McQueen—the War Lover—unwilling to leave his womb-cockpit, dies in a fiery crash, symbolizing his pathological consumption. Based on the book by John Hersey, the storyline condemns those primeval needs—found in some military men—that crave sexual pleasure in wartime violence.

What Did You Do in the War, Daddy?

United Artists, Directed by Blake Edwards, Released 1966

An irreverent, tongue-in-cheek caricature of the 1943 Sicilian campaign that ignores the thousands of American casualties and, instead, suggests the entire invasion resembled a dizzy, college fraternity drinking party. As the junior officer assigned to seize a hilltop village, Lieutenant James Coburn agrees to a surrender bacchanalia with the Italian troops left behind. (Lieutenant Coburn to *Il Duce*'s soldiers: "Until we find Major Pott and get this surrender thing worked out, we fake a battle.") Scheming with Captain Dick Shawn, the twosome keep the charade working—while duping some unsuspecting German soldiers—and eventually, after some Bugs Bunny adventures, their commanding general (Carroll O'Connor), proud as the proverbial peacock, acclaims them heroes. Along with a handful of similar films, the photoplay purports that Italy—a member of the Axis Pact—was nothing more than a happy group of fun-seeking, wine-sipping, pasta-eating nationals, who worshipped President Roosevelt, detested Benito Mussolini, and opposed belligerency.

When Trumpets Fade

HBO, Directed by John Irvin, Released 1998

A slow-moving, horrific, all-male combat tale reiterating the sacrificial nature of the frontal assault in which inexperienced American soldiers—the greenies—die rapidly as they move forward during the 1944 autumn Hurtgen Forest offensive. Ron Eldred is outstanding as a cynical U.S. private quickly promoted to sergeant, and then to lieutenant, who must lead untried GIs into a heavily fortified area where *Wehrmacht* troops—determined to keep the Allies from breaching their Siegfried Line—fight tenaciously. (Sergeant Eldred's reaction: "I am absolutely the wrong man—request permission for a Section Eight.") With many references to uncaring commanders, unstable squad members, and survival probability odds, much of the storyline points to the futility of conflict. Most harrowing scene: after a ferocious attack, only four GIs reach the German perimeter and, finally, destroy their large guns.

Where Eagles Dare

MGM, Directed by Brian G. Hutton, Released 1968

A puffed-up, implausible adventure yarn—featuring one mock heroic after another—that subliminally spoofs the black-and-white, two-dimensional propaganda films produced during the war. Portraying a British commando sent behind German lines to an elaborate Austrian Alps hideaway, Richard Burton seems a little pudgy to parachute from an airplane, leap across moving cable cars, and climb straight up fortress walls, while his taciturn partner (Clint Eastwood) looks nonplussed by this cloak-and-dagger mission. (Major Burton, explaining Eastwood's role in a complicated spy-versus-spy showdown: "He's an assassin — a member of the American intelligence organization known as O.S.S.") Eventually, the Allied team blows up Gestapo headquarters, rescues an American general, and — during a zany escape — wreaks havoc on the German war machine in a manner suggestive of a Looney Tunes Saturday-morning cartoon.

Windtalkers

MGM, Directed by John Woo, Released 2002

A high-octane, flames-everywhere, they're-coming-at-us-from-all sides, strictly male, special-effects extravaganza honoring the U.S. Marines' Navaho code talkers, whose esoteric combat messages resulted in many island victories during the war's closing months. Thirty-eight-year-old Nicolas Cage seems miscast as an intelligence sergeant assigned to protect or, if necessary, kill the Windtalkers rather then compromise their cryptic code during the Saipan offensive. Along with another noncom (Christian Slater), the two men guard their charges assiduously. (Sergeant Slater, pondering his orders: "We're here to kill Japs, not Marines.") With recurring scenes depicting both American and Japanese bodies disintegrating, hapless men on fire, bloody stabbings, frequent mutilations, a horrific decapitation, and uncanny marksmanship, the screenplay resembles many of the antics found in the Road Runner series, where this popular, anthropomorphic comic-strip hero bounces back from every conceivable mishap.

The Wings of Eagles

MGM, Directed by John Ford, Released 1957

A well-earned pat on the back for Commander Frank "Spig" Wead, the naval pioneer who — in the 1920s and 1930s — campaigned vigorously for an independent aviation section within his own branch of service. Once more, John Wayne kicks up a storm as a blunt-talking, chain-smoking, fly-by-the-seat-of-your-pants maverick who champions the fledgling aircraft carrier. After a devastating spinal-cord injury, he leaves the service and eventually becomes a successful Hollywood screenwriter but, following Pearl Harbor, bulldozes his way back into the navy. Within months, he implements the "jeep carrier" plan, a novel way to provide immediate replacements in the combat zone. (Commander Wayne, explaining the logistics: "Now backing them up, we have these jeep carriers, loaded with planes and crew.") With many action sequences, the film demonstrates, once again, the importance of naval airpower in the Pacific theater.

Yanks

Universal, Directed by John Schlesinger, Released 1979

A poignant, happy-go-lucky look at some lifestyle changes when large contingencies of American infantrymen arrive in a small Yorkshire town to train for the upcoming 1944 European invasion. Here, the Yanks flirt with local women, offer PX items for quick favors, use military equipment for personal transportation, and occasionally trade on the back market. Soon, a good-looking mess sergeant (Richard Gere), famous for his scratch cakes, falls for a shy shopkeeper's daughter. (Gere to girlfriend: "I've never met anyone like you before.") After some on-again, off-again romance, the twosome resolve all cultural differences on the eve of his Normandy departure, proving that love crosses all boundaries. With numerous references to wartime separation, uncertain future, and payroll disparities, the storyline accurately reflects an integral part of social history. Most realistic scene: a racial fight breaks out when some southern GIs, infuriated that a black soldier danced with a white girl, attack the helpless soldier, while the townspeople, unaccustomed to such behavior, stare incredulously.

Young Joe: The Forgotten Kennedy

ABC Circle Films, Directed by Richard Heffron, Released 1977

Another made-for-television Kennedy-family saga that traces the World War II navy career of the oldest scion from stateside preflight training, through the Caribbean, submarine patrol, and, finally, to a fatal August 1944 morning when the young lieutenant—eager for aerial combat—is accidentally killed during a secret English Channel airborne mission. Peter Strauss shines as the eldest son who moves in the shadow of the patriarch's vow that someday he will become the first Irish-Catholic U.S. president. Based on the Hank Searls' biography *The Lost Prince*, the Hollywood screenplay repeats Kennedy's noncombatant frustration, while his kid brother, John, a decorated navy PT boat officer, steals much of his thunder. (Young Joe, frustrated by his limited Normandy invasion participation: "It's been a month since D-Day—I might as well drive a bus.")

The Young Lions

Twentieth Century–Fox, Directed by Edward Dmytryk, Released 1958

A superbly crafted black-and-white CinemaScope production—based on the novel by Irwin Shaw—that carefully juxtaposes the lives of two Americans, from their basic training days to their European combat with a high-minded, idealist German officer, who slowly becomes disillusioned with the horror of Nazism. Dean Martin and Montgomery Clift are outstanding as two unwilling dogfaces who eventually become hardened combat veterans after their unit liberates a concentration camp. Now a *Wehrmacht* lieutenant, blond-haired Marlon Brando cannot fathom his superiors' brutality. (Brando to commander: "I don't think it possible to remake this world from the basement of a dirty little police station.") Eventually, the three soldiers converge on a German hillside and—in a somber allegorical ending—the Nazi dies from the rifle shots of the two GIs in a manner that suggests atonement for Third Reich misdeeds.

Zone Troopers

Empire Pictures, Directed by Denny Bilson, Released 1986

An eighty-eight-minute spoof of the many B-propaganda pictures that flourished during World War II. Here, Sergeant Tim Thomerson—trapped behind German lines during the Italian Campaign—stumbles upon an alien rocket ship and, after a series of science-fictional escapades, befriends the rodent-faced extraterrestrials who man this aircraft. Soon the two sides team up and—firing both Thompson submachine guns and space ray weapons—obliterate the *Wehrmacht* forces. (Newspaperman [Biff Manard], complimenting his alien friend's marksmanship: "That's cooking, Bughead.") Loaded with anachronisms and tongue-in-cheek homage scenes, this offbeat film in many ways parodies Hollywood's cliché-ridden portrayal of the Global Conflict. (Private Timothy Van Patten, discussing the alien's homeland: "Everybody knows there's no life on Venus. He's gotta be from Mars.")

Bibliography

Adams, Michael C. C. *The Best War Ever: America and World War II*. Baltimore: Johns Hopkins University Press, 1994.

Baker, M. Joyce. *Images of Women in Film: The War Years, 1941–1945*. Ann Arbor, Mich.: UMI Research Press, 1980.

Basinger, Jeanine. *The World War II Combat Film: Anatomy of a Genre*. New York: Columbia University Press, 1986.

Beigel, Harvey. *The Fleet's In: Hollywood Presents the U.S. Navy in World War II*. Missoula, Mont.: Pictorial Histories, 1995.

Biesen, Sheri Chinen. *Blackout: World War II and the Origins of Film Noir*. Baltimore: Johns Hopkins University Press, 2006.

Birdwell, Michael E. *Celluloid Soldiers: Warner Bros. Campaign against Nazism*. New York: New York University Press, 2001.

Boggs, Carl, and Tom Pollard. *The Hollywood War Machine*. Boulder, Colo.: Paradigm, 2006.

Braverman, John. *To Hasten the Homecoming: How Americans Fought World War II through the Media*. Lanham, Md.: Scarecrow Press, 1996.

Butler, Ivan. *The War Film*. New York: Barnes, 1974.

Cameron, Kenneth. *America on Film: Hollywood and American History*. New York: Continuum, 1997.

Chambers, John Whiteclay II, and David Culbert. *World War II, Film and History*. New York: Oxford, 1996.

Chapman, Ivan. *Private Eddie Leonski: The Brownout Strangler*. Sydney: Hale, 1982.

Clarke, James. *War Films*. London: Virgin, 2006.

Cripps, Thomas. *Making Movies Black: The Hollywood Message Movie from World War II to the Civil Rights Era*. New York: Oxford, 1993.

Dick, Bernard F. *The Star-Spangled Screen: The American World War II Film*. Lexington: University Press of Kentucky, 1985.

Doherty, Thomas. *Projections of War: Hollywood, American Culture, and World War II*. New York: Columbia University Press, 1993.

Dolan, Edward F. *Hollywood Goes to War*. Twickenham, England: Hamlyn, 1985.

Donald, Ralph R. "Savages, Swine, and Buffoons: Hollywood's Selected Stereotypical Characterization of the Japanese, Germans, and Italians in Films Produced during World War II." In *Race, Gender, Media: Considering Diversity across Audiences, Content, and Producers*. Edited by Rebecca Ann Linn, 193–98. Upper Saddle River, N.J.: Pearson, 2004.

Early, Emmett. *The War Veteran in Film*. Jefferson, N.C.: McFarland, 2003.

Eberwein, Robert T. *The War Film*. New Brunswick, N.J.: Rutgers University Press, 2004.

——. *Armed Forces: Masculinity and Sexuality in the American War Film*. New Brunswick, N.J.: Rutgers University Press, 2007.

Evans, Alvin. *Brassey's Guide to War Films*. Dulles, Va.: Brassey's, 2000.

Femina, Jerry Della. *From Those Wonderful Folks Who Gave You Pearl Harbor: Front-Line Dispatches from the Advertising World*. New York: Simon, 1970.

Freitas, Gary. *War Movies: The Belle & Blade Guide to Classic War Videos*. Bandon, Ore: Reed, 2004.

Friedrich, Jörg. *The Fire*. Translated by Allison Brown. New York: Columbia University Press, 2006.

Fussell, Paul. *Wartime: Understanding and Behavior in the Second World War*. New York: Oxford University Press, 1989.

Fyne, Robert. *The Hollywood Propaganda of World War II*. Metuchen, N.J.: Scarecrow Press, 1994.

Garland, Brock. *War Movies*. New York: Facts on File, 1987.

Guttmacher, Peter. *Legendary War Movies*. New York: Friedman, 1996.

Higashi, Sumiko. "World War II Newsreels and Propaganda Film," *Cinema Journal* 37 (Spring 1998): 38–61.

Holsinger, M. Paul, and Mary Anne Schofield, eds. *Visions of War*. Bowling Green, Ohio: Bowling Green University Popular Press, 1992.

Hoopes, Ray. *When the Stars Went to War: Hollywood and World War II*. New York: Random House, 1994.

Hurd, Geoffrey. *National Fictions: World War II on Films and Television*. London: BFI, 1984.

Hyams, James. *War Films*. New York: Gallery, 1984.

Jeavons, Clyde. *A Pictorial History of War Films*. Secaucus, N.J.: Citadel, 1974.

Jones, Ken D., and A. F. McClure. *Hollywood at War: The American Motion Picture and World War II*. New York: Castle, 1973.

Kagan, Norman. *The War Film*. New York: Pyramid, 1974.

Kerr, E. Bartlett. *Flames Over Tokyo: The U.S. Army Air Forces' Incendiary Campaign against Japan, 1944–1945*. New York: Fine, 1991.

Koppes, Clayton R., and Gregory D. Black. *Hollywood Goes to War: How Politics, Profit, and Propaganda Shaped World War II Movies*. New York: Free Press, 1987.

Langman, Larry, and Ed Borg, eds. *Encyclopedia of America War Films*. New York: Garland, 1974.

Marill, Alvin H. *Movies Made for Television: 1964–2004*. Lanham, Md.: Scarecrow Press, 2005.

Maslowski, Peter. *Armed with Cameras: The American Military Photographers of World War II*. New York: Free Press, 1993.

Matelski, Marilyn J., and Nancy Lynch Street, eds. *War and Film in America: Historical and Critical Essays*. Jefferson, N.C.: McFarland, 2003.

Mayo, Mike. *VideoHound's War Movies: Classic Conflict on Film*. Detroit: Visible Ink, 1990.

McAdams, Frank. *The American War Film: History and Hollywood*. New York: Praeger, 2002.

McKrisken, Trevor, and Andrew Pepper. *American History and Contemporary Hollywood Film*. New Brunswick, N.J.: Rutgers University Press, 2005.

McLaughlin, Robert L., and Sally E. Parry. *We'll Always Have the Movies: American Cinema During World War II*. Lexington: University Press of Kentucky, 2006.

Miller, Don. *"B" Movies*. New York: Curtis, 1973.

Moeller, Susan D. *Shooting War: Photography and the American Experience of Combat*. New York: Basic Books, 1989.

Nornes, Abé Mark, and Fukushima Yukio, eds. *The Japan/America Film Wars: Propaganda Films from World War II*. Chur, Switzerland: Harwood, 1993.

O'Neill, William. *A Democracy at War: America's Fight at Home and Abroad in World War II*. New York: Free Press, 1993.

Orris, Bruce. *When Hollywood Ruled the Skies: The Aviation Film Classics of World War II*. Hawthorne, Calif.: Aero, 1984.

Paris, Michael. *From the Wright Brothers to Top Gun: Aviation, Nationalism and Popular Cinema*. New York: Manchester University Press, 1995.

Parish, James Robert. *The Great Combat Pictures: Twentieth-Century Warfare on the Screen*. Metuchen, N.J.: Scarecrow Press, 1990.

Pendo, Stephen. *Aviation in the Cinema*. Metuchen, NJ: Scarecrow Press, 1985.

Perlmutter, Tom. *War Movies*. Secaucus, N.J.: Castle, 1974.

Polan, Dana. *Power and Paranoia: History, Narrative, and the American Cinema, 1940–1950*. New York: Columbia University Press, 1986.

Quirk, Lawrence J. *Great War Films*. New York: Carol, 1994.

Ray, Robert B. *A Certain Tendency of the Hollywood Cinema, 1930–1980*. Princeton, N.J.: Princeton University Press, 1985.

Renov, Michael. *Hollywood's Wartime Woman: Representation and Ideology*. Ann Arbor, Mich.: UMI Research Press, 1988.

Roeder, George H., Jr. *The Censored War: American Visual Experience during World War II*. New Haven: Yale University Press, 1993.

Rollins, Peter, ed. *Hollywood as Historian: American Film in a Cultural Context*. Lexington: University Press of Kentucky, 1983.

Rollins, Peter, and John O'Connor. *Why We Fought: America's Wars in Film and History*. Lexington: University Press of Kentucky, 2008.

Rubin, Steven Jay. *Combat Films: American Realism 1945–1970*. Jefferson, N.C.: McFarland, 1981.

Schickel, Richard. *Good Morning, Mr. Zip, Zip, Zip: Movies, Memory, and World War II*. Chicago: Dee, 2003.

Serene, Frank. *World War II on Film: A Catalog of Select Motion Pictures in the National Archives*. Washington, D.C.: National Archives, 1994.

Shull, Michael S., and David E. Wilt. *Hollywood War Films, 1937–1945: An Exhaustive Filmography of American Feature-Length Motion Pictures Relating to World War II*. Jefferson, N.C.: McFarland, 1996.

Sklar, Robert. *Film: An International History of the Medium*. New York: Abrams, 1993.

Slocum, J. David, ed. *Hollywood and War, the Film Reader*. New York: Routledge, 2006.

Spiller, Robert J. "War in the Dark," *American Heritage*, February/March 1999, 41–51.

Strada, Michael J., and Harold R. Troper. *Friend or Foe? Russians in American Film and Foreign Policy, 1933–1991*. Lanham, Md.: Scarecrow Press, 1997.

Suid, Lawrence. *Guts and Glory: The Making of the American Military Image in Film*. Lexington: University Press of Kentucky, 2002.

———. *Sailing on the Silver Screen: Hollywood and the U.S. Navy*. Annapolis: U.S. Naval Institute Press, 1996.

Suid, Lawrence, and Dolores A. Haverstick. *Stars and Stripes on Screen: A Comprehensive Guide to Portrayals of American Military on Film*. Lanham, Md.: Scarecrow Press, 2005.

Toplin, Robert Brent, ed. *Hollywood as Mirror: Changing Views of Outsiders and Enemies in American Movies*. Westport, Conn.: Greenwood, 1996.

Uklanski, Piotr. *The Nazis*. Zurich: Scalo, 2000.

Vidal, Gore. *Screening History*. Cambridge, Mass.: Harvard University Press, 1992.

Virilio, Paul. *War and Cinema: The Logistics of Perception*. New York: Verso, 1989.

Wetta, Frank J., and Stephen J. Curley. *Celluloid Wars: A Guide to Film and the American Experience of War*. New York: Greenwood, 1992.

Woll, Allen L. *The Hollywood Musical Goes to War*. Chicago: Nelson, 1983.

Index

About the Author

Robert Fyne, an English professor at Kean University, Union, New Jersey, teaches film and literature courses. Actively involved in numerous motion-picture organizations, Dr. Fyne has published extensively in *Film & History*, *North Carolina Historical Review*, *Wind/Literary Journal*, *Christian Century*, *Journal of Popular Film and Culture*, *Literature/Film Quarterly*, *France Magazine*, *Alaska Quarterly Review*, *Historical Journal of Film, Radio, and Television*, *Social Science Journal*, *Film Library Quarterly*, *New Guard*, and *Intellect*. Other World War II essays have appeared in anthologies including *The Columbia Companion to American History*. His 1994 book, *The Hollywood Propaganda of World War II* (Scarecrow Press), examines over four hundred wartime screenplays and their contribution to the victory effort. He is currently the book review editor for *Film and History*.